DIVISIONS OF WELFARE

DIVISIONS OF WELFARE

A Critical Introduction to Comparative Social Policy

Norman Ginsburg

SAGE Publications

London · Newbury Park · New Delhi

SAGE Publications Ltd
6 Bonhill Street
London EC2A 4PU

SAGE Publications Inc
2455 Teller Road
Newbury Park, California 91320

SAGE Publications India Pvt Ltd
32, M-Block Market
Greater Kailash – I
New Delhi 110 048

British Library Cataloguing in Publication data

Ginsburg, Norman
    Divisions of welfare: A critical introduction to
    comparative social policy.
    I. Title
    361.9

    ISBN 0–8039–8440–5
    ISBN 0–8039–8441–3 pbk

Library of Congress catalog card number 91–51088

Typeset by Photoprint, Torquay, Devon
Printed in Great Britain by the Cromwell Press Ltd,
Broughton Gifford, Melksham, Wiltshire

Contents

Preface and Acknowledgements

This book is the product of an extremely long period of gestation, born out of more than a decade of teaching in this field. The original impetus for it goes back to 1980 when I devised and taught a new undergraduate course in Comparative Social Administration at the University of Warwick. When I moved to South Bank Polytechnic in 1984, I was lucky enough to be able to continue teaching the course as an undergraduate option entitled Comparative Social Policy, while colleagues at Warwick continued to teach much the same course there. I am therefore extremely grateful to the many students who have taken the course over the years for their interest and the stimulating feedback I have received from them. I am also grateful to colleagues, co-examiners and external examiners at both institutions for the constructive criticism, support and advice I have received in connection with the course over the years. The bulk of the work which went into this book was done during three terms of sabbatical leave, two from the University of Warwick in 1982 and one from South Bank Polytechnic in 1990. I am extremely grateful to both institutions for those periods of leave.

I would like to acknowledge the generous access to information and sources on day care afforded to me by Jane Williams and Peter Moss at the Thomas Coram Institute. I am also particularly indebted to Judy Allsop, Avtar Brah, Mick Carpenter, Bob Deacon, Miriam David, Pat Ladly, Phil Lee, Susan Lonsdale, Laurence Marlow, Naseem Shah, Dave Taylor, Heather Wakefield and Fiona Williams for the advice and support they have given me over the years this book has been gestating. Finally I must express my gratitude to my publisher Karen Phillips and three anonymous referees of the original proposal for their constructive advice and criticism.

The main chapters of this book, each devoted to a case study of one country, were written in the summer of 1990. Since then, Sweden has applied to join the European Community, the Federal Republic of Germany has absorbed the five *Länder* of the former German Democratic Republic, and Mrs Thatcher has been ousted as Prime Minister by her own party; I have updated in the light of these changes. An unavoidable problem is that cross-national social policy analysis is usually based on data which is several years in arrears because of logistic difficulties. Aside from my own inadequacies, history does not stand still and cross-national policy analysis is still in its infancy.

Norman Ginsburg
Brockley

List of Abbreviations

British unless otherwise stated.

AFDC	Aid to Families with Dependent Children (US)
ALRA	Abortion Law Reform Association
AMA	American Medical Association
AMBC	Asian Mother and Baby Campaign
AMI	American Medical International
AMS	Swedish Labour Market Board
ATP	state earnings-related pension in Sweden
BMA	British Medical Association
CCT	compulsory competitive tendering
CDU	Christian Democratic Party (FRG)
CRE	Commission for Racial Equality
CSU	Christian Social Union (FRG)
DGB	trade union federation in FRG
DGH	district general hospital
DHA	district health authority
DHSS	Department of Health and Social Security
DSS	Department of Social Security
EC	European Community
ERA	Equal Rights Amendment (US)
ERS	earnings-related supplement
ET	Employment Training
FES	Family Expenditure Survey
FDP	Free Democratic Party (FRG)
FRG	Federal Republic of Germany
GDP	gross domestic product
GDR	German Democratic Republic
GNP	gross national product
GP	general practitioner
HMO	Health Maintenance Organization (US)
KV	sickness insurance funds (FRG)
LIS	Luxembourg Income Study
LO	Swedish trade union federation
MSC	Manpower Services Commission
NHI	National Health Insurance (US)
NHS	National Health Service
OASDHI	Old Age, Survivors, Disability and Health Insurance (US)
OBRA	Omnibus Budget Reconciliation Act, 1981 (US)
OECD	Organization for Economic Cooperation and Development
RAWP	Resource Allocation Working Party

SA	social assistance
SACO	white collar union federation in Sweden
SAP	Swedish Social Democratic Party
SB	Social Assistance (Sweden); Supplementary Benefit (UK)
SERPS	State Earnings Related Pension Scheme
SMA	Swedish Medical Association
SMP	Statutory Maternity Pay
SI	Sickness Insurance
SPD	Social Democratic Party (FRG)
SSI	Supplemental Security Income (US)
TEC	Training and Enterprise Council
UIB	unemployment insurance benefit
YTS	Youth Training Scheme

1
Analysing and Comparing Welfare States

This book attempts a critical appraisal of modern social policy in four Western states. In the chapters on each welfare state there is a strong emphasis on factual data about social policies, largely from official government statistics, but the approach is very far from being just an exercise in the presentation of data. In the selection and presentation of data, conscious biases have been exercised in order, wherever possible, to ventilate some critical themes about the origins, purposes and outcomes of social policy in Western societies, particularly in relation to the key social divisions of class, 'race' and gender. Needless to say, it is easy to ask such critical questions, but frequently extremely difficult to answer them on the basis of available data. In many ways all we have are pinpricks of light in a number of areas, which are bathed in gratefully and exploited as fully as possible. The reader will hopefully be wary of instances where the data is overinterpreted or even massaged. This chapter is devoted to examining some of the methodological, conceptual and theoretical issues which such policy analysis raises, in order to explain the approach taken in the rest of the book.

The terms 'social policy' and 'the welfare state' are virtually synonymous. They are conventionally used to describe government action in the fields of personal and family income, health care, housing, education and training, and personal 'care' services. 'Government action' embraces not only direct provision of benefits and services, but also the regulation and subsidy (including fiscal reliefs) of the various private forms of welfare. These latter include occupational welfare provided by employers, welfare provided by for-profit, charitable, trade union, community, religious and other voluntary organizations, as well as that provided informally by family members, friends and neighbours. Clearly the boundaries of social policy extend into areas which are conventionally ascribed to 'economic policy' (e.g. employment, industrial, monetary and fiscal policy) and other areas of 'public policy' (e.g. immigration, law enforcement, industrial relations and penal policy). The concept of 'policy' is also usefully extended in at least two other directions. First, it must cover the activities of agencies to whom governments and legislation frequently delegate responsibility for social policy – quangos, regional and local government, and so on. Administrative, professional and local government discretion often create enormous complexity in defining what policy actually amounts to. Second, the term 'social policy' should cover areas of inactivity by government and its agencies in relation to social issues. Thus 'government inaction, or nondecision, becomes a policy when it is pursued over time in a fairly consistent way against pressures to the contrary' (Heidenheimer *et al.*, 1990: 5). This is particularly apparent in areas such as family policy, where governments uphold the privacy of 'the family', while inevitably, at the same time, intervening in many ways into family life.

From whatever value perspective it is pursued and however its boundaries are defined, the study of social policy involves analysis of three basic elements – the origins, the substance and the impact of policy, or as Heidenheimer *et al.* (1990: 3) put it, 'how, why and to what effect . . . governments pursue particular courses of action or inaction'. Pursued from a radical and critical perspective, policy analysis should attempt to keep all three elements in play, although this is a difficult juggling act. To examine the origins of policy is to understand the processes of policy change with a view to understanding how to shift policy in a more radical direction. In examining the substance of policy it is necessary to look critically behind the ostensible aims and functions of policy. Above all it is essential to examine the impact or outcomes of policy in terms of critical parameters such as class, 'race' and gender inequality without taking for granted benign intentions or successful implementation of policy. Analysis of the impact of social policy is therefore discussed first, followed by brief discussions on the origins and the substance of social policy.

The Impact of Social Policy

Both supporters and detractors of the welfare state would agree that one of its purposes is to heal fundamental social divisions or at least to mitigate social inequalities. This is essential to the idea or ideology of the welfare state, but such outcomes cannot be taken for granted. There is considerable evidence that, in fact, the welfare state institutionalizes class, gender and racial divisions and inequalities. Yet it is also true that without the welfare state, the extent of class, 'race' and gender inequalities and divisions would in most instances be even more substantial. This contradictory nature of the welfare state in both mitigating and furthering social inequalities and divisions is a key theme of this book. We start from the premise that in the United States (US), the Federal Republic of Germany (FRG – known as West Germany until 1990), Sweden and Britain the welfare state operates in the context of a 'patriarchal and racially structured capitalism' (Williams, 1989: xiv). Of course there are many other important social divisions upon which welfare states have a critical impact and around whose welfare needs social movements have mobilized. These would include divisions by age, physical impairment, intellectual impairment, sexual orientation, religious affiliation, and national identity. Such divisions in industrial societies are just as universal as those of class, 'race' and gender. The choice of class, 'race' and gender is largely dictated by the contemporary politics of welfare states and the social science data which reflects that politics, in which these divisions have played a pre-eminent role. It is therefore assumed here that three of the key social divisions of welfare are those of class, 'race' and gender – concepts upon which some brief reflection is required.

Class and Class Divisions of Welfare

In a capitalist society the great majority of the population is primarily dependent for its present and future welfare on the selling of labour power, that is the potential to work in exchange for wages. This dependence may be direct in the case of a worker or former worker, or indirect in the case of a worker's dependants. Wages are used to purchase, amongst other things, the welfare necessities of life. Labour power is purchased by employers and employing organizations (capital), over whom the workers collectively (the working class) have limited effective control. Through party political and trade union organization and many other forms of popular pressure (the class struggle) the working class has frequently been able to exert a degree of informal and formal influence over capital, both at the workplace and through the state by taxation and regulation of capital. Capital's sole reason for existence is to make profits and to survive the harsh pressures of capitalist competition. Hence legal and bureaucratic regulation of capital by the state is required to achieve a measure of 'fair' competition. Modern capital *may* also require the state to ensure that the education, health and welfare of the working class is sufficient to meet the demands of the labour process. Above all capital requires the working class to be available for disciplined, paid employment. The welfare state is therefore also the result of capital's requirements for the reproduction of labour power. The combination of the working class struggle for welfare and capital's requirements for the reproduction of labour power have produced the welfare state. The term 'welfare state' covers both the direct provision of welfare benefits and services by public agencies, and the subsidy and regulation of occupational, for-profit, voluntary, charitable, informal and other forms of private welfare.

Capitalist economies inevitably experience booms and slumps – periods of profits growth and expansion, and periods of profits decline and recession. The welfare state is obviously more secure in periods of growth and expansion, though capital is always seeking out new areas for profit in the area of welfare services itself. In some circumstances this can develop into pressure for the privatization of parts of the welfare state. Whatever the state of the economy, the welfare state under capitalism is never entirely secure or stable. Particularly during recession and mass unemployment, capital may seek retrenchment of the welfare state, when the welfare needs of the working class are most pressing. On the other hand in such periods, capital may support the use of social welfare to counter working class anti-capitalist sentiment and agitation.

Such a Marxian 'class analysis' assumes therefore that 'capital' struggling for profits and fair competition, and 'the working class' struggling for a decent standard of living, have played a major role in shaping the welfare state. It is readily apparent however that such an analysis unravels with some difficulty and complexity when applied, for example, to the actual sociological and political divisions of the working class by income, skill, type of employment, status, 'race', religion, gender, locality and so on. In pursuing a class analysis of the impact of the welfare state more precisely, it is customary to use more neutral Weberian concepts of occupational social class and to use data on income distribution and poverty which can be interpreted in terms of a social class analysis. Official statisticians and sociologists in Britain, Sweden and the FRG have deployed classifications of occupational divisions for many years, but unfortunately they are constructed on different bases. There is no widely accepted definition of occupational social class for the US, though 'race' is widely used as a key parameter of social stratification. Occupational social classifications use criteria such as skill, status, and source of income. Frequently the working class in a Weberian sense is equated with manual and lower-status white collar workers, while the middle class(es) are identified as those in managerial and professional occupations. Of course when households are classified in this way, the occupation of the so-called 'head of the household', usually a man, is used, which gives such classifications an inevitable sexist bias. The aim of the modern welfare state, at least within liberal democratic ideology, is to mitigate welfare inequalities between the middle class and the working class thus defined. However, welfare states differ quite significantly in the degree to which this is achieved. It is also the case that the middle class have everywhere benefited extensively from the welfare state, and are politically well equipped to defend those benefits if and when they are threatened. It can be plausibly argued that the overall impact of the welfare state under capitalism on the social class distribution of welfare has been to stabilize and thus reinforce the class structure, at least in the post-war boom decades. Nevertheless the dismantling of the welfare state would, almost inevitably, deepen social class inequalities catastrophically.

'Race' and the Racial Divisions of Welfare

Capitalism was built upon colonialism and slavery and is sustained by modern imperialism in the form of the continued exploitation and dependency of the peoples of the so-called Third World. Migrant workers, their descendants and the descendants of slaves are to a varying extent colonized internally in Western societies by processes of racialization. Such processes are of course much older than capitalism, and certainly cannot be understood or explained fully by reference to slavery, colonialism and the power of modern capital, as the history of anti-semitism, for example, shows. Nevertheless the domestic interests of capital have coincided with these processes, particularly in the recruitment of cheap, migrant labour from poor, formerly colonized societies and from formerly enslaved groups. Ideologies of racial superiority, enhanced by colonialism and modern imperialism, have also fostered racial division of the working class, which saps its potential for collective strength in pursuing the reform and transformation of the capitalist system.

The concept 'race' is used here as a political and sociological category, whose meaning is established in concrete historical and political circumstances, and is therefore subject to change. Racial differences are not a constant or objective phenomenon. Real biological differences frequently inform the construction of racial difference, but they are not necessary to the process. In other words,

> 'race' has to be socially and politically constructed and elaborate ideological work is done to secure and maintain the different forms of 'racialization' which have characterized capitalist development . . . It is struggle that determines which definition of 'race' will prevail and the conditions under which they will endure or wither away. (Gilroy, 1987: 38–9)

Hence, in the contemporary welfare states examined here, different groups are significantly racialized – African American and Hispanic people in the US, Asian and Afro-Caribbean people in Britain, Turks and other Southern European people in the FRG. The US is the only state where data on 'race' and welfare needs and provisions is extensively collected, but there is some useful data for Britain and the FRG.

Liberal democratic welfare states in the modern era generally claim to be undermining racial inequalities and racialized processes of social control. Yet serious policies which follow up such intentions have only been implemented in a few states (such as the US and Britain) where anti-racist movements have been able to exert some real pressure. The lived experience of ethnic minorities and the sociological evidence both suggest that racialized processes are embedded in modern welfare states. These processes cannot by any means be explained solely in terms of explicit racism in legislation (e.g. immigration laws), and overt subjective racism in bureaucratic and professional practice. Nor can they just be explained satisfactorily in terms of the structural, socioeconomic requirements of capital as outlined above. The term 'institutional racism' is useful to identify policy and administrative processes in the welfare state, which result in relatively adverse treatment of ethnic minorities. Institutional racism takes many forms such as stereotyping ethnic minority clients, failing to recognize their particular welfare needs or to consider them legitimate, and accommodating to overt racist pressures in the wider community. The impact of contemporary social policy on racial inequalities is quite different in each welfare state, but in all of them social welfare has both mitigated and reinforced racial inequalities and institutional racism.

Patriarchy and Gender Division

Patriarchy means simply male domination, or the subordination of women. Here a universal concept of patriarchy is assumed, for as Dahlerup (1987: 95) explains,

> the fact that male dominance seems to be somewhat universal speaks in favour of constructing a universal concept. A universal concept of patriarchy implies that male dominance is not just an effect of, for instance, capitalist society, or a left-over from feudalism, but an independent structure of its own.

Patriarchal gender division is certainly a fundamental characteristic of individual welfare in industrial societies. Welfare states have played an important role in both reinforcing male supremacy, and, under pressure from women's movements, in transforming it to some extent. Convention-ally in capitalist societies since the advent of the modern poor law, social policy has been built around the concept of the family wage and the patriarchal division of labour in the family. In this model, the married male breadwinner earns a family wage sufficient to meet the subsistence and other welfare needs of his dependants, including his wife who works at home unpaid to care full-time for children and other family members in need. Poor law and means-tested assistance systems have given deterrent, stigmatized relief to families which deviate drastically from the norm. Contributory social insurance was established under pressure from the male-dominated labour movement, to provide a semblance of the family wage to the sick, the old, the unemployed and widows to protect them from the degradation of poor relief. The family-wage model is patriarchal because it puts women financially in a wholly dependent position, which reinforces men's overwhelming private economic power in the family, bolstered by the wider patriarchal culture. In reality men's wages have usually been insufficient to support their families adequately, which has fuelled the pressure from working class men and women for the welfare state. Paradoxically the very elusiveness of the family wage 'may have deepened popular commitment to the family-wage ideology, which came to represent respectability and stability for working and middle class alike' (L. Gordon, 1988: 619). Thus patriarchal social insurance based on the family-wage model was a cornerstone of the New Deal welfare reforms in the US and the Social Democratic welfare reforms in Sweden in the 1930s, and the Beveridge and Adenauer welfare reforms in Britain and the FRG in the 1940s and 1950s.

The material inadequacy of the family wage and the impoverishment of lone mothers have always helped to encourage working class women to find paid employment, as well as putting women into the forefront of the struggle for the welfare state. Demands for maternity rights, safe birth control, decent benefits for mothers, particularly lone mothers, and so on were just as central to the first phase of feminism around the turn of the century as they have been in the recent past. The development of the welfare state since the Second World War has generally been accompanied by substantial growth in women's paid employment, particularly employment within the welfare state itself, as well as by increasing numbers of lone mother families. To a limited extent this has shifted the locus of women's economic dependence away from male breadwinners and onto the state, both as employer and as provider of benefits and services. Patriarchy has been transformed in the sense that, under the welfare state, more women shoulder the dual burden of unpaid welfare work at home and lower-paid, lower-status paid employment in the labour market. The development of the welfare state has therefore made a central contribution to the modern reconstruction of patriarchy. A 'feminization of poverty' is sometimes said to have occurred in recent decades with increasing numbers of lone mothers and older women in poverty, that is outside the patriarchal family. This perhaps reflects a process in which women's poverty has become less hidden within the patriarchal family than it was in earlier periods. The increasingly visible poverty of lone mothers and older women outside the patriarchal family reveals the inadequacies of welfare systems based on the patriarchal family model.

Of course patriarchal gender division is not just enforced through ideology and policy concerning women's incomes; it is also maintained, for example, by obstructing their control of their fertility, by condoning male violence and by the reluctance of welfare states to relieve some of the burdens of caring, particularly for young children and the growing numbers of infirm elderly people. Women have struggled hard to resist and challenge both traditional and modern patriarchal processes in social policy. Hence the struggles for women's right to an independent income, for abortion on demand and against sterilization abuse, and for day care for young children are highlighted in this book as central examples of policy conflict over gender division and patriarchy in the welfare state. The available data on gender division and inequalities in welfare is clearly limited by the widespread use by official statisticians of the family household as a unit and the concept of the head of household. Data on fundamentally important areas like day care and abortion is not really gathered on a comparative basis. Nevertheless the pressures created by the modern women's movements have helped to generate more and more useful sources of information for critical policy analysis.

The Origins of Social Policy

Analysing policy origins requires an examination of the political and social pressures, the forces of agency, which push governments into policy formation. Mainstream policy analysis offers several schools of thought on how the welfare state came into being and how social policy is shaped. These give primacy respectively to

1   parliamentary party politics, both of the right and the left, in response to pressure and interest groups as well as direct electoral pressures (*party pluralism*)
2   corporatist negotiation between government, capital, organized labour and other corporate bodies such as the medical profession (*corporatist pluralism*)
3   the institutional capacity of the state itself in the shape of the civil service, and other public administrative structures and traditions (*state capacity*)
4   political class struggle pursued by trade union movements and parties of the left in advancing the interests of the working class (*neo-Marxism/socialism*).

In the policy analysis in subsequent chapters, we draw on and refer to these mainstream traditions where appropriate to the particular national and policy context. With the possible exception of the neo-Marxist model, such mainstream approaches tend to portray policy as being delivered 'from above' by establishment organizations and their leaders. In certain interpretations, one establishment figure such as Bismarck, Beveridge, Per Albin Hansson, Roosevelt, Kennedy, or Thatcher may be portrayed as a key initiator of policy change.

Radical approaches naturally tend to emphasize policy change as a response to pressures 'from below'. As well as conventional lobbying, pressure groups and interest groups, these pressures are also represented by more radical social movements and self-activity, and occasionally by agitation and uprising. Women's movements, civil rights movements, welfare rights movements and anti-racist movements in recent decades have been particularly significant in relation to the policy areas covered here. For the US perhaps the most celebrated example of such an analysis of policy change is the work of Piven and Cloward (1971; 1977). They argue that popular resistance and organization by poor people in the US, particularly the unemployed and the industrial workers in the 1930s and the civil and welfare rights movements in the 1960s, pushed governments into major programmes of social policy reform. Piven and Cloward have been criticized for not recognizing that 'the welfare-rights movement was a women's liberation movement' (L. Gordon, 1988: 623) too, and that women's demands for abortion rights and affirmative-action programmes were a complementary part of the radical challenge to the policy establishment. In Western Europe too, such popular struggles and social movements are undervalued in many accounts of the origins of social policy. Unquestionably what sociologists have called the 'new social movements' since the 1960s have been in the forefront of the pressures for welfare state expansion (Olofsson, 1988). Besides the women's movement, in Western Europe such new social movements have included the squatters, the student movements, the welfare rights movements and occasionally cataclysmic urban uprisings or riots. In some senses there is nothing particularly new about these movements, which are just the latest wave of radical and popular movements which have shaped social policy throughout modern history. The relationship of such movements to organized labour has been close in some respects and at some moments in history, particularly in Western Europe. However, frequently labour movements have distanced themselves from poor people's movements and radical, new social movements. Trade unions have advocated and defended elements of the welfare state when it is perceived to be in their interests to do so, but at other junctures such intentions have been undermined by divisions over workers' perceived political and economic interests. The relationship between popular struggles and movements on the one hand, and political and trade union organizations on the other hand, is raised by the continuing debate about welfare corporatism. Welfare corporatism envisages a contract between the citizenry and the welfare state to ensure that welfare and employment needs are adequately catered for in exchange for industrial peace and reasonable freedom of manoeuvre for capital. This contract is regularly negotiated between trade unions (representing the citizenry), employers and government. Such a system has apparently flourished in Sweden and Austria, and has been advocated strongly for Britain by writers such as Mishra (1984) and Lee and Raban (1988). Socialist theorists such as Korpi (1983) and Stephens (1979) see Swedish welfare corporatism as the essence of the democratic class struggle and the gradual transition to socialism. Some feminists, such as Adams and Winston (1980), advocate social democratic, quasi-corporatist feminist social policies on the Swedish model for the US. Some black activists in the US such as Wilson (1987) have put forward a programme for social democratic corporatism, as the means of achieving effective implementation of equal rights and employment rights legislation in order to redress the widening racial inequalities in the US. There are however several weaknesses in the corporatist vision of social policy. The first problem concerns representation; sometimes corporatist regimes, notably Weimar Germany, rest on too narrow a social base, so that for example the organized, male working class benefits, leaving the less powerful elements of the working class out of the social contract. Second, the corporatist welfare state is likely to inhibit relatively autonomous activity around welfare needs, the popular struggles which have always pushed the welfare state forward. It will almost inevitably try to stifle, control and divert such pressures into bureaucratic avenues.

Radical social movements of many kinds tend to be 'hidden from history' partly by their very nature and partly because of the establishment bias of historians and social scientists. This book attempts to keep the influence of pressures 'from below' in focus, though it is equally important not to overinflate their power. Another key theme is therefore that social policy emerges out of a continual conflict involving pressures 'from above' emanating from established economic and political forces in power and pressures 'from below' arising out of unmet welfare needs and movements advocating them.

The Substance of Social Policy

The substance of social policy covers the structure and functions of policy, or, if you prefer, its nature and purposes. Obviously policy substance is analysed empirically in terms of public finance, legislation, and adminis- tration of welfare (public and private), or, in other words, 'provision, providers and payment' as Higgins (1986: 226) puts it. Governments and policy analysts are adept at producing factual information on these matters, but this often gives relatively little to bite on in terms of the definition and the incidence of the welfare needs to which policy is responding, a question which rapidly leads back into the discussion of the impact of policy dealt with above. However, behind empirical questions about the substance of policy lie fundamental issues about its functions and purposes, that is what 'pulls' governments into social policy action or inaction. There are at least three ways of looking at this, elements of all three of which are taken up in later chapters.

First, the *idealist* approach, frequently adopted by political scientists, suggests that each welfare state has been shaped by a clash of ideologies out of which has emerged an institutionalized consensus or dominant ideology. A social policy consensus or welfare ideology reflects a semi- permanent, hegemonic resolution of the active political processes already discussed. Such an approach frequently produces a typology of welfare states and/or welfare ideologies, such as that adopted in this book to analyse the particular character of social policy ideology in each state. Conventionally such typologies are constructed on the basis of empirical data on welfare expenditures, rights and outcomes analysed in the context of the prevailing political hegemony. Looked at from critical perspectives on 'race', class and gender, the function of social policy is the interpre- tation and application of the political consensus in order to contain or restructure class, gender and 'race' relations. The functions of particular policies can then be assessed for the extent to which they maintain or transform the prevailing consensus. In this book the modern welfare consensuses in the four states under examination are characterized as Social Democratic (Sweden), the Social Market Economy (Federal Republic of Germany), Voluntarism and Liberalism (the United States) and Liberal Collectivism (Britain).

Second, more *sociological* approaches essentially theorize social policy as functioning to deal with the problems of order, social integration and social discipline in industrial societies. For example at moments of crisis, states have sometimes seized upon social policy reform in the attempt to engineer national solidarity – Bismarck in the 1880s, the Swedish Social Democrats in the 1930s, the Beveridge Report, Johnson's Great Society programmes of the 1960s. Even in the less solidaristic context of the present day, the more universalistic elements of the welfare state such as the British National Health Service continue to evoke a popular sense of national pride. The view that the substance of social policy represents the social rights of citizenship is a Fabian variant of the nationalist approach. Extending the social rights of citizenship, that is the coverage of needs and individuals, functions to promote social solidarity. Such views of the welfare state continue to have strong support in capitalist societies, particularly in Western Europe, but they have been heavily condemned by the New Right and the new social movements. The libertarian New Right see citizenship rights as imposing economic dependence of individuals on the state and a bureaucratically defined solidarity, thereby undermining the social disciplines imposed by markets, as well as individual and voluntary initiative. The new social movements suspect the concept of citizenship in practice as implicitly excluding many people, including migrant workers, lone mothers, dependent wives, long-term unemployed people and so on.

From a critical perspective a sociological function of the welfare state is the maintenance and legitimation of social divisions, notably class, patriarchal and racialized social relations. Substantively, social policy functions to impose labour discipline on the working class, to reproduce labour power on behalf of capital, to reinforce the patriarchal family and women's dual burden, and to reproduce the internal colonization of racialized groups. Such a critical, functionalist approach to policy analysis offers enormous insights and is frequently adopted in this book, but it also has severe limitations, as critics of neo-Marxist analysis of the welfare state in particular have pointed out, for example Lee and Raban (1988: 125–8). Essentially the limitation boils down to the emphasis on the continuity and inevitability of these functions, which underestimates the state's capacity for policy change and the pressures which social movements and class struggle bring to bear on social policy making and implementation. When used in an undiluted form, critical functionalism implies an unyielding logic of capitalism, patriarchy and racism. The critical analysis of policy substance should reveal that such 'logics' are constantly modified and shaped by the immediate political and economic context. These problems are aired further in the section on methodological issues below.

The third form of substantive policy analysis can be labelled *economic* approaches. Here social policy is conceived as a subdivision of economic policy, and the purposes of social policy are therefore largely subservient to the dictates of economic forces and economic policy making. In the real world of most Western governments, this is certainly the dominant view of social policy. Conventional economic analysis of social policy has been dominated by two schools of thought since the 1930s, commonly described as neo-classical microeconomics and Keynesian macroeconomics. Keynesianism was ascendant in the post-war boom years, while neo-classicism has seen a great revival since the stagflationary recession of the mid 1970s in such modern forms as monetarism and supply-side theory. Both traditions continue to exert enormous influence over social policy making. Neo-classicism starts from the premise that unrestrained markets tend to maximize welfare, except under special circumstances where 'externalities' (self-destructive effects of free-market competition) intervene or where 'the public good' is of paramount importance (e.g. national defence). Substantive policy is therefore analysed by neo-classical economists in terms of the extent to which it either undermines or contributes to the economic efficiency of private enterprise by limiting externalities and promoting the public good. Keynesianism is more intrinsically favourable towards the welfare state. Social policy is considered as an element of fiscal policy (government taxation, expenditure and borrowing) which is a key tool for regulating the whole national economy in order to counter inflation and unemployment, and to generate economic growth. Hence the welfare state is manipulated, expanded and contracted in order to stabilize the economy. Substantive social policy is therefore analysed by Keynesians in terms of whether it undermines or enhances macroeconomic equilibrium. Increased welfare expenditure may be used to generate economic demand and hence employment and economic growth. A reduction in welfare expenditure may be used to damp down inflationary economic demand and economic overactivity. Keynesians would argue that the growth of the welfare state from the 1940s to the 1970s generally reflected successful, expansionary macroeconomic management, and that the restraint of welfare state growth since then has contributed to the lowering of inflation. Neo-classicals would generally be more sceptical of the former claim. There is, of course, a lot of common ground between the two schools of thought, particularly as applied in practice by governments.

Neo-Marxist, anti-racist and feminist analyses of social policy tend to avoid pure economic approaches because of their functionalism and abstraction from human, social relations. Modern Marxian economics, however, in its critique of the neo-classical and Keynesian traditions, suggests that the post-1930s expansion of the welfare state has been part of the institutionalization of the 'Fordist regime of accumulation'. Under this regime improved real wages and increased welfare expenditure have 'both reconciled workers to the intensification of labour associated with Fordist methods of production [assembly lines etc.] and provided the rising mass consumption' (Clarke, 1988: 65) which has absorbed the growing volume of consumer goods pouring off the assembly lines. The limits of the Fordist regime have emerged since the mid 1970s, as capital has become unable to raise productivity sufficiently to counter the inflationary costs of ever rising consumer demand and the vastly increased costs of technological change. Cuts in real wages and in social expenditure can only provide a respite, as capital struggles to establish a new, post-Fordist regime of accumulation. In this analysis, the substantive development of social policy is intimately bound up with the fundamental disequilibria of capitalist economies, and the attempts of capital to overcome them.

Another central theme of this book is therefore that social policy and welfare expenditure have been crucially shaped by the crises, slumps and booms of capitalist economies. In the West, there have been three key periods in which the ideology of welfare has fundamentally shifted, all of which have been moments of international economic crisis – the 1870s, the 1930s and the 1970s. Hence the development of social policy is intimately connected with attempts, often deeply conservative, to resolve capitalist economic and consequent social crisis. The crisis of the 1870s eventually ushered in Bismarckian social insurance in Germany, New Liberalism in Britain and Progressivism in the US, a period of reform which peaked in the first decade of the twentieth century. The crisis of the 1930s generated the New Deal in the US, the fascist welfare state in Germany, the Social Democratic welfare transformation in Sweden and somewhat belatedly the Beveridge reforms in Britain. These ideological shifts towards various forms of welfare collectivism begun in the 1930s were consolidated in the post-war decades sustained by the economic boom. The expansion of the welfare state came to an end, and the welfare states have been reshaped to some extent in order to conform with more stringent and disciplinary capitalist requirements. The welfare state under capitalism is not irreversible, contrary to the intimations of Block (1987) and Therborn and Roebroek (1986). It is a movable feast, though even the neo-conservative project requires an authoritarian, regulatory welfare state to underpin the privatization of welfare services and benefits. The recessions of the mid 1970s and early 1980s saw considerable restructuring of industrial relations and social policy in the Western welfare states,

> on the basis of a fragmentation of the working class in the attempt to confine the aspirations of the working class within the limits of capital by confining wages and social expenditure within the limits of profitability. (Clarke, 1988: 86)

The fragmentation of the working class, enhanced by neo-liberal economic and social policies in some states, may take different forms, but racial and gender divisions are common to almost all industrial societies. The exploitation of such divisions has been fiercely resisted and it is by no means obvious that racial and gender inequalities have actually worsened over the past two decades in the states examined here. However, in those states such as the US and Britain where neo-liberalism has made its greatest impact, the fragmentation of the working class by income, status and occupation has become more pronounced, instanced by the wide use of the term 'underclass' to describe people living in poverty, whether benefiting from a welfare safety net or not. The recession of the early 1990s is likely to further these processes.

Methodological Issues

So far we have sketched out three areas of social policy analysis, within which a variety of analytical approaches, both mainstream and critical, have been indicated. The term 'mainstream' is used here to denote the work of liberal (in the American sense) and social democratic writers who are hegemonic in the West in the disciplines of sociology, political science and economics. The term 'critical' is used here to denote Marxist, feminist and anti-racist analysis, bearing in mind that there is enormous variation of perspective on social policy within these three, as discussed in detail for example in Williams (1989). In the mainstream, questions of 'race', gender and class (in the Marxian sense) are, at best, of peripheral concern. Needless to say, the literature on social policy analysis is dominated by debates within and between the mainstream disciplines, and also between them and Marxism. While feminist work and anti-racist work have established themselves to some extent as subdivisions within the main-stream disciplines, as yet they appear to be distinctly ghettoized from mainstream social policy analysis. The analytical discussion of the origins and substance of social policy offered above is essentially derived from debates in the mainstream and in Marxism, and it is far from clear how adequately they can be applied to feminist and anti-racist policy analyses. Clearly it is insufficient simply to tack on the latter to established conventions.

The distinction between idealist, sociological and economic forms of substantive policy analysis, as drawn above, is not meant to convey these as necessarily competing or mutually exclusive approaches. This book draws on key themes from each as already indicated. It almost goes without saying that an idealist welfare consensus or ideology of welfare is a fundamental element in forging sociological integration or social reproduc-tion, and also embraces assumptions about economic policy and ideology. Ideally a political economy of the welfare state has to keep all three forms of analysis in play. However the separation of the analysis of policy origins and policy substance implied from the start of the chapter is artificial and problematic, simply because policy analysis in practice inevitably carries assumptions about both origins and substance, whether this is made explicit or not.

Agency and Structure

In the discussion of policy origins the focus is on 'agency', the concrete institutions and human pressures shaping social policy. This implies that the substance of policy emerges from the resolution of power conflicts between the 'actors' or 'players'. Such a resolution will reflect the interests of and the balance of power between those forces of agency, whether the emphasis is on political parties, pressure groups, the class struggle, radical social movements or other significant players. In reading off the actual purposes and implementation of policies directly from the process of, say, 'political choice' (e.g. Heidenheimer *et al.*, 1990) or 'working class mobilisation' through social democratic politics (e.g. Stephens, 1979), the undertowing effect of the deep structures of economic development or ideological power is inevitably missing.

In the discussion of policy substance the focus is unquestionably on 'structure' (i.e. functionalist), that is suggesting that social policies fulfil functions essential for the maintenance of the political consensus, social integration and/or economic equilibrium and growth. Social policies therefore emerge of necessity to meet essential social and economic needs which increasingly cannot be met by unaided voluntary and private means. In critical analyses, the implication is that the welfare state functions to reproduce capital and capitalist social relations, patriarchal economic and social relations, and racialized economic and social divisions. Functionalism is open to the criticism of being ahistorical, deterministic and denying the possibility of radical change.

At a theoretical level, many Marxists and social theorists such as Giddens resolve the agency–structure problem by proposing that 'the notions of action [agency] and structure *presuppose one another* [emphasis in original] . . . [and have a] dependence which is a dialectical relation' (Giddens, 1979: 53). Nevertheless, in going about practical policy analysis, the methodological questions of agency and structure pose particular problems for critical approaches. On the one hand, the origins of policy and welfare reform must be sought in the activity and struggle of working class movements, women's movements and anti-racist pressures. On the other hand, it is difficult to concede that the patriarchal, capitalist and racist imperatives structurally embedded in the Western welfare states can be shed, short of a radical transformation to a quite different political economy. Critical analysis is therefore open to the accusation of 'wanting its cake, and eating it' – celebrating social policy reform and defending the welfare state as positive gains of pressure from below, while in the same breath portraying the functions of the welfare state as fundamentally oppressive. For socialists in relation to social policy, this dilemma was perhaps first confronted in the 1880s when Bismarck promulgated his social insurance schemes for organized workers, while at the same time criminalizing working class political organization. The measures aimed to stem the rising influence of Marxism within the workers' movement by conceding that an authoritarian capitalist state was capable of social reform in favour of the working class, or in this case its most politically and economically organized elements. Bismarck exploited the division among socialists between fundamentalists who denied the possibility of progressive reform and pragmatists pressing for piecemeal progressive reform of the state. The pragmatists were significantly strengthened by Bismarck's reforms, not least because they gained considerable bureaucratic power in the administration of the insurance schemes, while in reality only an élite of the working class benefited. Welfare reform, ever since, has often raised such dilemmas for socialists. For feminists in the Western welfare states, comparable dilemmas have been raised by the sex discrimination and equal opportunities measures of recent decades. On the one hand it can be argued that patriarchal power has not been significantly undermined except possibly for some middle class women. The emphasis on 'equal rights' feminism, particularly in the US, has not fundamentally challenged institutionalized sexism in the labour market, the home and the welfare state. On the other hand it can be argued that the women's movement has generated a gathering momentum behind such policies, which has at least opened up the possibility of the withering of patriarchy. In the US, and to a much lesser extent in Western Europe, similar dilemmas have also been raised by the civil rights and 'race relations' reforms since the 1960s. On the one hand it can be argued that such measures have failed to achieve significant positive changes in racial inequalities and racism institutionalized in the public and private sectors, while benefiting a small ethnic minority elite. On the other hand it can be argued that, subject to further reform and more effective implementation of present policies, irreversible changes in breaking down racial inequalities and racialized processes have been achieved. Here we will examine briefly some examples of critical policy analysis which have attempted to resolve the agency–structure questions.

In relation to a class analysis of social policy, attempts to resolve the agency–structure problem have been usefully described as a 'reconciled' (Jones, 1985: 47) or 'compromise' (Lee and Raban, 1988: 133) Marxist viewpoint, which attempts to reconcile the apparent contradictions of class struggle and capital logic. Hence Gough (1979: 65) suggests that periods of progressive welfare reform are explained by 'a coincidence of interests' between the welfare functions required by capital and the working class political pressures for the welfare state, but 'the respective importance of each varies over different policy issues'. As Gough implies, the question has to be resolved differently for particular policy examples and historical moments in different welfare states. Piven and Cloward (1971) is an outstanding example of a reconciled analysis which applied Marxian functionalism to the patriarchal and racist administration of welfare benefits in the US. They showed how the welfare benefits system was used in the southern states to push poor people, particularly black women, into low-paid employment. They also document how this system was, to some extent, overturned by the civil and welfare rights movements of the 1960s. As these struggles have continued the welfare system has become more liberal and less punitive, but the enforcement of low-paid employment in a gendered and racially structured labour market remains at root a function of the system.

Feminist analysts of social policy have also sought to reconcile agency and function. For example, according to L. Gordon (1988: 628–9) 'promoting the family-wage system is a better overall explanation of the social-control functions of the welfare state than has been previously offered . . . [but] the welfare state has, on balance, increased women's power'. Gordon emphasizes that the welfare state cannot successfully implement traditional patriarchal functions in the face of the reality of labour markets and of women's resistance. In her analysis of British social policy, Pascall (1986) puts a predominant emphasis on the functions of the welfare state in reproducing women's dependence and the social control of women's lives. However she also notes that 'one difficulty with such arguments is the danger of portraying women as victims of outside structures – whether of capitalism or of patriarchy' (Pascall, 1986: 238). Hence the vital significance of women's campaigning and protest over social policy issues. West European feminists such as Hernes (1987) and Borchorst and Siim (1987) have reconciled agency and structure by suggesting that the women's movements of recent decades have succeeded to some extent in transforming gender relations into a new form of patriarchy. According to Sassoon (1987: 180),

> these transformations in the nature of women's subordination and in our relative freedom, and the new contradictions which are arising, are missed by any functionalist view, with or without a Marxist label, which defines the relationship between women and the state in terms of how state policy maintains the nuclear family or acts to keep women in the home . . . Women are at one and the same time freer *and* enmeshed in a new web of dependence.

In the new patriarchy most women experience the dual burden of paid employment and unpaid domestic caring, less financially dependent on men perhaps but more dependent on state services.

Anti-racist analysis of contemporary social policy in Britain and the US has hardly dwelt on theoretical questions about agency and function. In the US attention has focused on the urgent debate about the real impact of the reforms achieved in the Second Reconstruction in the 1960s. Even the most critical analysts accept that African Americans made 'significant strides during the civil rights movement of the 1960s' (Pinkney, 1984: 177) and that the Second Reconstruction was by no means a 'splendid failure' unlike the First after the abolition of slavery (Marable, 1984b: 208). Yet radical writers like Pinkney and Marable certainly imply a structural or functionalist perspective in debunking the liberal myths of significant and continuing black economic and welfare progress. Hence

> the demand for racial parity within a state apparatus and economy which is based on institutional racism and capital accumulation at the expense of blacks and labour is fatally flawed from the outset. Racism and capitalist exploitation are logical and consistent by-products of the American system. (Marable, 1984b: 211)

Marable (1983) and Pinkney (1984) describe how the reforms of the 1960s helped to create a privileged black elite, brought very modest benefits to the mass of the black working class and contributed to the expansion and the disciplining of the urban underclass. Marable's analysis has understandably been described as 'structuralist' (Hochschild, 1988: 172), yet at the same time he puts enormous emphasis on the activity and resistance of African Americans in creating the Second Reconstruction and developing the possibility of the Third. In Britain anti-racist policy analysis has largely concentrated on the important task of elucidating and challenging racialized processes in particular policy fields, such as immigration, policing and housing. Resistance and pressure from the black communities and anti-racist movements have unquestionably had some positive impact on the welfare state. Yet racism continues to be structurally embedded in the labour market, the national 'culture' and the welfare state. As Williams (1989) has shown, several anti-racist schools of thought have emerged in British social science which reconcile the agency–structure questions in contrasting ways. If racism is essentially structurally functional, then racist processes have to be understood and challenged at the broadest cultural and macroeconomic levels (e.g. Gilroy, 1987; Miles, 1989). If racism is located essentially in institutionalized processes and in the actions of individuals and communities, it must be analysed and challenged in terms of local politics and community resistance (e.g. Ben-Tovim *et al.*, 1986; Ball and Solomos, 1990). Clearly these are differences of emphasis in relation to action and structure; they are by no means necessarily mutually exclusive.

The critical policy analysis adopted here attempts to reconcile some of the methodological and political dilemmas raised by the questions of agency and structure. There is no logical inconsistency in emphasizing agency in analysing the origins of policy, and structural functions in analysing the implementation and impact of policy. The welfare state in a patriarchal and racially structured capitalism is obviously capable of significant reform in favour of workers, women and racialized minorities, particularly for their most organized or most privileged elements. However such reforms only come about as a result of serious and sustained social and political pressures from those groups. Reforms, such as those mentioned above, restructured and transformed class, 'race' and gender relations in a long-term, positive direction, but such transformations are not irreversible nor do they necessarily open the way to the end of capitalism, patriarchy or racism. On the contrary it is manifestly clear that, particularly in periods of capitalist economic crisis, such progressive welfare reform is reversible, and that the welfare state can contribute to an adverse reinstatement of class, 'race' and gender divisions.

Comparing Welfare States

The very suggestion of 'comparative' analysis of social policy is problematic because it conjures up the hope that social scientists have developed rigorous methods and established schools of thought for comparing welfare states. Nothing could be further from the truth. Twenty years ago the field of study barely existed, though writing and research have expanded considerably since then. Attention has been particularly focused on the historical and political origins of benefits systems and on comparing aggregate public expenditures on social needs. In areas such as family policies and on questions such as the implementation and impact of policies, we only have a few pinpricks of light. In particular on questions of 'race', racial inequalities and racialized processes of social control, there is remarkably little critical, cross-national material. The outstanding exception is the work of Stephen Castles and his collaborators on migrant workers in Western Europe (Castles, 1984; Castles and Kosack, 1973). This work reviews the migration process, the citizenship status and the labour market position of racialized minorities in Western Europe. It shows that governments and racist popular pressures have denied full citizenship to racialized minorities, implying a strong convergence amongst all the states. Yet the data also suggests enormous differences in the welfare status of racialized groups, for example between Germany, Sweden and Britain. However, as yet, there has been no attempt to theorize these cross-national differences and the experiences of racialized groups in the modern welfare states.

Students of cross-national social policy under capitalism are faced with several kinds of literature. First, there is an increasing amount of useful data from international agencies and databases, such as that used for the statistical appendix in this book. The most important and accessible sources are perhaps the Organization for Economic Cooperation and Development (OECD), the European Commission (EC) and the Luxembourg Income Study (LIS). Such organizations have reworked national government statistics to put them on a comparable basis. The student is of course left to analyse and theorize the data, though obviously it contains its own biases shaped by the kinds of statistics which governments collect. Also agencies like OECD and the EC are not primarily concerned with comparative social policy. Their interest in the field is in examining the relationship between social policy and the regulation of public expenditure and labour markets. Such data tends to concentrate on direct public services and benefits, so that fiscal, occupational and private welfare forms are sometimes neglected, not least because governments often do not collect good data on these. Many critical parameters in terms of policy outcome like class, 'race' and gender feature marginally at best in most of this empirical data.

Systematic Comparison of Social Security Systems

Another form of cross-national material attempts to develop quantitative indices and concepts for comparing the origins and performance of welfare states. It is therefore perhaps the most deserving of the title 'comparative' in the eyes of social scientists. Here analysts use published and unpublished data from national government and international agencies such as those discussed above to develop comparative hypotheses about the development and impact of welfare states. Hence such analyses are very much subject to the critical limitations already mentioned regarding definitions of social welfare and of social divisions. We will discuss, briefly, three prominent examples of the genre. Wilensky (1975) compared social security spending as a proportion of GNP in sixty-four states for 1966. He concluded that 'economic level', that is GNP per head of population, 'overwhelms regime type as a predictor of social security effort' over the long term (Wilensky *et al.*, 1985: 9). In other words differing welfare ideologies and political regimes amongst nation states are much less significant than different levels of economic development, and related differences in demographic structure, in explaining differences in social security spending. Wilensky thus takes a structural functionalist position and supports the thesis of convergence, which suggests that industrialization and economic growth encourage convergent welfare state forms, despite differences in political ideology. Structural functionalist comparison such as this has become unfashionable in the wake of the sociological critiques of functionalism and of 'end of ideology' theses. However the inability of Western states to reverse fundamentally the growth of the welfare state, despite lower levels of economic growth, may lend some support to the thesis.

In direct contrast to structural functionalists, analysts who emphasize that 'politics matters' have attempted to derive a quantitative relationship between welfare spending and the political composition of governments in the West. The thesis here is that political forces of agency, particularly party politics, have had a predominant influence over welfare state development, and that therefore comparative political differences account in large measure for differences in welfare expenditure. Hence, for example, Alber (1983) compared social security expenditure and the political complexion of governments in thirteen Western states over the years 1949 to 1977 using quantitative indices. He found that 'left cabinets tended to increase the social expenditure ratio markedly stronger than cabinets which excluded socialist parties or centre-left coalitions' (Alber, 1983: 166). Such a view is sometimes described as the 'class mobilization' thesis, suggesting that the development of the welfare state is closely linked to the mobilization of the working class for parties of the left. Castles (1982) related social expenditures on education, income maintenance and health care in eighteen OECD states to a number of political variables. He found that 'partisan control of government' was a key determinant of patterns of social expenditure in the 1960s and 1970s, 'with strong parties of the Right acting as an impediment to expansion and social democratic and other parties, jointly or separately, serving as a stimulus' (Castles, 1982: 85). The restraint of welfare state growth in the 1980s has been more marked in states with predominantly conservative governments, so that recent experience lends some support also to this thesis. Both the structural functionalist and the class mobilization theses in these quantitative forms have naturally been subject to criticism for their insensitivity to the social and political histories of individual welfare states, limitations which are of course recognized by their authors (e.g. Castles, 1982: 88; Wilensky *et al.*, 1985: 12). Taking account of this kind of criticism but upholding a 'politics matters' approach, Esping-Andersen (1990) uses seven quantitative indices for measuring the accessibility, coverage and redistributive impact of benefits systems and four quantitative indices of 'welfare regime', that is characteristics of the political economy of welfare states. Applying these to the eighteen OECD states, reasonably close correlations are established between the nature of the benefits systems and the political regime types. The performance indices for pensions, sickness and unemployment benefits cover such critical questions as the balance between private and public pensions systems, the degree of universal access to benefits, and the extent of differential benefits for different social groups. One of these indices is the scale of 'de-commodification', that is the extent to which pensions, sickness and unemployment benefit schemes allow aged, sick and unemployed workers to survive economically outside the labour market. The de-commodification index therefore quantifies the extent to which social security benefits exempt such workers from offering their labour power as a commodity (Esping-Andersen, 1990: 54). Table 1.1 gives the de-commodification scores for 1980 for eighteen OECD welfare states, which Esping-Andersen divides into three clusters – the Anglo-Saxon and Scandinavian states at the extremes and the continental West European states in the middle range.

Table 1.1   *The rank order of welfare states in terms of combined de-commodification in old age pensions, sickness benefits and unemployment insurance, 1980*

State	De-commodification score
Australia	13.0
United States	13.8
New Zealand	17.1
Canada	22.0
Ireland	23.3
United Kingdom	23.4
Italy	24.1
Japan	27.1
France	27.5
FRG	27.7
Finland	29.2
Switzerland	29.8
Austria	31.1
Belgium	32.4
Netherlands	32.4
Denmark	38.1
Norway	38.3
Sweden	39.1
Mean	27.2

Source: Esping-Andersen, 1990: Table 2.2

The indices used to assess regime type take account of both economic development and political power, including indices very similar to those used by Wilensky and Castles. Esping-Andersen's model offers little support for the structural functionalist view, because 'economic development is negatively correlated with de-commodification' (Esping-Andersen,

1990: 52) and has little or no explanatory power in relation to the other indices of benefits systems' performance. The three political factors which all offer significant correlations with benefits systems' performance are the degree of 'left power' (working class mobilization) in government, electoral support for Catholic conservatism, and the extent of absolutism (authoritarian rule, limited franchise) in the history of each state. Aggregating these political indices produces three clusters of political regime types, which Esping-Andersen describes as 'liberal', 'conservative' and 'socialist', as in Table 1.2.

Table 1.2   *Clustering of welfare states with strong degrees of conservative, liberal and socialist regime attributes*

Strong liberal	Strong conservative	Strong socialist
Australia	Austria	Denmark
Canada	Belgium	Finland
Japan	France	Netherlands
Switzerland	FRG	Norway
United States	Italy	Sweden

Source: Esping-Andersen, 1990: Table 3.3

The liberal welfare states tend to have benefits systems in which stigmatized means-tested assistance has a central role, social insurance benefits are modest and private benefits are promoted by the state. The liberal political regimes are characterized by a relative absence of both working class mobilization for the left and of Catholic and absolutist mobilization for the right. Comparing Tables 1.1 and 1.2, the US, Canada and Australia fit well with the typology. For other states, such as the UK and Japan, low de-commodification does not appear to correlate well with liberal regime type. The conservative welfare states emphasize social insurance over both means-tested and private benefits, but in forms which tend to maintain firm class and status distinctions, so that income redistribution through benefits systems is low. Such regimes tend to be characterized by a Catholic conservative tradition and absolutist tendencies in their political histories. Comparing Tables 1.1 and 1.2, Italy, France, FRG and to a lesser extent Austria fit reasonably well with this model. The socialist (or social democratic) states have achieved the most universal and most class redistributive benefits systems, modifying the class structure but by no means removing it. Labour market measures rather than benefits are deployed to discipline and support the unemployed and those threatened with unemployment. The political regime is characterized not only by strong working class mobilization in government, but also by the ability of social democratic parties to form 'class coalitions' with other groups such as farmers. Clearly the correlation between de-commodification and socialist regime is strongest in the Netherlands, Denmark, Sweden and Norway, but the model fits less well for states such as Finland and Belgium.

It almost goes without saying that this typology is based on correlations which merely suggest tendencies rather than direct relationships. Clearly too Esping-Andersen's comparative model has a limited application to the issues with which this book is concerned. 'Race' and gender play no part in his quantitative analysis. Questions, for example, around gender discrimination and assumptions of women's dependence built into benefits systems are not included in the performance indices, nor is women's political mobilization included amongst the regime type indices. Nevertheless the model carries strong implications about the class divisions of welfare, or what Esping-Andersen describes as 'the welfare state as a system of stratification'. The indices of benefits systems' performance suggest strong division along social status and occupational social class lines, although these concepts are not explicitly developed on a quantitative basis. The index of working class mobilization carries with it the implication that class (in a Marxian sense) shapes welfare politics very directly. The Esping-Andersen model is only applied to pensions, sickness and unemployment benefits and to labour market policies. It has not been applied to policy areas such as health care, family benefits and services, education, housing and so on. Also, while the model does take into account private and occupational benefits, fiscal welfare, such as tax reliefs on pensions contributions, cannot be accounted for. Of course most of these limitations are imposed by the absence of relevant data from national governments. Despite the limitations, Esping-Andersen's model is the most successful attempt thus far to develop a quantitative approach to a class analysis of comparative social policy. The following chapters of this book take an example of each of the three types of welfare state generated by the model, with the addition of Britain, a welfare state which reflects an odd mixture of the 'socialist' and 'liberal' types.

Structured Diversity: Comparing Social Security Systems

Beyond the quantitative literature discussed so far, qualitative comparative analysis of social policy is dominated by a 'structured diversity' approach, which emphasizes the diversity or even the uniqueness of each welfare state in its national social and historical context. The diversity may be structured by domestic political processes, cultural values, economic forces, demographic factors or whatever. The last two decades have seen a growing number of such texts, sometimes confining themselves to single policy areas and/or a few states. Notable examples, which all offer their own structural emphases, are Rimlinger (1971), Rose and Shiratori (1986), Ashford (1986), Friedman *et al.* (1987), Morris (1988), Castles (1989), Heidenheimer *et al.* (1990), Baldwin (1990) and Mishra (1990). Whether this kind of literature deserves the accolade 'comparative' is a matter of debate, since methodical and/or theoretical comparison is often either underdeveloped or absent. Many of these texts devote a chapter to each welfare state, which in itself tends to emphasize diversity and uniqueness, especially if the chapters are written by different people! All of them are written broadly within the mainstream pluralist or social democratic perspectives of political science. This book too adopts a 'structured diversity', state by state method which has been eloquently advocated by Castles (1989: 12–13), who argues that the

> investigation of particular cases is not a return to the particularistic over-determination of single nation histories . . . the logic of comparative explanation does not suddenly disappear when we are treating intentional, institutional and historical variables. Learning from a particular national experience will always take particular forms, but patterns of human action and purposes, especially as moulded by the fact of living in societies constrained by common structural parameters, are likely to manifest certain intrinsic similarities as well as residual differences.

Here as in most other structured diversity approaches, it is sometimes left to readers to assess these intrinsic similarities and residual differences in the light of their own knowledge and experiences of welfare states. It is suggested in particular that the diversity of welfare states is structured by the common features of 'race', class and gender divisions and of capitalist economic development already outlined.

Comparing Health Care Systems

Most of the cross-national research on social policy discussed so far concentrates on social insurance and social assistance benefits. Cross-national research on health care policy is for the most part empirical and descriptive in nature, being primarily 'addressed to policy planners, who pay more attention to pragmatic goals' (Wilensky et al., 1985: 48). However the diversity of public interventions in health care, of power struggles within health care systems and of health status outcomes is striking. There has been relatively little analysis or theoretical discussion about the extent to which cross-national factors have shaped this diversity. The key political dimensions for comparative analysis which suggest themselves from policy analysis of national health care systems are, on the one hand, the influence of the political context (i.e. the welfare consensus) and, on the other hand, the influence of the medical profession. Indeed most accounts of the origins and administration of health care systems focus on the conflicts and the establishment of consensus between national governments (or health bureaucracies regulated by the state) and medical professional organizations. There are sharp differences of interpretation as to the relative importance of such exogenous and endogenous players (see Wilensky, 1975: 51–2). In the state by state analysis, here, it is suggested that both the medical profession and national politics have played a critical role, the relative influence of each being shaped by the national context. Comparative analysis of the increasingly significant movements of health care consumers and workers barely exists, but the women's health movement is widely recognized as having exerted an international influence on health care provision. The gay movement must surely take the credit for pushing the health care issues surrounding AIDS onto policy agendas. Although mainstream policy analysis of health care seems dominated by pluralist, political choice perspectives, there are a number of socioeconomic dimensions which structure the diversity of health care systems. First, all the Western welfare states witnessed a rapid rise in public expenditure on health care as a proportion of GNP in the post-war boom decades, followed by varying degrees of restraint since the mid 1970s (Tables A.20, A.21, A.22). This is linked in part to another 'structural' dimension, namely the cross-national influence of scientific medical knowledge and technology, allied with the interests of increasingly transnational pharmaceutical and medical technology corporations. Health care can be usefully conceived as a major industry, the hospital as a factory, fundamentally shaped by the development of industrialism, the macroeconomy and the industrial class struggle. The functionalism and reductionism of such an analysis, which obviously underemphasizes national differences in health care, is unfashionable. Yet the evidence from the states examined here suggests that health care is being increasingly commodified as techniques of management and cost control, for example, are imported from industry. Such structural convergences in health care policy have to be kept in mind in pursuing critical comparison.

Comparing Family Policies

Family policy is a much less clearly demarcated area of welfare state intervention than health care and social security. It is also only quite recently and rather reluctantly that governments have been forced to consider the impact of social policies on the achievement (or lack of it) of equal opportunities and equal rights for women. 'The family' continues to be considered as a private area of civil society, into which the state should only intervene at moments of crisis. The Nazi and Stalinist experiences with explicit family policy continue to give the very idea a bad name. This ideology of non-intervention in the family coexists very awkwardly with the modern array of social policies, almost all of which carry direct implications about, for example, the rearing of children and the care of other 'dependants' such as the infirm elderly. This book confines itself to examining selected aspects of family policy, namely income maintenance and labour market policies in relation to women, child benefits, abortion, pre-school day care and parental leave. Cross-national study of family policies and the impact of social policies on women has been particularly circumscribed by the inadequacy of national government statistics and cross-national incompatibility of parameters (e.g. definitions of day care and part-time employment). In some critical areas such as access to abortion services, sterilization abuse and the demand for day care, governments may be reluctant to collect good data for political reasons. The cross-national diversity of family policies, at least in the areas specified above, has been structured by a number of common functions and political concerns of the modern capitalist state, some of which have a longer history. These include:

1   care and control of poor families deviating from or unable to sustain the patriarchal norm, mostly lone parent families
2   fertility control measures, more or less explicitly targeted at poor people and racialized groups
3   pronatalism, that is the use of family policy measures to attempt to increase the birth rate, sometimes targeted away from poor people and racialized groups
4   interventionist family policy as a means of promoting state investment in child development or children as 'human capital'
5   the deployment of women's paid and unpaid labour, in and out of the labour market.

The relative prominence of these functions or concerns varies considerably from state to state and in different historical periods. A wide range of social forces have shaped such policies including the churches, charities, women's organizations, the medical profession and educationalists. Although party politics has generally not featured a great deal in family policy making, the wider political context and the welfare consensus have inevitably shaped the form and content of family policies. In recent years, several women writers have developed comparative analyses of family policies, predominantly dealing with the relation between women's paid employment and family policies and taking up the methodological questions about agency and structure discussed above.

Adams and Winston (1980) compared a range of policies affecting the paid employment of women in Sweden, the US and the People's Republic of China. They conclude that neither the level of economic development nor direct pressure from social movements and political parties was very significant in explaining governments' family policies. They develop what might be described as a 'state capacity' explanation, suggesting that the key difference between the US and Sweden is the differing ideological and administrative capacities of their governments to adopt 'full employment' policies, and interventionist and centrally coordinated approaches to family policy. Ruggie (1984) compared policies on women's paid employment and on day care in Britain and Sweden, reaching broadly similar conclusions to Adams and Winston. According to Ruggie (1984: 19) 'the explanation . . . for the differences in British and Swedish policies for women is grounded in a theory of state/society relations . . . the nature of these relations varies according to the particular state formation.' Ruggie applies a conventional dual typology of welfare states to these areas of family policy. British policy is analysed as an example of the 'liberal welfare model' in which, at the policy making level, traditional ideas about women's role remain pre-eminent and labour market policy for women is market-led. Sweden's policies are analysed as an example of 'the corporatist welfare model' in which active intervention in the labour market to promote women's paid employment and even gender equality is legitimate. Ruggie's 'corporatist' model corresponds to Esping-Andersen's 'social democratic' regime type. Although he does not analyse family policies, Esping-Andersen (1990: 27) notes that the 'conservative' welfare states (not considered by Ruggie) are 'strongly committed to the preservation of traditional family-hood. Social insurance typically excludes non-working wives, and family benefits encourage motherhood. Day care and similar family services are conspicuously underdeveloped.' The analysis of family policies in the US, Britain and the FRG presented below suggests that differences in family policies between conservative and liberal regimes are in fact relatively insignificant in comparison to the differences with social democratic regimes. The application of comparative typologies derived from analysis of benefits systems does not provide a very good fit for the analysis of family policies. Kamerman and Kahn (1978: 3) have made a useful distinction between welfare states with an *implicit* family policy such as Britain, the US and perhaps the FRG, and those with an *explicit* family policy such as France and Sweden.

In contrast with the analyses above, Norris (1987) offers evidence in support of the view that party politics matters, at least in relation to some aspects of family policy. Norris sought correlations among the OECD states between indices of the economic and social positions of women on the one hand, and macroeconomic, party political and social variables (e.g. the strength of Catholicism) on the other hand. She found that GNP per capita correlated with the proportion of women in paid employment, while party political complexion of governments did not. Social democratic governments, however, had a significant positive impact on women's earnings as a proportion of men's and also on breaking down occupational segregation by gender in the labour market. Right-wing governments (rather than Catholicism) correlated with restrictive legal rights to abortion and limited day care provision. Access to abortion services was, however, clearly correlated with the strength of Catholicism as well as GNP per capita. Using a large sample of states and a range of indices thus suggests a more complex structured diversity in the comparative positions of women and in comparative family policies than indicated by state capacity analyses. Rubery (1988) indicates some other aspects of this diversity. Comparing Britain, France, Italy and the US she found no association between public expenditure on benefits and services for families, and either the level of lone motherhood or the proportion of women in paid employment. This points to the possible ineffectiveness of family policies in some of its aims, or at least the contradictory functions which such policies frequently embrace. The treatment of lone mothers is a vivid illustration. They may be encouraged to find paid employment and not to depend on benefits, while at the same time the virtues of full-time parenthood are extolled by welfare agencies and politicians. In comparing women's labour market position in the four states, Rubery concludes that it is impossible to say which is better or worse for women. Thus societies which offer more flexible employment forms, providing opportunities to combine domestic with wage work, may also offer lower pay and status, associated with these types of employment (for example part-time work in Britain; informal sector work in Italy). Opportunities to maintain employment continuity and status over the family formation stage (for example in France and Italy), have to be set against the disadvantages of taking on full dual burdens of domestic and wage labour, or may only be taken up because of the availability of family assistance based on unpaid female labour. Reliance on state welfare provision may provide a more equitable basis for women to enter the labour market, but where this provision is linked, as in France, to strong state support for the ideology of the family and motherhood, it has contradictory impacts on women's labour market and social roles. (Rubery, 1988: 280–1)

Clearly the labour market strategies of women and employers, as well as governments, vary enormously according to aspects of the socioeconomic, demographic and cultural context, apart from the state's capacity and direct political factors. The state by state analysis here can only throw some shafts of light on this diversity.

Summary and Organization of the Book

Cross-national policy analysis, as attempted here, adopts a critical, structured diversity approach. Welfare states are uniquely shaped by their political, cultural, social and economic context within a nation state. However, social policy is also structured by common elements shared by wealthy Western states, notably the context of patriarchal and racially structured capitalism. All the welfare states have had a contradictory impact on class, 'race' and gender divisions. They owe their origins to a combination of pressures from those advantaged and those disadvantaged by the social structure prominently divided by class, 'race' and gender. The substance of social policy is structured by a number of ideological, sociological and macroeconomic requirements necessary to the continued survival of modern capitalism, which are historically redefined under changing economic and social circumstances. Most importantly, welfare states have been significantly restructured in periods of international economic crisis, the inter-war years and the period since 1974.

The main chapters of this book are case studies of four welfare states, Sweden, the Federal Republic of Germany, the United States and Britain. The discussion covers the decades since the inter-war restructuring, but concentrates as far as possible on the contemporary period. The US, the FRG and Sweden are often held up as clear examples of three contrasting forms of welfare regime, Esping-Andersen's (1990) 'three worlds of welfare capitalism'. Britain is included as a fourth case study, being something of a hybrid and illustrating the significance of diversity and uniqueness amongst welfare states. Each case study is structured around five headings: ideology and welfare expenditure; income maintenance policies and outcomes; 'race' and racial inequalities; women and family policies; the health care system. This structure evolved as a pragmatic solution to the inevitable problems of integrating critical perspectives into the empirical material of conventional policy analysis without losing a sense of structural, cross-national commonalities in the diversity. Three policy areas are focused on: income maintenance, family and health care. Income maintenance or social security policy clearly lies at the heart of the welfare state. Considerations of the class, 'race' and gender dimensions of income inequality, poverty and labour market processes are essential to critical policy analysis. Family policies clearly reflect the patriarchal structure of welfare states, and the examples of abortion, lone motherhood and day care have been particular foci of struggle by contemporary women's movements. Health care systems exhibit enormous cross-national diversity in their financial and administrative forms. Yet there are comparable structural conflicts around resources, management and health status inequalities. The data used here has been trawled from international agencies, government statistics and social science research sources, as discussed above. The limitations of the available data are colossal, such as the unknown extent of unmet needs, incompatible definitions for comparative purposes, absence of critical data on class, 'race' and gender divisions, and many other forms of bias shaped by established social science and government norms. The reader must decide what has the ring of truth.

2
Sweden: the Social Democratic Welfare State

Most enthusiastic advocates of the welfare state under capitalism see Sweden as having achieved the closest to the ideal. For most of the post-war period Sweden has achieved healthy economic growth, 'full' employment, and one of the highest standards of living in the world, combined with the largest, most expensive and possibly most egalitarian state welfare system in the West. It is almost as if the Swedes have obstinately defied gravity – or in this case the 'logic' of capitalism. Detractors on the free-market right suggest that this has been achieved by creating a particular form of authoritarianism at the expense of individual, family and entrepreneurial freedoms, a system whose rigidity may eventually be self-destructive. On the left, many Marxists and feminists would point out the limitations of the achievement in view of the enduring structures of class and patriarchy in modern Swedish society, suggesting that the Swedish welfare state only modestly blunts the oppressions and inequalities which capital and patriarchy exploit. With the growth of the global economy, the emergence of the united capitalist states of Europe and the faltering of the Swedish economy in the 1980s, the survival of the present Swedish welfare state is increasingly coming into question.

There is no dramatic turning point from which the modern welfare state in Sweden can be said to have begun. Policy history in Sweden is a story of gradualism, a slow but fairly inexorable development of social welfare. As many analysts point out, this reflects a political tradition of compromise and coalition in an ethnically and confessionally homogeneous society, which has not been engaged in imperialist excursions or wars since the industrial revolution. The clearest moment of ideological shift towards the welfare state occurred in the 1930s when the Social Democratic Party (SAP) for the most part abandoned both Marxist and neo-classical or deflationary economic policies in favour of Keynesianism. Initially on the basis of counter-cyclical economic policies involving public works and food price subsidies, the SAP was able to dominate Swedish coalition governments from 1932 onwards, with the exception of a period of centre-right coalition government from 1976 to 1982. During the 1930s what has been described by Korpi (1978; 1983) as a historic compromise between capital and labour was forged: on the one hand, private capital was guaranteed economic freedom, particularly from the threat of nationalization; on the other hand, beyond the economic sphere, the Social Democrats, in the name of the people rather than the working class, had overwhelming influence over state policy. In the 1940s and 1950s there was in fact only modest growth of the welfare state, albeit largely on a universalist and progressive class redistribution basis. The 1960s and 1970s saw rapid expansion of welfare benefits and services on a more neutral distributional basis, solidifying middle class commitment to the welfare state. Policies were also shaped by the pressure to recruit more women into paid employment. The gathering problems of stagflation, unemployment and growing union militancy from the late 1960s prompted governments to adopt a stout Keynesian defence of the welfare state until the early 1980s, keeping unemployment relatively low. The Swedish response to the fiscal crisis of the state and recession in the 1970s was therefore quite different from most other capitalist welfare states. Since the recession of the early 1980s, however, the growth of the welfare state has been all but halted with governments gradually moving towards more stringent anti-inflationary wage and public expenditure restraint policies.

Ideology and Welfare Expenditure

The Social Democratic Hegemony

It is fruitless to search for a clear theoretical or programmatic statement of the Swedish Social Democratic conception of the welfare state. It has to be reconstructed from the pragmatic, piecemeal development of social policy over the last century. Policy formation by the Social Democrats since the 1930s has been shaped by two broad influences – populism and socialism. Populism entails seeking a popular mandate, a broad appeal within the electorate, and thus coalition and compromise with social groups and interests structurally hostile to socialism. Socialism involves the develop-ment of economic democracy, political accountability, social equality and the advancement of working class interests. Having dominated govern-ment for so long, the Swedish Social Democrats have continually wrestled with the contradictions between populism and socialism. Commentators often convey the ideology of Swedish Social Democracy either as being essentially socialist, for example Korpi (1983) or Stephens (1979), or alternatively as having abandoned socialism in favour of a progressive liberal collectivism, for example Tingsten (1973). Neither is the case; socialist ideology and rhetoric remain the rationale for the party's existence and a benchmark for ideological renewal, but populist pragmatism and political realism shape much of the party's policies in government.

In the 1930s, three elements of this welfare ideology came to promi-nence. First, 'the People's Home', to describe the future welfare society, was characterized by 'equality, concern, cooperation and helpfulness' (quoted by Korpi, 1978: 84). This famous phrase was coined by the party leader Per Albin Hansson in 1928. The emphasis on 'the people' signalled consciously the party's intention to move beyond an emphasis on the needs of the working class. The party was soon to form a successful coalition with the Farmers' Party. Later in the 1950s the SAP dropped its alliance with the farmers, turning to the growing ranks of white collar workers and professionals as allies of the blue collar working class. The word 'home' implied the re-creation of a 'sharing, just community on a national basis . . . a person would not take more than his or her share, but neither would anyone stand outside the system of community provision' (Heclo and Madsen, 1987: 158). The 'People's Home' connects directly with a second idea, that of 'solidarity' as a limit to competition and inequality. This translated into a keen emphasis on universal, flat-rate benefits as the underpinning of the welfare state in the 1940s, and also trade union commitment to solidaristic wages policy, adopted in the late 1930s. This emphasizes that wages should be related to workers' performance rather than capital's profitability, and also that pay differentials should be minimized. A third element of Social Democratic ideology from the 1930s is the commitment to Keynesian counter-cyclical economic policies, particularly the use of infrastructural public employment and labour market policies to limit unemployment. In practice in the 1940s and 1950s the principles of the Social Democratic ideology of the welfare state were essentially the commitment to full employment and the provision of universal flat-rate benefits as protection against fundamental risks of sickness, low income etc. This had of course much in common with Beveridge's Liberal Collectivist conception of the welfare state as incorporated by Labourist social democracy in Britain.

During the 1960s pressure built up on the leadership of the SAP to renew socialist commitment to equality of outcome in terms of both class and gender. This was inspired by the student movement, the rediscovery of poverty within the welfare state, the rebirth of feminism and other radical, new social movements. A turning point was reached in 1969 with the party's adoption of a policy document calling for increased social equality, arguing that this was the primary issue faced by the labour movement. It said that

> an equalization of living conditions is a means for attaining altered human relations, a better social climate . . . Those who are left behind, with insufficient resources to contribute to the common good, represent an obstacle to both efficiency and desirable social change . . . In the Social Democratic conception, there is no reason that extreme differences in endowments, in health, in intellect, or in work capacity should lead to an assignment of standards and life chances that differentiate some from others. (quoted by Heclo and Madsen, 1987: 174–5)

The report highlighted wage and salary differentials, poverty, unemployment and gender inequalities as issues which should be tackled more energetically, arguing that the welfare state should build upon Beveridgean universalism 'through "targeted" reforms for groups with special difficulties' (Heclo and Madsen, 1987: 178), that is those who had been left behind in the post-war economic boom. This 'equality movement' had a considerable impact on SAP ideology and policy making in the 1970s, above all perhaps with the introduction of sharply progressive income tax in 1971. It led to a great expansion of services and staffing within the welfare state with some modest success in improving equality of outcome.

During the 1970s the energy of the rejuvenated trade union wing of the labour movement was focused on the question of 'economic democracy', the achievement of more popular direct control of private industry and commerce without nationalization or socialization. The proposal was to establish trade union controlled 'wage-earner funds' out of a substantial profits tax; the funds would build up stock holdings in leading companies, thereby gaining substantial leverage over their management and investment policies. The pressure for 'economic democracy' in part reflected concern about the growth of structural unemployment and workers' inability to influence decision making in increasingly transnational firms, which resulted in long-term deterioration in the welfare of working class communities. In 1983 with the labour movement in retreat in the wake of the recession, the government implemented an extremely watered down version of the wage-earner funds, largely funded by workers' contributions and unlikely to have much influence over capital's decision making (Pontusson, 1987). In the 1980s the movements for equality of outcome and for economic democracy have declined in their influence, as the SAP leadership has increasingly adopted a 'new realist' posture under ideological pressure from the New Right and the fiscal crisis of the state. The attack on anti-capitalist ideology in the SAP was led by Kjell-Olof Feldt who was the Minister of Finance from 1982 to 1990. As far back as 1984 he complained that 'anti-capitalist agitation still plays a role in the Labour movement' (Linton, 1984). On April 17th 1989, interviewed by *The Financial Times*, he said that the market economy 'is a dynamic and efficient economic system, which produces the best results in this imperfect world . . . as long as it is influenced by the democratic forces operating in a free society'. Reading behind his public statements and his policies, it is clear that he was 'trying to drag Sweden forward through a radical programme of "free-market" reforms' (Woodall, 1990: 15), including tax and benefit cuts, higher unemployment and the encouragement of private for-profit health and welfare services. Despite Feldt's resignation in early 1990 in response to the SAP leadership's failure to support his policies, the influence of such new realist, pro-capitalist or market socialist views is gaining ground in the SAP. In the 1990s the party therefore faces something of a serious ideological crisis over future social and economic policy.

Welfare Expenditure

Not surprisingly Sweden has the highest level of public expenditure on social welfare amongst the capitalist states. In 1981, the last year for which comparable statistics are available, real social expenditure (Table A.1) accounted for 33.5 per cent of GDP, compared to 15.9 per cent in 1960 which was not far above the OECD average in that year. Until the 1960s the actual levels of welfare expenditure in Sweden lagged far behind what one might have expected from the Social Democratic hegemony. Therborn (1989: 220–2) explains what he calls this 'social lag' in terms of the tradition of low taxation due to non-belligerence, fiscal conservatism and workers' resistance to indirect taxation. The OECD figures also reveal that the growth of welfare spending as a proportion of GDP growth in Sweden in the years 1960–75 was not far above the OECD average, but in the years 1975–81 real social welfare spending increased four times as fast as the economy as a whole, twice as fast as the OECD average in that period (Table A.1). In other words, Swedish governments protected and expanded the welfare state during the 1970s recession, reflecting a progressive interpretation of Keynes, unlike most other capitalist welfare states. Ironically, for all but one year of the 1975–81 period the SAP was in opposition, though the centre-right coalition did not deviate significantly on welfare spending policy. Public expenditure as a whole was down from a peak of 68 per cent of GDP in 1982 to 61 per cent in 1989. According to Woodall (1990: 15),

> the burden of public-spending cuts since 1982 has fallen particularly heavily on investment projects, and public infrastructure is falling apart in some cities. There are also serious staff shortages in education, health care and the police. Common complaints are that there are too few state nursery-school places and that waiting lists for operations such as hip replacements or eye cataracts can be more than two years long. True, compared with London, say, most public services seem to be running fairly well . . . But Swedish voters perceive a deterioration in their services.

The Swedish welfare state is of course financed by very high levels of personal and corporate taxation compared with most other Western states. Although income and wealth taxes are steeply progressive, a skilled industrial worker on an average wage in the late 1980s incurred local and national income tax at about 40 per cent of gross income (Swedish Institute, 1988), a figure which has gradually come down from around 50 per cent in the late 1970s. Employers pay a 43 per cent payroll tax for social welfare contributions, which it may be argued either is effectively a deduction from wages or inflates prices. Social insurance contributions by employees are only significant in financing unemployment benefit. Otherwise the welfare state in Sweden is financed largely from direct central government, local government and payroll taxes (Olsson, 1989: Graphs 2 and 3). A massive tax cutting reform is due to be implemented in 1990 and 1991, which the government claims will preserve its progressive effects. Indirect and wealth taxes are due to be increased, but the tax reform will undoubtedly have to be paid for by more cuts in public spending. The future of welfare expenditure in Sweden will no doubt reflect the outcome of the ideological struggle within and beyond the SAP as discussed above.

Income Maintenance Policies and Outcomes

Income Inequality and Poverty

Table A.2 gives an indication of the comparatively enormous significance of cash benefits from the welfare state as an element of gross incomes in Sweden. In 1980 cash benefits contributed 29.2 per cent of average gross income, compared to 17.2 per cent in the UK, 16.5 per cent in the FRG and a mere 8.0 per cent in the US. To pay for this, income tax took 28.5 per cent of average gross income (that includes public and private transfers, property income and so on, as well as income from employment), compared to between 13 and 17 per cent in the other three states. Evidence for the comparatively progressive effects of this income taxation and income maintenance regime in Sweden comes from statistics on the distribution of disposable household income, adjusted for household size (Tables A.3 and A.4). In 1972/3 and 1980 the bottom 20 and 40 per cent of the distribution had very much higher proportions of total disposable/net incomes than in most of the other capitalist welfare states, while the top 20 per cent had significantly smaller proportions. Gini coefficients (Table A.5) also indicate that Sweden has consistently had one of the most equal disposable income distributions in the West, very significantly more equal than the other countries in this study. Recent data from Olsson (1986: Table 23) and Åberg *et al.* (1987: Table 8.11) suggests that the Swedish welfare state, at least up to the early 1980s, continued to redistribute incomes on a relatively progressive basis. Åberg *et al.* (1987: 140) conclude that 'the tax and transfer systems seem to have a more redistributive effect in 1980 than was the case in 1967', but most of the change occurred in the late 1960s and early 1970s in the wake of the tax reform of 1971 and the development of the state earnings-related pension. From the mid 1970s to the early 1980s (and probably since then) there was little significant change in income distribution (Olsson, 1986: 58; Åberg *et al.*, 1987: 151). The professional and managerial classes have been able to maintain their position, in part because of the large and increasing proportion of women in this class who are in full-time paid employment, compared to the other occupational social classes (Åberg *et al.*, 1987: 136). Using an indicator called 'the household consumption surplus' which 'indicates how much money households have available after deducting from disposable income those expenditures required to maintain a certain basic standard' of welfare including housing, Åberg *et al.* show that the distribution of consumption has become less equal since the 1960s. The professional and managerial class has benefited increasingly and differentially from various tax reliefs, particularly on mortgages, to enhance its living standards relative to the lower classes, over and above the basic necessities. When wealth and consumption are taken into account the professional and managerial class 'despite a long-term income equalization, has succeeded in holding on to its solid lead in economic resources . . . probably mostly due to the use of tax relief and the high level of inflation during the 1970s' (Åberg *et al.*, 1987: 150). The same is likely to be true for the 1980s, probably more so.

Table A.6 indicates that in 1980 5.0 per cent of the Swedish population were poor, using the economic distance poverty measure. Not surprisingly this was the lowest amongst the four states examined here, though not that much lower than the FRG at 6.0 per cent. There is apparently little other data on poverty in Sweden. There are no national scale rates for means-tested social assistance, and anyway, as Olsson (1987: 73–4) points out in relation to Sweden, 'the humiliating nature of means-tested social assistance makes it . . . extremely difficult to use as an indicator of both relative and absolute poverty'. Unlike the situation in many other welfare states, most lone mothers and low-income old people in Sweden do not have to resort to social assistance because of the development of the pensions and benefits systems. Nevertheless these groups together with the long-term unemployed are in relative poverty in modern Sweden. Here we shall examine the position of social assistance claimants, the unemployed and women in the income maintenance system to analyse the position of the relatively poor within the welfare state.

Old Age Pensions

The statutory old age pension schemes accounted for 85.5 per cent of old age pension payments in 1980 in Sweden, which is unsurprisingly a much higher proportion than the average amongst capitalist states (Table A.8). On top of the statutory pension, about half of Sweden's old age pensioners receive payments from an occupational or private insurance pension. There are two statutory pension schemes, a basic flat-rate payment supplemented by an earnings-related scheme for higher earners called ATP. All Swedish citizens and foreigners settled on a long-term basis are entitled to the basic, flat-rate pension which was introduced in 1948; a much lower, universal statutory pension had been in existence since 1913. The flat-rate pension was annually indexed to prices as early as 1951, but in fact its real value against retail prices increased by 350 per cent between 1949 and 1984 (Olsson, 1986: Table 8). In this important respect, Sweden contrasts vividly with the other countries in this study in having a universal payment to old people which lifts them out of primary poverty. This has been of particular significance for women, who have greater longevity and are unlikely to have had an occupational pension until recently. The earnings-related statutory pension (ATP) was passed by a single parliamentary vote in 1959, after a long and furious conflict, still perhaps the most significant debate in the history of the modern welfare state in Sweden (Heclo, 1974). It was a victory for the notion of a universal, state earnings-related pension as advocated by the Social Democrats and the trade union movement, and against the notion of state regulated occupational and/or private pensions, as advocated by the centre-right parties. The social insurance schemes dominate pensions provision much more completely in Sweden than in the other three states examined in this book, with private pensions accounting for less than 5 per cent of total pensions expenditure in 1980 (Table A.8). The movement for the ATP, whose inegalitarian basis many socialists opposed, helped to forge the integration of the white collar unions into Swedish Social Democracy during the 1950s. Thus the SAP managed to extend its support amongst the growing ranks of 'the new middle strata' and give them a material stake in the welfare state (Stephens, 1979: 179). The distinction between labourism and socialism is illustrated very clearly by the 1959 pension reform, which showed that 'even welfare reforms that have no redistributive function may still have mobilising effects that strengthen labour's position' (Pontusson, 1984: 80). The ATP only started to make a significant contribution to old people's incomes in the 1970s. It gives an index-linked payment of 60 per cent of average earnings in the worker's fifteen most lucrative years up to a certain ceiling, provided there have been thirty years' pensionable earnings. The payment is reduced pro rata for less than thirty years' service. Nonetheless this level of payment and the eligibility conditions are much more generous than most statutory pension systems. By the mid 1980s 59 per cent of pensioners were receiving an ATP pension. A supplement to the basic pension was added in 1969 to help those with low or no ATP. By the early 1990s over 90 per cent of men and 65 per cent of women should be receiving the full ATP (Olsson, 1986: Table 10).

Notwithstanding the universality and generosity of the statutory pensions schemes, there are of course significant, structural inequalities in incomes amongst old age pensioners in Sweden. The most affluent are those private sector white collar employees covered by occupational or private pensions, followed by public sector employees with occupational pensions, and then by skilled workers with occupational pensions. On the lower rungs are the pensioners solely dependent on the statutory schemes, with those at the bottom on just the basic pension. These latter include a number of self-employed people, farmers and others who have not fulfilled the eligibility conditions for ATP. Nevertheless compared to the UK and the US, old people in Sweden as in the FRG derive relatively little (11.1 per cent) of their income from paid employment (Table A.9). Perhaps the single most striking achievement of the Swedish benefits system is that only 0.1 per cent of elderly people are poor, after transfers are taken into account (Table A.6), compared to 9.3 per cent in the FRG, 18.1 per cent in the UK and 20.5 per cent in the US.

Not surprisingly with the development of ATP and occupational pensions, income inequality amongst the elderly has increased in recent years, particularly between men and women. As Åberg *et al.* (1987: 130) explain, many 'women in particular receive lower pensions as a rule because they have often been housewives . . . [and] do not reach the maximum 30-year gainful employment rule.' Having said that, the relatively high level of women's earnings compared to men's in Sweden and the relative generosity of the pension eligibility rules put women in a comparatively much better position in Sweden than in the other countries in this study. Åberg *et al.* (1987: Table 8.7) compare the incomes of Swedish pensioners by gender and occupational social class in the years 1967 and 1980. The class differentials in pension income amongst women remained largely unchanged in the period. Amongst men the pension gap between blue collar and white collar workers narrowed, but the gap between these two classes and the professional and managerial class remained more or less the same. Clearly as long as wage and salary differentials are structured along class and gender lines, structural differences in income in old age will remain while pensions are paid on an earnings-related basis. Hence the Swedish pensions system reflects and maintains class and gender inequalities to a considerable extent, but blue collar male pensioners have improved their relative position in the last twenty years.

Social Assistance

Means-tested social assistance is administered by local authority social services departments as part of the social work system. Rates of payment are determined locally and benefit is frequently part of a casework package. The scheme was known as poor relief until 1956 when it was reformed and renamed social assistance; in 1982 it was reformed once again and renamed 'Socialbidrag' (SB, Social Benefit). In 1963 the proportion of the population claiming social assistance fell to an all-time low of 3.5 per cent, since when it has fluctuated between 4 and 7 per cent. Average levels of benefit are modest at between 3 and 4 per cent of the average gross industrial wage, a quarter of the basic pension level, though supplemented by child and housing allowances (Olsson, 1987: Table 4). Until the last twenty years, most claimants were elderly or poor families, but by the 1980s claimants were predominantly single, young and often childless. Hence the poverty rate amongst non-elderly households without children at 7.0 per cent is highest in Sweden amongst our four welfare states (Table A.6). Amongst the factors prompting claims for SB, social workers cite unemployment, mental and/or physical illness and alcohol/drug problems. According to Gould (1988: 104),

> one other factor associated with the increase in SB claimants [between 1981 and 1985] was that of refugees and immigrants from outside the Nordic area. While some of the local authorities reported around 10 per cent of all households in this group, in Stockholm it was claimed that it accounted for 40 per cent of the actual growth in numbers.

Ethnic minorities are likely to be more dependent on SB because of their differential vulnerability to unemployment and their failure sometimes to fulfil eligibility criteria for mainstream benefits covering sickness, old age, unemployment and disability. SB payments can be made to supplement low wages, and for families with only one wage earner 'it is becoming more difficult . . . to avoid relativistic poverty' (Nasenius and Veit-Wilson, 1985), even if lone parent benefits lift many of these families above the social assistance level.

Gould (1988) gives a fascinating account of a major dispute over the administration of SB in a poor neighbourhood in Stockholm in 1984. It concerned the age-old dilemma in the administration of poor relief between, on the one hand, disciplining and deterring the claimant in order to sever their dependence on the state and encourage independence and self-help, and, on the other hand, the more benevolent, liberal view that claimants should have an inalienable right to the means of subsistence. The 1982 reform of SB explicitly sought a middle way between the two views, which seems to have been interpreted with different emphases in different social work departments. In one Stockholm office under a lot of pressure from claimants, the social workers opted for a more deterrent approach, encouraging many claimants to empower and organize themselves and their lives without resort to SB. Many of these claimants allegedly had drug and/or alcohol abuse problems. In the context of Sweden's very strong puritan, temperance tradition, the view that deterrent state 'pressure and even force might be the best way of getting them to help themselves' (Gould, 1988: 118) had considerable popular support on the left as well as the right. Nevertheless resistance from claimants prompted an official inquiry, which produced a compromise report. By 1986 it seems that the social workers had moderated their strategy, the number of successful claims had increased and the number of social work posts had been increased. Thus this appears to be a classical example of successful resistance by poor people to disciplinary, deterrent relief policy, and an equally significant example of resistance by welfare workers to under-resourcing of the welfare state. The social assistance system in contemporary Sweden functions both to discipline and to maintain an underclass, apparently of quite a disparate social composition – young post-materialists or drop-outs, older long-term unemployed single people, ethnic minorities and others who have slipped through the statutory income maintenance system.

Unemployment and Labour Market Policies

At first glance unemployment in post-war Sweden has been exceptionally low, and by any measure has been consistently lower than in the other countries studied here (Table A.10). The official or 'open' unemployment figures are based on the number of insured unemployed as a proportion of the workforce insured against unemployment, but do not include either the insured or the uninsured on training, job creation and other labour market schemes. This is a remarkably narrow definition of registered unemployment, because there are young people, women and others who have not worked in insured employment long enough, if at all, to come into the reckoning. 'Open' unemployment in the post-war period has fluctuated between 1 and 2.5 per cent except in the years 1982–4 when it reached an all-time peak of 3.5 per cent. The world economic downturns in the mid 1970s and early 1980s produced comparatively modest and short-lived increases in 'open' unemployment in Sweden. However if workers covered by the various state labour market schemes are included, the unemployment rate is more than tripled. In 1988 the 'open' unemployment rate was 1.6 per cent, but if those on labour market schemes are included, the unemployment rate rises to 5.0 per cent (OECD, 1989b: Diagram 22). This still does not include those who are seeking or available for paid employment but are ineligible for the benefits and not catered for by the labour market schemes. If one includes early retirees, 'discouraged workers' who do not register and reluctantly part-time employees, OECD (1989b: 62–3) suggest that 'the pool of under-utilised labour was about 14 per cent of the labour force in 1984' though it has declined significantly since then. Labour shortages in some industries and some parts of the country were met by the arrival and recruitment of migrant workers in the 1950s and 1960s, and by the recruitment of many more women into paid employment since the 1960s (see below).

Until recently at least, a key component of Swedish employment policy has been the 'solidaristic wages policy' adopted in the 1930s by the trade unions in their national, centralized bargaining with the employers. The principle is that 'all wage differentials motivated by differences in profits or "wage-paying ability" between regions, industries or firms should be removed' (Bjorklund and Holmlund, 1990: 23) or 'equal pay for equal work' regardless of the profitability of a firm or an industry. Thus inefficient firms, propped up by low wages, are driven out of business, while efficient and profitable firms are not burdened with wages pushed up by aggressive trade unionism. With more than 80 per cent of the labour force organized in trade unions, the annual wages bargain has played a central role in employment policy. During the 1980s the solidaristic wages principle has to some extent fallen by the wayside in a context of increased unemployment, faltering real wages and more aggressive strategies from employers and trade unions.

An inevitable consequence of wages solidarity is that the redundant workers from inefficient firms should be retrained or redeployed with the assistance of the state. Hence in the 1940s the state Labour Market Board (AMS) was established, an agency which helped smooth the way for the dynamic restructuring of Swedish industry by private capital, particularly in the 1950s and 1960s. The AMS has presided over a range of measures. First, the employment service matches the unemployed to vacancies on a national basis. All vacancies and layoffs have to be notified by law to the service which pays substantial mobility and relocation grants. The latter increasingly took the form of serious financial inducements until being cut back in 1987. A substantial proportion of the unemployed have been encouraged to migrate to the boom areas in the south of the country, often quite reluctantly, with the consequent break-up of established communities. Second, there are AMS training schemes (beyond the in-house training by employers) organized in training centres and schools. Third, AMS oversees job creation measures including relief-work projects, temporary employment subsidies and recruitment subsidies. Finally, there are extensive special measures for the occupationally handicapped, often involving the subsidization of wages in the open labour market. The expenditure on these 'active' labour market programmes is more than double the expenditure on unemployment benefit and amounts to nearly 2 per cent of GDP, the highest level of such spending in the OECD. A very substantial proportion of the expenditure on active labour market measures, fluctuating between 30 and 50 per cent during the 1980s, has been devoted to the occupationally impaired. Another unique result of these measures in comparative terms is that only 8 per cent of the unemployed in 1988 were jobless for more than a year, compared to about 50 per cent on average in the European Community.

The unemployment insurance benefit (UIB) system is a clear exception to the universalism and direct public sector provision generally characteristic of the Swedish welfare state. UIB is administered by voluntary societies under the control of the trade unions, and financed by government, trade union and employer contributions. In 1950 only a third of the labour force was thus covered, but this has risen to over 80 per cent in the 1980s. Benefits are paid for up to twelve months under fairly tight eligibility conditions; contribution and benefit levels vary considerably from one UIB society to another. For example 'members with higher unemployment risks (e.g. musicians) pay higher contributions than those with lower unemployment risks (e.g. metal workers)' (Kerans *et al.*, 1988: 136–7). With increased government subsidy of the societies inaugurated in 1974, eligibility rules have become less severe, UIB society provisions more uniform, and membership of a society became compulsory for all trade union members. Although UIB is both taxable and earnings-related, Sweden is only surpassed in its generosity to the insured unemployed by Luxembourg and Denmark according to OECD (1989b). Hence disposable income for UIB recipients is reduced by between 12 and 29 per cent by unemployment (OECD, 1989b: 82). In 1980 average UIB payments were 78 per cent of average gross industrial wages (Olsson, 1987: Table 4).

UIB remains under voluntary administration by the unions for a number of reasons. First, the generally low levels of unemployment combined with the high levels of union membership mean that pressure for a government takeover of the societies is not significant. Reflecting this, second, the UIB societies have been seen by the unions since the nineteenth century as an important means of recruiting and keeping members. Heclo (1974) describes the central role played by the Swedish trade unions in the development of support for the unemployed over the last century in comparison with the relative negligence of the British unions. From the trade union viewpoint the advantage of the voluntary system is that members are served by work colleagues whom they trust, the unions go out of their way to render a service to their members, and beneficiaries are likely to perceive themselves as ongoing members of their respective union. The unions, in turn, are able to keep a close tab on the working conditions of their members, as well as having regular contact with the unemployed. (Kerans *et al.*, 1988: 132–3)

The trade unions continue to defend the system because 'in a country with no tradition of a closed shop, services to members are very important for the maintenance of union support and identification' (Kerans *et al.*, 1988: 138). In 1974 an unemployment assistance benefit was introduced for the uninsured; with certain eligibility conditions, it is only payable for up to six months and the flat-rate payment is very modest. Nevertheless by the 1980s the number of beneficiaries was more than double the number of those on UIB, the great majority of these being young people. As Vogel (1987: 266) suggests, there is a growing number of young people in their twenties and of women of all ages who are in and out of paid unemployment, and ineligible for UIB, though they may claim unemployment assistance benefit.

Over the last twenty years Swedish governments have built up large public sector deficits to finance the 'full employment' commitment by direct subsidies to industry, expansion of employment in the welfare state and the active labour market policies, all of which absorbed a great deal of unemployment. By the late 1980s with rising inflation and industrial militancy, the commitment to 'full employment' through measures such as we have described has been questioned more confidently by the new realists. OECD (1989b: 55) attribute Sweden's higher than average inflation to the low level of unemployment and the tight labour market, which gives the trade unions enhanced wage bargaining power. They suggest that an increase of 1 per cent in the official level of unemployment (a massive 67 per cent increase in terms of people) would reduce inflation in Sweden to the OECD average (OECD, 1989b: 71). Woodall (1990: 9) concludes that 'to anyone else but the Swedes, that would seem a small price to pay', but it is not yet clear whether this trade-off of unemployment and inflation is so precise, and even if it is, what interpretation will be put on it by Swedish governments in the 1990s.

Women, the Labour Market and Income Maintenance

The position of women in the Swedish labour market is distinct in several respects, as documented for example in OECD (1985a). The female proportion of the paid labour force (Table A.12), from being below the average amongst the capitalist states after the war (26.3 per cent in 1950), rose to being the second highest after Finland in the 1980s (48.0 per cent in 1987). By 1987 79.4 per cent of adult women below retirement age were 'economically active' in paid employment or training, a ratio approaching that of men. This is by far the highest level of female economic activity amongst our four states (Table A.13). The lower economic activity of women in the immediate post-war years in part reflects the fact that Sweden was a non-combatant in the war, so that the demand for women's paid employment was much lower. Since the 1960s women have been keenly recruited into paid employment, not least through the active labour market measures. In 1970 married women constituted 46 per cent of those on AMS training schemes, compared to 14 per cent ten years earlier (Wilson, 1979: 79). Since the early 1970s women have had parity with men (though no more than that) in terms of participation in and support from the various AMS schemes described above.

Women's hourly earnings as a proportion of men's have risen steadily in the post-war period to reach 90 per cent in 1981, by far the highest in the OECD states. This data however comes from the LO, the blue collar trade union federation, and does not cover by any means all sectors of women's paid employment. According to Ruggie (1988: 183), 'using samples of full-time, full-year workers in all unions, women's pay as a proportion of men's appears to be lower than previously thought – in 1981 it was 80.5 per cent overall.' In 1981 46.4 per cent of women employees worked part-time, the second highest proportion of female part-time employment among the OECD states (OECD, 1985a: Table 1.3). Social benefits and employment protection are reduced significantly for those who work less than twenty-two hours a week, but it is not clear what proportion of women part-time workers are affected by this. With the growth of part-time employment women's weekly earnings in comparable occupations may be as much as 30 per cent less than men's, before taking occupational segregation into account. Registered unemployment has been considerably higher amongst women than men, a gap that increased in the 1970s and narrowed in the 1980s, as women benefited from labour market measures and unemployment hit male-dominated industries. Comparison of unemployment levels between men and women is problematic, as hidden unemployment is much higher amongst women. Nevertheless on the OECD basis, female unemployment has been consistently higher than male unemployment throughout the post-war period (Table A.14). An official survey found that 90 per cent of women aged between twenty and fifty-nine wanted paid employment, but only 80 per cent had achieved it (Vogel, 1987: 270). The final important feature of women's position in the Swedish labour market is vertical and horizontal occupational segregation, which follows a pattern in some respect similar to that of other Western countries: 89 per cent of secretaries, 94 per cent of nursing auxiliaries, 78 per cent of shop assistants and 90 per cent of cleaners are women (Scriven, 1984). Compared to other states, however, women are much less prominent in 'unskilled' factory work in the private sector and extremely prominent in public sector employment in the welfare state. According to Esping-Andersen (1990: 202), in the period 1965–85 'women accounted for 87 per cent of total health-education-welfare employment growth in Sweden'. He concludes that the past two decades have seen the upgrading of women's employment from 'junk-jobs' in private industry to higher-status and better paid jobs in the welfare state. This has however resulted in increased horizontal occupational segregation by gender, with women increasingly concentrated in clerical work and welfare work. In this respect, when compared to the US and FRG,

> Sweden emerges as the most gender-segregated among the three countries. More than half of the women are locked into typical female jobs, while very few women have penetrated the sanctuaries of male dominance. Post-industrialization in Sweden only augments the problem. (Esping-Andersen, 1990: 212)

It would therefore seem that women in Sweden have not been used so much as substitutes for male workers in industry. They have been the beneficiaries in paid employment terms of the expansion of welfare services in the 1960s and 1970s as part of counter-cyclical Keynesian economic policies. Perhaps above all as an employer the Swedish welfare state has affected women's welfare over the past two or three decades. Positive discrimination in the active labour market measures, sex equality legislation and belated trade union pressure have had some success in improving women's wages and salaries relative to men, but such pressures have had little positive effect on horizontal and vertical occupational segregation (Ruggie, 1984: Chapter 4). The increase in part-time paid employment of women, much of it in low-paid service sector jobs, seems to reflect a growing marginalization of women workers who are 'functioning once again as an industrial reserve army . . . and this fact is being masked by the rhetoric of family values' (Ruggie, 1988: 185) which is discussed further below.

The extent of paid leave (for sickness, holidays, parenting etc.) is an outstanding achievement by Swedish workers, with women taking two to three times as much paid leave as men. Esping-Andersen (1990) and Woodall (1990) refer to this rather pejoratively as 'paid absenteeism'. On any given day 20 per cent of women workers are on paid leave of one kind or another, reaching a level of 30 per cent in the public sector. For mothers with children under three, the proportion was 47.5 per cent, four times the national average for all workers. Esping-Andersen (1990: 156) on this basis suggests that in Sweden 'a very large share of what normally is regarded as labor time is in fact "welfare time" ' illustrating that 'the employers' control of the purchased labor-commodity is heavily circumscribed'. However the increasing amount of sickness leave taken by women is probably also a direct result of stress-related illnesses including alcoholism and depression, as described by Ruggie (1988: 186). The levels of sickness leave amongst both men and women are much higher than in most other capitalist states, possibly reflecting a relatively generous and open-ended sick pay scheme. In 1990 the Social Democrat government announced a reform to make employers responsible for the first two weeks of sickness to cut down alleged abuse, despite strong opposition from the trade unions.

Unravelling the links between women's position in the labour market and their eligibility for income maintenance benefits is never easy. Nevertheless, given Swedish women's overwhelming representation in insured paid employment, their eligibility in their own right for pension, sickness, unemployment and other welfare benefits linked to that employment must be commensurate, and much better than in states with a significantly lower level of female paid employment such as the FRG. The relatively advantageous position of Swedish women compared to their sisters in other countries is still limited of course by their lower earnings and higher levels of unemployment compared to Swedish men and the high level of part-time paid employment amongst women.

Ethnic Minorities and the Welfare State

Migration

The Swedish people are widely described as having one language, a single Lutheran religious tradition and a common culture and history, without recently being colonialists or being colonized. Native Finns, Lapps, Jews and Gypsies form long-established, relatively small ethnic minority communities. Recently the Lapps have fought a losing battle with the state over grazing rights and access to land in the far north of the country. Prior to the 1930s Sweden experienced large-scale emigration, especially from poor, rural areas, particularly to the United States. In the 1930s the Social Democratic ideology of the People's Home and expansionary socioeconomic policies were legitimated in part by their declared purpose to reverse the falling birth rate. The building of the welfare state was clearly linked to the recovery of national identity and purpose. The fear of national population decline mingled with 'a mild sort of nationalism', according to Gunnar Myrdal (1938: 204), the influential Social Democratic sociologist. Writing for an American audience in 1938 he was highly ambiguous on the question of whether immigration would be part of a solution to 'the population question' (Myrdal, 1938: 203). In the same context, he also wrote that

> we are just as much, and even more, interested in the physical, intellectual and moral quality of the population as in its quantity. Now at least in Sweden with its homogeneous population, quality does not depend on racial differences. (Myrdal, 1940: 203)

Myrdal later became a very significant advocate of liberal race relations reform in the US. Here in the Swedish context he was hinting at a social eugenic attitude to race and immigration which was then, and is still today, a significant element of Social Democratic ideology both in Sweden and elsewhere, even if it is rarely made explicit.

From the mid 1950s to the late 1960s migrant workers came to Sweden, mostly from Finland but also from Yugoslavia, Greece, Turkey and Italy. According to Widgren (1982: 153) most of them came on their own initiative, presumably referring to the Finns. Finnish workers gained the right of unhindered entry to Sweden in 1954, when Iceland, Denmark, Norway, Finland and Sweden established the Nordic free labour market. Swedish offices for the collective recruitment of workers were established in Ankara, Athens, Rome and Belgrade. These were all closed down by the end of the 1960s, except the Yugoslav one which closed in 1977. From 1967 onwards the government used existing immigration laws to limit, increasingly severely, the number of non-Nordic immigrants, so that 'since 1974 there has been practically no immigration into Sweden of non-Nordic workers' (Widgren, 1982: 153). Non-Nordic immigration since 1974 has consisted of the families of already-settled immigrant workers and political refugees (defined much more liberally than most states) from many parts of the world, including Latin America and South Africa. The regulations on admitting relatives of foreign residents are much more liberal than those of the UK and the FRG. Also in the early 1970s immigration from Finland was put on a more controlled basis, which in effect means that a Finnish migrant worker has to have a job in Sweden fixed through the state employment service before being allowed entry. The recession of the early 1970s led to a considerable exodus of Finnish workers; according to Widgren (1982: 149), '36 per cent of all Finnish immigrants who had arrived in 1970 left Sweden in 1972.' Thus by the mid 1970s, as elsewhere in Northern Europe, a formidable immigration control system had been established, allowing entry to a regulated number of Finns, relatives of established immigrants and political refugees, but nobody else. This policy was subsequently consolidated into Immigration Policy Acts of 1975 and 1976. According to Hammar (1984: 29), in the day-to-day practice of immigration control at the borders, immigration officers have been instructed since 1976 to identify non-Nordic people by their physical appearance, clearly an explicit form of institutional racism. The legitimation of immigration control is presented in terms of enabling 'underemployed national groups to have access to the labour market' (Widgren, 1982: 151) and 'the protection of the Swedish labour market' (Hammar, 1984: 28). Yet these considerations emerged well before the modest increases in open unemployment in the 1970s, and could equally well have applied in the 1950s for example to the recruitment of women. Another official argument for immigration control made in the late 1960s was that 'if the number of resident immigrants became too large it would become impossible to guarantee them a reasonable standard of living' (Hammar, 1984: 41). Implied here are fears about the possible creation of an underclass which might allegedly overburden the welfare state.

The Status of Ethnic Minorities

In 1981 about 12 per cent of the Swedish population were of migrant origin, of whom about half were Finns, and projections suggest that 'by the year 2000, 20 to 25 per cent of the Swedish population will consist of people closely linked by origin to other countries' (Castles, 1984: 64). With a residence permit, the status of the migrant worker and his/her family is fairly secure. The number of migrants without legal status is probably small because all residents have to have an identity number, and the extent of the informal economy is limited by the efficiency of the tax gathering system. The police, however, have been criticized for stopping people of non-Nordic appearance for identity checks. After five years' residence in Sweden, a foreigner can apply for and get Swedish citizenship (two years for Nordic citizens). Naturalization policy is much more liberal than most other capitalist states, though few of the non-Nordic residents apply for it, perhaps because they feel reasonably secure without it and because dual citizenship is not allowed.

Up to the mid 1960s there were no positive social policy measures specifically directed towards migrant workers and their families, who it was assumed would assimilate with the support of the welfare state. Between 1964 and 1974 a long process of public discussion and consultation took place on whether the assimilationist ideology should continue or whether multiculturalism should be adopted. Eventually the Immigration Policy Act of 1975, which closed the doors to non-Nordic workers, embraced a liberal, multiculturalist ideology towards Sweden's immigrant and ethnic minority communities. The policy has three goals: equality of living standards, cultural freedom of choice, and political solidarity between the indigenous Swedes and ethnic minorities. Thus the state has promoted ethnic minority political, social and cultural organizations and activities, including on a limited scale bilingualism in schools, and in 1976 foreigners with at least three years' residence were given the vote in local and regional elections. In terms of equality in the labour market, in living standards and in welfare, it is extremely hard to assess the relative position of the ethnic minorities in Sweden. Survey evidence cited by Widgren (1982: Table 9) shows that foreign workers experienced much more dangerous and unpleasant working conditions; in the 1980s the open unemployment rate amongst foreign workers was double the rate for the labour force as a whole. There is little evidence of effective measures to achieve equality of access to and use of the welfare state in relation to the needs of the ethnic minority communities. There is no equivalent to the Commission for Racial Equality in Britain, although racial discrimination was explicitly outlawed in the new constitution of 1976. However, ethnic minority trade union representatives and local politicians are becoming increasingly numerous and vocal in pressing forward such issues. At the same time in recent years, there has been a marked increase in overt racism and racist politics in Swedish society which has been documented and described by Larsson (1991). This includes racial attacks and harassment as well as discriminatory behaviour by the police, public officials and landlords.

There is therefore some evidence that the new ethnic minorities in Sweden, mostly originating from the migration of workers in the 1950s and 1960s, do constitute a racialized underclass in Sweden, particularly the Southern Europeans. The extent to which the welfare state has furthered or undermined this process is unclear. Certainly immigration control policies developed since the late 1960s, while being more liberal *vis-à-vis* those already settled, are institutionally racist in discriminating against non-Nordic and, to a lesser extent, Finnish migrants and also in only requiring visas for entrants from Asia, Africa and Eastern Europe.

Women and Family Policies

Ideology and Family Policy Reform

Swedish social policy is famous for its relative 'liberalism' (as opposed to conservatism) *vis-à-vis* some of the key aspects of family policy, reflecting widely held, long-established values amongst the population. For example, the legal status of illegitimacy was abolished in 1917, liberal divorce reform was introduced in 1920, homosexuality was decriminalized in 1944 and compulsory sex and birth control education was introduced in schools in 1956. Historically public support for lone mothers and their children has been comparatively generous, and cohabitation has been treated relatively tolerantly. Compared to most other Western states, defenders of a traditional patriarchal view of marriage and the family as an almost sacrosanct private institution have had much less influence. The origins of these liberal values lie deep in Sweden's cultural and socioeconomic history (Myrdal, 1945: Chapter III). By the 1980s, over 35 per cent of children were born to unmarried parents, 30 per cent of families with children under eighteen were lone parent families (90 per cent being lone mother families) and over one in two marriages ended in divorce, twice the rate in Britain. Swedish family policies have also been shaped by a mixture of other ideological traditions, similar to those which have shaped policy in other states. These include the advocacy of birth control particularly for the working class as a means of combating poverty associated with large families. Such neo-Malthusian ideas had enormous influence around the turn of the century in establishing widespread use of modern birth control techniques by the early 1920s. The mixture also includes different variants of the feminist tradition, bourgeois, libertarian and socialist, which have had two great waves of political influence in Sweden as elsewhere. The first wave peaked with the achievement of women's suffrage in 1919, and the second wave emerged in the 1960s.

In the inter-war years, pronatalist thinking came to prominence as Sweden's birth rate became the lowest in Europe. As already discussed in relation to emigration and immigration, the declining population size in these years was a major political issue linked directly to fears of national decline. Swedish pronatalism does not embrace a rejection of birth control, but alongside the notion that 'every child should be a wanted child' the view was widely accepted that the state should try to encourage people to have a modest number of children. After coming to power in 1932 the Social Democrats began to integrate aspects of these various ideologies into their own response to the 'population question' as it was called. This ideological synthesis was performed by Alva and Gunnar Myrdal in 1934 in their book *Crisis in the Population Question*, which was later published in an expanded English version as Myrdal (1945). The authors argued that population policy and socialist socioeconomic policies should be inextricably entwined so that the nation and the family would protect each other and thrive. The fall in the birth rate was attributed by the Myrdals to improved birth control, the decline of child labour and above all the increased and unjust financial burden of child rearing on parents. The latter were portrayed as contributors to the upkeep of the nation who were impoverished by that contribution. The goals of social policy should be to increase fertility by 25 per cent, to encourage 'medium-sized families', to improve the 'quality' of the next generation by radical improvements in child welfare, to reduce illegitimacy and to encourage marriage, while at the same time emphasizing the voluntary nature of parenthood in a democratic society. These goals were planned to be achieved by a very wide range of collectivized services and benefits in all areas of human welfare. The Myrdals take pains to distance their ideas from the policies being implemented at the very same moment in Stalinist Russia and Nazi Germany. Indeed initially 'the Social Democratic press attacked the Myrdals' position as nationalistic and even militaristic, and some Conservatives [saw] . . . a backdoor effort to promote socialism' (Adams and Winston, 1980: 183) but pronatalist concern prevailed in the end. Their programme unquestionably put a strong emphasis on universal social welfare measures, not to be directed just at the working class or poor people alone, yet they also expressed a strong commitment to using family welfare benefits and services to break down class inequalities, particularly amongst children. The Myrdals' approach to family policy is predominantly child-centred and resembles the view of children as valuable human capital in which the state should invest heavily to secure its future. The programme was certainly not feminist in orientation and the effects of family policy on women's position in society are not directly confronted. Nevertheless Myrdal (1945: 121) acknowledged that

> defending the right of the working woman to marry and have children becomes a protection of, and not a threat against family values . . . The forced celibacy or sterility among wage-earning women is a sign of society's incapacity to adjust itself to modern conditions. A population policy of democratic vision thus creates a new stronghold for married women's fight for their right to work.

Thus the Myrdal programme of reform included parental leave and benefits, socialized day care and encouragement of men to take a greater share of domestic labour. Many elements in the programme thus went way beyond the confines of the Social Democrats' actual policy making in the 1930s and 1940s. The importance of the Myrdals' book was that 'population policy suddenly became a lever for socialists for far reaching sociopolitical reforms in collaboration with the conservatives, who were prepared to bank on the preservation of the Swedish national stock'

(Liljeström quoted by Scott, 1982: 13). Population policy alongside Keynesian counter-cyclical public expenditure policies became the legitimation for the expansion of the welfare state, and to a large extent that remains true today.

Family policy reforms in the 1930s in the wake of the Myrdals' report included free maternity care in public clinics, special public housing schemes for large families, rent rebates according to family size, child tax allowances, marriage loans, guaranteed maintenance for some lone mothers and employment protection for mothers. In 1948 universal child benefit was introduced to replace the inegalitarian child tax allowances. Child benefit is not statutorily indexed to inflation, but it has largely kept pace with retail prices (Olsson, 1986: Graph 20), adding about 5 per cent per child to the gross earnings of an industrial worker. In the 1950s statutory provision of birth control and family planning advice by the health service and statutory maternity leave were introduced. Notably absent from this list is liberal abortion reform, and day care and nursery education for the under sevens (primary school starts at the age of seven), both of which represented too much of a challenge to traditional ideology. The effects of the reform on the birth rate are debatable; it stabilized as elsewhere during the mid 1930s, probably linked more to economic recovery and the fall in unemployment.

A second wave of discussion of family policy reform began in the mid 1960s. Pronatalism remained on the agenda, particularly amongst conservatives concerned that most parents were increasingly limiting themselves to having one child. Family poverty was also of growing concern, with the rediscovery of poverty amongst families with dependent children, particularly amongst lone mother families. Of much greater significance than these two factors and in contrast to the 1930s, the new feminism of the women's movement together with concern about the implications of and needs created by the growth of women's paid employment were both firmly on the political agenda (Liljeström, 1978). These two pressures, which of course are closely linked, contributed to what is called the 'sex-role equality' movement, an element of the wider movement for social equality of outcome in the welfare state which radicalized the Social Democrats in the 1960s.

Beginning in the early 1960s a largely female group of sociologists, economists and psychologists documented the effect of women's paid employment on the family and on children, and also the impact of patriarchy in the home and in paid employment on women's job opportunities. They advocated the break-up of the sexual division of labour in the home, and policies of equal opportunities and affirmative action outside the home in the welfare state and in employment. The Social Democrats' women's organization took up these ideas in 1964, and they were eventually incorporated into the party's *Programme for Equality* adopted in 1969. The document was by no means, however, a feminist manifesto, for as Scott (1982: 7) explains, just as Sweden's early social measures were accepted because they were presented as the solution to a 'population crisis' . . . so the sex-role equality program was assimilated because it was part of an 'equality program' that had something for everybody . . . Thus some of the more fiercely debated measures relating to the status of women (or the status of men) were packaged so that the inclusion of women was only implicit.

Among the many policy reforms ensuing from the sex-role equality movement have been liberal abortion law reform, extensive statutory parental leave, and a great expansion of day care, all of which are examined in detail below. Also unemployment benefit was extended to non-contributor housewives. Possibly most significant of all, in 1971 independent taxation rules were introduced for men and women, which made it 'more profitable for a wife to work even at a part-time job than for her husband to take on a few extra hours' (Scott, 1982: 72).

Lone Mothers

The position of lone mothers provides a good illustration of the achievements and the limits of family policy in contemporary Sweden. In 1983 19.0 per cent of families with children under eighteen were lone parent families (Table A.16), around 90 per cent being lone mother families. The proportion of lone parent families is much higher than in Britain and the FRG, but somewhat less than in the US. Only 9.2 per cent of lone parent families in Sweden are poor, which is a very much lower proportion than in the other welfare states examined here. In 1979 86 per cent of Swedish lone mothers had paid employment, a very much higher proportion than in the other countries studied in this book, and much higher than the proportion of married mothers in paid employment (Table A.17). The net income of lone parent families in Sweden is as much as 87 per cent of that of two parent families, when household size is corrected for (Table A.18), which is a much higher proportion than in the other three states, particularly the US. Yet it would be quite mistaken to assume that the welfare state in any way encourages the establishment of lone parent families. On the contrary 'surveys and statistical analyses show unequivocally that lone parents are economically disadvantaged in many respects' (Kindlund, 1988: 76). In 1981 20 per cent of lone mother families were dependent on social assistance, compared to 9 per cent of lone father families and 3 per cent of two parent families. There is no guaranteed minimum income for lone parents, but Advanced Maintenance payments were introduced in 1937 and subsequently considerably improved. The index-linked, flat-rate payment is about one and a half times the rate of child benefit but 'payment is conditional on the custodial parent assisting in efforts to establish paternity' (Kindlund, 1988: 89), so that by no means all lone mother families benefit. About 14 per cent of Swedish children in both lone parent and reconstituted families benefit from maintenance advances, which are paid with child benefit. The government recovers about a third of the expenditure from fathers. Lone mother families in Sweden are therefore probably more generously supported by the welfare state than in any other country in the world, yet they are far from having achieved equality with two parent families. The welfare state merely succeeds in lifting most of them out of dependence on means-tested assistance.

Abortion

Until the liberal reform implemented in 1975, the struggle over abortion rights was waged as fiercely in Sweden as in most other countries. In 1934, amidst great concern about apparently increasing numbers of illegal abortions, a government committee suggested that in certain circumstances abortion should be decriminalized. These circumstances included not only cases of rape and hereditary problems, but also social indications such as where mothers in extreme circumstances were 'worn-out', living in 'dire poverty', likely to suffer career damage or likely to be 'disgraced' by the shame of unmarried motherhood, or where the birth of a child threatened a permanent relationship. However the Population Commission set up to translate the Myrdals' ideas into policy, rejected the Abortion Committee's report, arguing that the social problems confronted by mothers should be mitigated and prevented by other benefits and services of the welfare state, particularly birth control. The only social indication for legal abortion which the Population Commission approved was for the 'worn-out mother', for whom the birth of another child would be life-threatening. The Population Commission view prevailed and legislation in 1938 only decriminalized abortion where there was serious danger to the mother's life or health, which was interpreted by doctors very conservatively. In the same year, 1938, legislation forbidding the sale and distribution of contraceptives was repealed, which prompted one of the pioneers of sex education, Elise Ottesen-Jensen, to comment that 'the beautiful principle of voluntary parenthood which the Population Commission upholds in the contraceptive question kicks the legs out from under itself in the abortion question' (quoted in Liljeström, 1974: 43). The very limited sociomedical indication for legal abortion was relaxed slightly in 1946 in the context of a sharp struggle over the issue between the Conservatives and some Liberals on one side, and women's organizations and the blue collar trade union federation on the other side. The number of illegal abortions was estimated at more than double the number of legal abortions in the 1940s and 1950s, but in order to get a legal termination a woman had

> to convince the doctor . . . of her own weakness and inability to handle her own affairs. She had to bow down to the diagnostic rules of the game and assume the role of an insufficient, depressive or neurotic . . . She could not be competent, responsible and mature. (Liljeström, 1974: 59)

During the 1960s with the rise of the women's movement and changing social and medical attitudes, the number of legal abortions with social indications began to rise, until by 1974 as the reform legislation was going through parliament, illegal abortion had all but disappeared. Yet it took ten years for the Swedish government to enact a liberal reform of the abortion law. In 1965 a government commission was appointed, which in 1971 reported that women should have the right to early, safe and legal terminations, but that abortion should be regarded not as a form of birth control, but rather as 'a last resort'. Eventually legislation went through parliament in 1974 and came into force at the beginning of 1975. The law gives women the right to a termination up to the eighteenth week of pregnancy unless a doctor believes that it would put the woman's life or health at risk. After the twelfth week a social worker has to investigate the woman's circumstances in order to inform the doctor's decision. A doctor's refusal to perform an abortion before eighteen weeks is always referred to the Board of Health for review. After eighteen weeks, all decisions are referred to the Board of Health, informed by a social work investigation. Abortion is illegal if the foetus is viable, except where the woman's life is threatened, but the definition of viability is left to medical discretion.

The 1974 abortion law reform appears to have won wide acceptance in Sweden, and the issue seems to have disappeared from the political agenda as a result. The number of abortions has remained roughly the same since before the Act, at a level of twenty per thousand women aged fifteen to forty-four, comparable with that in the UK. A very significant achievement of the legislation and of the health service is that 95 per cent of terminations are performed by the thirteenth week of pregnancy, which is much safer for women and much cheaper for the health service. This compares very favourably with the situation in other states.

Day Care and Parental Leave

The growth of women's paid employment from the 1960s onwards and the concomitant rise of the sex equality and women's movements have made a striking impact on social policy concerning the parenting and care of children, particularly pre-school children, that is those under seven years old. By 1983 the great majority (82 per cent) of mothers of pre-school children had paid employment, in sharp contrast to the situation in the other three states examined here (Table A.15). Policy has developed in two directions, first by greatly increasing public investment in day care and second by giving parents very substantial statutory rights to paid parental leave to care for children. These two obviously complement each other, the one supporting out-of-home care particularly for parents in paid employment, and the other supporting parental care in the home. It is noticeable that both policies are designed primarily to benefit parents in paid employment and their children, rather than being universally of benefit to all, whether the parents are in paid employment or not. This no doubt reflects the very high proportion of women in paid employment in Sweden, though it is perhaps surprising that the child care debate has not been more child-centred.

The Parental Insurance scheme was introduced in 1974 and has been improved regularly since. The basic entitlement is twelve months' leave at 90 per cent of gross earnings funded by social insurance, a period which can be shared between the parents as they wish. The parent has to have worked six months for the same employer, or twelve of the preceding twenty-four months to qualify. Parents cannot take leave simultaneously but it can be divided up into intermittent blocks. According to Rapaport and Moss (1989: 10),

> a further six months of unpaid leave is available and the entire eighteen months will become paid at 90 per cent earnings from 1991; in effect this will extend to around twenty months because people on parental leave are also entitled to annual leave . . . in practice most parents took leave in a full-time block immediately after the birth of their child. Since July 1989 the time limit for taking leave has been extended until a child is eight.

The government would like parents to spread leave over a longer period and/or use it on a part-time basis. Other leave entitlements at 90 per cent of gross earnings are 'fifty days pregnancy leave, ten days paternity leave, ninety days per year per child under twelve to care for a sick child or to care for a child if his/her normal caregiver is ill [average leave in 1985 was seven days per sick child], and two days leave per year to visit a child's nursery or school' (Rapaport and Moss, 1989: 11). All these other leaves are funded by social insurance, and are available to all employees without qualifying restrictions. Finally parents have the right to work a six hour day in paid employment until the child is eight. Unfortunately there are no official statistics on the take-up rates of parental leaves, but they can be assumed to be high, as reflected in the 'absenteeism' figures discussed above. In 1986 83 per cent of fathers took paternity leave, but father usage of the other leaves is modest, except for leave to care for sick children, of which fathers took 44 per cent of the days in 1985. Hence in 1984 in the first six months of the child's life, fathers took only 1.9 per cent of the leave days, rising to 9 per cent in the period after the first six months. Between 1974 and 1980 fathers' usage of parental leaves increased relative to mothers', but since then there has been a modest decrease. Sundqvist (1987: 151) attributes this to 'the economic situation', that is falling real incomes and less employment security. Role reversal in Swedish families is clearly very unusual. Rapaport and Moss (1989: 38) gained the impression that 'fathers in Sweden take a greater share of family responsibility than . . . in the UK . . . [but] there is insufficient evidence to confirm this.' Government equal opportunities policy in the 1990s will attempt to encourage more take-up of parental leave by men. Overall it is very clear that Swedish social policy is comparatively interventionist in encouraging parental care of children, in contrast to mere ideological exhortation by policy makers and politicians more typical of other states.

Public provision and funding of day care for children, both after-school for older children and pre-school for children under seven, has probably been the most significant new service development in the Swedish welfare state over the past two decades. As usual with day care, changing definitions and parameters make precise quantitative measures of the expansion impossible. In 1967, according to Berfenstam and William-Olsson (1973: Table 13), children under seven *with parents in paid employment* were overwhelmingly cared for privately, mostly at home by nannies, relatives or partners, but also by private childminders. Only 16 per cent of them attended full-time or part-time nurseries or nursery pre-schools. By 1987 of *all* children under seven, 53 per cent were still cared for privately, again largely at home, but the other 47 per cent were cared for by salaried childminders or municipal day care (Broberg and Hwang, 1991: Table 5.6). In 1987 34 per cent of the under threes received care in municipal nurseries or from salaried childminders. The government aims by 1991 to provide a public day care or salaried childminder place for all children over eighteen months old whose parents are in paid employment, studying or training.

Behind these figures lie the two major developments of the last two decades, the development and expansion of both an administratively integrated municipal day care service and a municipally salaried child-minder service. The day care service includes nurseries, mothers' clubs and part-time kindergartens. Provisions vary widely amongst local authorities, some of whom provide few or no places for the under threes. Most local authorities also organize salaried childminding schemes:

> Childminders get a fixed monthly salary, but on condition they look after at least four children full-time or provide the equivalent hours of care for children attending part-time; many have to look after eight–ten part-time children to get their salary. One reason so many children attend organised childminding schemes on a part-time basis is that many municipalities only admit children needing full-time care to nurseries, arguing that nursery places are too costly only to be used part-time. (Broberg and Hwang, 1991: 78)

This account certainly gives the impression that municipal childminding is extremely hard work, done (almost exclusively by women) for a very modest salary. Fees paid by parents cover between 10 and 15 per cent of the cost of municipal nurseries and salaried childminders, and are usually income-related. Lone parent families are prioritized for nursery places, but children of immigrant parents are underrepresented in municipal day care (Broberg and Hwang, 1991: 90).

The dual provision of salaried childminding and municipal day care reflects a long-established political division of opinion, which has remained prominent on the political agenda over the last two decades (Adams and Winston, 1980: 99; Broberg and Hwang, 1991: 96–8). On the political right both the Conservative and Centre Parties have opposed the expansion of municipal day care, regarding the public investment in it as discriminating against parents who stay at home with their children. These parties have argued that the state should encourage more parents to stay at home with a universal child care allowance. Parents could then make a choice between staying at home or buying day care, only modestly if at all supported by public subsidy. Non-socialist local authorities have tended to favour salaried childminding as a more flexible and familial form of day care. There has been considerable tension between more traditionally minded local authorities and the central government over the expansion of municipal day care (Ruggie, 1984: Chapter 6). The non-socialist parties have focused on the class inequalities which have emerged in the use of municipal day care. According to Broberg and Hwang (1991: 130), 'the higher the parents' educational and occupational status, the earlier they place their children in day care outside the home.' The blue collar trade union federation (LO) considers this is due to the limited opening hours (6.30 a.m. to 7 p.m.), and have long argued for twenty-four hour municipal day care to be available. In fact, however, these class differences in usage probably reflect more a difference in cultural attitudes towards parenting, to which the non-socialist parties have appealed with some success. On the other hand middle class parents in rural and/or traditional local authority areas complain about shortage of nursery places, where priority for places goes to lone parents and poorer children.

The expansion of publicly funded day care in Sweden, like any development of the welfare state, has thus brought into focus a number of class and gender issues. Publicly funded day care is by no means universally available to all who want or need it; much of it is on a part-time basis and it is not clear whether this is what mothers want or whether it is determined by employers' demand for part-time workers and the limited public resources for day care.

The New Patriarchy?

A number of contrasting analyses of Swedish family policy have been put forward. Most analysts agree that the reforms since the 1960s are linked directly with the demand and opportunities for women's paid employment. Ruggie (1984: 299) for example explains the expansion of day care in Sweden compared with its stagnation in Britain in terms of 'the differences in the role of the state toward women workers' linked to 'the respective' status of labor and its relation with the state'. Ruggie stresses the significance of Swedish corporatism, the partnership of the labour movement, the employers and the state, in the promotion of employment opportunities for women. As a result 'perhaps the most significant development concerning women workers in Sweden is the tendency toward "universalization" of the category of worker . . . the distinctions among workers based on class, occupation and sex, are breaking down and becoming less determinant of workers' opportunities and rewards' (Ruggie, 1984: 340). This scenario is perhaps somewhat overoptimistic in the light of the evidence on gendered segmentation of the labour force, but it reflects a widely held view that the forward march of women in Sweden has been closely intertwined with the forward march of socialism and the labour movement. Ruggie (1984: 24) dismisses feminist interpretations, which she says cannot 'adequately account for the differences that are evident in policies for women in Britain and Sweden'. Adams and Winston (1980) however explain such differences between the US and Sweden in terms of different feminist strategies in the two countries. They describe Swedish women as having pursued 'social feminism' through social policy reform, while women in the US have pursued 'equal rights feminism' through legal and constitutional reform. Adams and Winston suggest that Swedish women have chosen to advance their cause from within established political and social organizations rather than through more autonomous forms of organization. Social feminism in Sweden has thus played a significant role throughout Swedish civil society, not just in the Social Democratic and labour movements. As Adams and Winston (1980: 157) point out, 'it can hardly be argued that the welfare state is a response to the needs of working women because most of the Social Democrats' welfare programmes were introduced before women entered the labor force in significant numbers.' Women's activism in shaping the population policies of the 1930s so that they were implemented without a strong ideology of domesticity has been a feature of Swedish family policy, which distinguishes it significantly from the Stalinist and Nazi variants being implemented at the very same time.

The successful incorporation of social feminism into mainstream politics may have held back the development of a more critical and more radical feminist movement. Scott (1982: 158) suggests that self-organized, autonomous feminist initiatives such as rape crisis centres, shelters for battered women, self-help women's health clinics are rare in Sweden. The word 'feminism' is more widely associated with a revolutionary, 'separatist' view than in most other Western countries. Yet the need for such organizations appears to be just as strong, and they have begun to emerge in the 1980s (Morgan, 1984: 661–3). As Scott (1982: 157–8) says,

> it is a paradox of the Swedish welfare state that it has absorbed so many feminist demands, and yet women in Sweden appear to find it even more difficult than they do elsewhere to keep 'from being devoured by equality under the terms of a male value system' . . . Men feel that they have 'done a great deal for women' . . . but they expect it all to be done in the framework of existing male institutions.

Such analysis of the limits of the Swedish welfare state in undermining patriarchy has been extended recently by a number of Scandinavian women writers. Hernes (1987) sees Scandinavian welfare corporatism as a reconstitution of patriarchy in male-dominated corporate institutions, upon which women are particularly dependent. Women are much more reliant on the welfare state for paid employment than men, and their daily lives depend much more directly on the services and benefits of the welfare state than do men's lives, because women still carry the greater burden of unpaid domestic and caring work. Yet real power in the·upper reaches of welfare administration and in the wider corporate institutions is predominantly in the hands of men. Hernes (1987: 76) suggests therefore that 'one can describe the Scandinavian state form as a tutelary state for women, since they have had a minimal role in the actual decision-making process concerning distribution.' Borchorst and Siim (1987: 154) also suggest that, as a result of the substantial gains for women from the development of the welfare state, patriarchal power is now maintained by 'the institutionaliza-tion of women's dual roles as mothers and workers', which has left men free to consolidate their power in public and private corporate institutions. The Scandinavian welfare state has thus had a contradictory impact for women, sweeping away some of the traditional patriarchal assumptions about the primacy of women's unpaid domestic work, but establishing a new form of patriarchal citizenship for women in partnership with the welfare state as both employer and provider (Siim, 1987 and 1988).

The Health Care System

Finance and Administration

Technically speaking Sweden does not have a national health service akin to that of the UK or Italy. This is because the bulk of health care services and finance is not under direct central control, but is under the control of the upper-tier, elected local authorities – the county councils. In addition out-patient consultations and GP services are financed through regional, semi-autonomous sickness insurance funds. All residents of the country, whether contributors or not, are entitled to hospital, out-patient and primary care. Patients pay a fee for GP and out-patient consultations; in 1984 the charge was £5 for a private doctor (registered with the insurance fund) and £4 for a public doctor. There are prescription charges, and subsidized fees for dental care. Hospital care is free, though long-stay, chronic patients have to pay £3 a day. Navarro (1975: 74) is surely quite correct to point out that 'it is misleading to refer to the funding of the Swedish health system as an example of national health insurance' because access to the system is not based on contributory eligibility rules and 90 per cent of the funding comes from local and national taxation.

Using a different parameter one could argue that public sector health care is more comprehensive than in Britain. Thus in 1984 public expendi-ture on health care in Sweden constituted 91.4 per cent of total health care spending, the second highest amongst OECD countries, compared to 88.9 per cent in the UK (Table A.19). There are only two small private clinics offering acute medical treatment, and only 5 per cent of doctors operated totally in the private sector in 1985. As M. Gordon (1988: 210) explains, 'although patients . . . go to private practitioners, the great majority of the practitioners were associated with hospitals or public dispensaries, and their private fees supplemented their basic salaries from public sources.' Britain and Sweden were amongst only six (out of twenty-three) advanced capitalist states offering 100 per cent public coverage for hospital care as early as 1960. Most striking in comparison with Britain is the proportion of national resources devoted to health care (Table A.20). In the UK in 1984 health care spending accounted for 5.9 per cent of GDP, compared to 9.4 per cent in Sweden, a proportion only exceeded by the US. In terms of total health care spending per capita (adjusted for purchasing power parity) Sweden spent $1445 in 1984, compared to an OECD average of $917 (OECD, 1987: Table 20); see also Table A.21. In the years 1960–75 the growth of health care spending as a proportion of GDP growth was fastest in Sweden amongst eighteen OECD countries, but by the 1980s it was amongst the lowest (Table A.22). According to the Swedish National Board of Health and Welfare, in the 1980s 'the State has imposed heavy spending restraints on the county councils [who provide the bulk of health care] with the effect that medical spending has been cut from 9.7 per cent of GNP [in 1982] to 9.1 per cent in 1986' (quoted by Diderichsen and Lindberg, 1989: 222). This suggests that like the FRG and Britain, Sweden has been quite successful in containing health care costs in the context of the fiscal crisis of the state.

Predominant administrative and financial power in the Swedish health care system lies with the twenty-six county councils who run the hospitals and much of the primary care through out-patient clinics. The post-war boom years saw a massive investment in new hospitals; hospital-based scientific medicine was hegemonic, with much less investment in primary care and preventive health measures. In order to rationalize this growth, in 1962 central government introduced legislation which prescribed in detail national rules and standards for the provision of hospital care. Government grants for new hospital building and training of physicians were used to encourage compliance. By the late 1960s, 'primarily because of considerable unrest among the populace over ever increasing local taxes' (Navarro, 1975: 5) which largely finance the hospitals, the health care planning machinery was strengthened and began to have significant effects. Hence the slowdown in growth since the early 1970s. In 1982 central bureaucratic control of the county councils was significantly diminished. The 1962 legislation was abandoned in favour of decentralized administration, in which

> detailed central regulation and close supervision is . . . replaced by broad planning and coordination . . . The state now relies on two means of directing the activities of the county councils: by giving special grants for the kinds of health programmes it wishes to see . . . and by framing special conditions in the state insurance system which make the county councils more interested in certain programmes . . . State grants have been channelled into psychiatric care as well as preventive care. (Lane and Arvidson, 1989: 86–7)

This reform diminishes the direct power of central government over the management of health care, but, of course, in this system local politicians are under acute pressure to limit costs, because of their impact on local taxation. Hence during the 1980s there have been few new programmes and an increasing emphasis on economic efficiency. There is a move towards making clinicians directly accountable for their budgets, called the 'base unit system'. This may generate better financial discipline and accountability, while 'the autonomy of the health professionals seems to be retained if not increased at the clinical level' (Lane and Arvidson, 1989: 94). The complexities and contradictions of decentralization and cost consciousness in health care are enormous.

Power Struggles in the Health System

On the face of it health care issues in Sweden seem to be very depoliticized, in the sense that overt political or social struggles around health care issues seem to be rare. This may reflect the fact that, comparatively unusually, the health service is formally under the control of locally elected politicians. Inevitably this means that the consumer, trade union and professional politics of health care is carried on within established local party political structures. The politics of health care is therefore directly incorporated into mainstream politics. To the outside observer, it appears in fact that decision making about priorities, resourcing, industrial relations and so on are highly bureaucratized and largely dealt with by central and local government administrators in partnership of course with the medical profession.

Ever since the ascendance of Social Democracy in the 1930s there has been an ongoing struggle between government and the doctors over the status and remuneration of the profession, behind which lies the universal conflict over clinical autonomy and attempts by the state to control professional behaviour. The Social Democrats came to power in the 1930s with a commitment to establish a national health service in a context in which only 30 per cent of doctors were employees of the county council hospitals. Medical care was dominated by private practitioners operating from their own offices or from the public hospitals on a fee-for-service basis. By the 1970s, as mentioned above, the great majority of doctors were salaried employees of the public health care system. This transformation did not come about without conflict, which came to a head in two instances. First the government commissioned a report, published in 1948, on out-of-hospital and out-patient medical care. In fact the five members of the commission could not agree, which is extremely unusual in Sweden, but the minority report by the Director General of the National Medical Board, Axel Höjer, reflected Social Democratic thinking. Höjer's view, in his own words, was that

> all medical care services needed by the individual should be offered free of charge at the time of treatment. It should be *the duty of the community to deliver this by means of an extended and (comprehensively) regulated organisation*, including and coordinating public health, hospital care, preventive medicine on an individual basis and ambulatory medical care. Especially ambulatory medical care, which has largely been left to medical doctors' private initiative . . . should be extended and regulated by public provision. (quoted by Serner, 1980: 101)

In other words Höjer wanted a fully salaried, publicly employed medical profession, a system which integrated preventive, curative and care services, free at the point of consumption. His vision was not unlike that of his contemporary in Britain, Aneurin Bevan. Like Bevan, his proposals ran into severe opposition from the medical profession, represented by the Swedish Medical Association (SMA). As Anderson (1972: 78) explains, 'Höjer was a declared Socialist, and even in Sweden, such a label does not sit comfortably with the medical profession.' The Social Democrats did not mobilize sufficient public and trade union support for the Höjer proposals; their behind-the-scenes, bureaucratic strategy for reform failed. The SMA were more successful in rejecting Höjer than the BMA were in attempting to reject Bevan. Hence when finally in 1955 the government implemented compulsory health insurance to cover ambulatory care, the out-of-hospital doctors continued to work on a fee-for-service, private basis with patients reimbursed for a certain proportion of the fee from the insurance funds.

During the 1950s and 1960s the nature of the medical profession changed; the old guard who stoutly defended solo practitioner status gradually retired. The concentration of new investment on in-patient care in the citadels of the system, the county hospitals, led to the atrophy of general practice. More and more doctors were hospital-based and salaried. Internal conflict in the SMA centred around income inequalities among hospital doctors, particularly between those who benefited from the fee-for-service work and those who did not. This coincided in the 1960s with the emergence of the 'equality movement' amongst the Social Democrats. Thus in 1970 the corporate rationalizers in the health care bureaucracy succeeded in making the hospital doctors totally salaried and in abolishing the fee-for-service basis for ambulatory care. This was called the 'Seven Crowns Reform', named after the original flat-rate fee of around 70 pence. In fact a two tier flat-fee system emerged, with a higher charge to see a doctor on a 'private' appointment basis, and a lower fee to queue to see a doctor on a 'public' basis. As already discussed, since 1970 the great majority of the medical profession have in effect become salaried civil servants. Indeed in 1971 the doctors, alongside other members of the public sector professionals union, SACO, went on strike very briefly in a salary struggle with the government, which was broken by emergency legislation. The doctors had finally entered traditional collective bargaining, and so some of Höjer's principles had come to fruition. Inequality in access to ambulatory care was sharply reduced, as the cost barriers which deterred those on low incomes came down. Salary differentials amongst specialists were diminished, to give more priority to lower-status specialties such as psychiatry and geriatrics. The Seven Crowns Reform was one of the major achievements of the equality movement within the Social Democratic Party, and its successful implementation 'demonstrated how little power the Swedish medical profession exercised' (Starr and Immergut, 1987: 237).

During the 1970s and 1980s the relationship between Social Democracy and the SMA appears to have been more harmonious, though not without significant conflicts. In 1979 the counties sought to force doctors to move to underresourced areas, to which the SMA responded with a campaign for 'the protection of free enterprise', but in general doctors seem to have collaborated with the planners. Most recently in 1982 the SMA resisted aspects of the decentralization of health service management, described above. An important element of this managerial reform was the clear separation of management responsibility from clinical responsibility, and the notion that final medical responsibility lay with the county council rather than with particular physicians. The SMA lost this battle, but paradoxically, with the virtual freeze on real growth in health care spending in the 1980s, the county councils have had limited room for manoeuvre in shaping clinical priorities and detailed spending. The conflict between the corporate rationalizers (the politicians and administrators) and the medical professionals continues in the county hospitals' corridors of power.

Health Status and Health Inequalities

The health status of the Swedish people is unquestionably one of the highest in the world. The infant mortality rate has consistently been amongst the lowest in the Western world, 6.8 per thousand live births in 1985. Life expectancy is amongst the highest in the West, significantly better than that in the other capitalist states focused on in this book. On these parameters Sweden performs about the same as Switzerland (OECD, 1987: Tables 8 and 9). Using a composite ranking of seventeen age- and sex-specific mortality rates for ten advanced capitalist states in the mid 1970s, Maxwell (1981) ranked Sweden in first place, some way ahead of Switzerland which is a comparatively low spender on health care (Table A.23). Such statistics are perhaps largely a reflection of the very high living standard in Sweden rather than the welfare state in general or the health care system in particular, though Maxwell's findings indicate some possible differential impact of the social democratic welfare state.

As in Britain, during the 1970s three critical and interrelated issues came to prominence in health policy in Sweden: diminishing resources, rising technological demands and costs, and faltering performance in terms of health status and health inequalities. The 'technocratic ideology' which emphasizes a hospital-based, curative, high-tech approach to health care is particularly hegemonic in the Swedish health service. Hence, in-patient hospital care is much more predominant than in the US or Britain, and ambulatory care correspondingly much less common. This has begun to change with out-patient primary care doubling its budget share in the 1980s. The emphasis on hospital technology may be explained in part by the keen commitment of the Social Democrats to technological rationality as the handmaiden of industrial and social progress applied to health care (Diderichsen, 1982: 195). By the mid 1970s political opposition to such assumptions, applied to nuclear power for example, was gaining momentum in the shape of the green movement. The Social Democrats' overconfident commitment to nuclear power was a major factor in their defeat in 1976.

So the familiar dilemma of increasingly articulated health needs and growing pressure to limit resources led not only to administrative decentralization in 1982, but also to a renewed attention to preventive health care and equality of health outcomes. Unlike in Britain, it does not appear that these issues were particularly pressed forward by the public sector unions and the left, because they have never been particularly prominent in public debate (Carr-Hill, 1989: 40). Nevertheless social scientists and epidemiologists in the 1970s discovered significant inequalities in mortality and morbidity. Le Grand (1989) examined the variation in mortality amongst the population as a whole in a large number of industrial societies. He found that although Sweden had relatively low overall inequality of mortality amongst children and infants, for adults the Swedes did no better than the average variation in mortality in thirty-two countries. Data on social class differences in mortality is inadequate since the government does not recognize such parameters, but on the basis of the limited evidence Erikson (1987: 56) concludes that 'there are some, albeit rather small, differences in mortality between social classes in Sweden.' Valkonen (1989) suggests that adult mortality in six countries including Sweden is correlated with levels of education for both men and women, suggesting another aspect of the effects of class. Using data from the Living Standard Surveys of 1968, 1974 and 1981, Kjellström and Lundberg (1987) found significantly higher incidence of health problems amongst women, elderly people and the blue collar working class, with their degree of disadvantage remaining largely unchanged since 1968. As in other industrial societies, women in Sweden suffer more ill health than men, despite their greater life expectancy. The use of health care services by the less healthy groups in the population increased significantly over the period, suggesting perhaps that inequalities would otherwise have widened. Nevertheless access to health care remains more difficult for pensioners, housewives and the unemployed compared to those in paid employment (Diderichsen, 1982: 194). This may reflect the fee-paying basis for ambulatory care and the fact that poorer people have to queue and wait longer for appointments, than those who can afford the higher fees to see a doctor on a 'private' appointment basis. The limited evidence suggests that the welfare state as a whole may have had only a limited effect in curbing class and gender inequalities in health status.

During the early 1980s expert reports commissioned by the government on these issues prompted the passage of the 1985 Health Policy Bill which recognized that

> special attention should be paid to those groups of society who are at greatest risk . . . manual workers and the low-level salaried employees; immigrants, long-term unemployed, people living alone, divorced men and among children of parents with low incomes and social and mental problems. (quoted by Dahlgren and Diderichsen, 1986: 536)

Surprisingly the health problems of women are not specifically mentioned. The Bill also advocates extra resources for prevention, public health, epidemiology and primary care. The Bill is a rather uneasy compromise between three radically different forms of policy prescription – conservative, social democratic and a radical public health approach. Conservatives, including the Swedish Conservative Party, emphasize competition and privatization to increase real resources and individual responsibility for health problems related to lifestyle. Mainstream Social Democrats still emphasize the benefits of scientific medicine allied with rational cost-effective planning and management in the public sector, and the importance of medical technology and drugs for Sweden's exports. Improvement of economic growth would generate more resources for health care and lower unemployment, seen as a major contributor to health problems. The radical public health movement advocates a fundamental switch of priorities towards primary care and preventive measures, targeting the less healthy groups. They would shift the policy emphasis from individual lifestyle changes towards highlighting corporate and public responsibility for ensuring informed choices for all groups. The first Public Health Report subsequent to the Bill (reprinted in Diderichsen and Lindberg, 1989) hesitantly moves a little way towards the radical position, but it seems unlikely that the Bill signals a really dramatic shift in health policy and priorities in Sweden.

Conclusion

Since the 1930s, the Social Democratic hegemony has shaped the Swedish welfare state so that it is very significantly different from the other welfare states examined in this book. The hegemony is based on a degree of collaboration between organized labour, capital and the state which has not existed in other welfare states. In this partnership, private capital continues to exercise control over industry, finance and commerce without much threat of political interference. The Swedish economy is owned and controlled by private interests to an astonishing extent, when one considers how frequently Sweden is described as a socialist country. One family, the Wallenbergs, has effective control of more than a third of the total value of the Stockholm stock exchange. Yet this extremely dynamic capitalist economy has thrived alongside the development of an extensive welfare state. Over the years since the 1930s, the welfare state, as we have seen, has succeeded in ameliorating class and gender inequalities in welfare, though also reconstructing and even sustaining forms of class, gender and racial inequalities and oppression. The Social Democratic hegemony would suggest that the successful development of the welfare state and of the capitalist economy is a symbiotic process, but this is impossible to prove. Since the 1970s, as in other countries, private capital and even some Social Democrats have come to believe that the welfare state is a serious drag on further economic growth. On the left, it is argued that the unfettered activity of private capital has created extra burdens for the welfare state in terms of unemployment, retraining, social dislocation, early retirement and so on. Unquestionably in the 1990s the Social Democratic hegemony is going to bear its greatest pressures since the 1930s. This became clear in February 1990 when the Social Democrat government resigned after failing to get an austerity package through parliament, which included a two year wage freeze and a ban on strikes in exchange for continued support for the welfare state. The government withdrew the wage freeze and strike ban, but still now proposed higher indirect taxation, cuts in social benefits and postponement of the planned extension of parental leave in 1991. Behind these struggles lie a number of issues similar to those facing other welfare states.

First there is the question of the impact of the welfare state on the working class. There seems to be a growing perception amongst the Swedish working class that the welfare state may differentially benefit the professional and managerial groups and that the working class may pay in taxes a disproportionate contribution towards the costs of the welfare state. This argument is commonly made about the welfare states of Eastern Europe and elsewhere. An understandable reaction is to call for wage increases and tax cuts to put money into workers' pockets with which they can buy the welfare services and goods that they need without having the state dictate to them how their needs should be fulfilled. Such an argument has come to the fore in the day care debate for example. Another related issue is the question of the remoteness and authoritarianism of the welfare state. This has come to prominence around questions such as the rights of social assistance claimants, drug addicts, parents of children taken into care (Gould, 1988) where the Swedish welfare state has tended to adopt fairly authoritarian practices. There are increasing pressures for more effective welfare rights, better advocacy for clients and more consumer participation. This again is related to a third aspect – the emergence of the new social movements over the past twenty years. To some extent the strength of the Social Democratic hegemony may have held back some of these movements, for example the autonomous women's movement as discussed above. Nevertheless the anti-nuclear-power movement and the peace movement have had an increasing impact on the political scene in recent years. In 1988 the Green Party exceeded the threshold of 4 per cent of the vote for the first time and thereby achieved parliamentary representation. Their philosophy of decentralization and consumer power may have an impact on the Social Democrats. Finally it is apparent that Swedish corporations are investing more and more overseas, as a reaction to the very high levels of corporate taxation at home and also to be established players inside the single European market of the EC.

The Social Democrat government of 1982–91 attempted to respond to these pressures, while at the same time trying to counter inflation and to protect the welfare state, which is unquestionably still very popular in its present form. It is therefore extremely premature to talk of the crumbling of the Social Democratic hegemony, though clearly a significant adaptation has already taken place in that the growth of the welfare state has been ended in the 1980s. The new centre-right government formed in 1991, like it predecessor in the 1970s, will probably not lead to radical change. In the long term, however, the likelihood is that the hegemony will adapt to new capitalist and international realities, moving towards the new realism of the social market economy model in the absence of a feasible socialist model.

3

The Federal Republic of Germany: the Welfare State in the Social Market Economy

The Federal Republic of Germany (FRG) came into being in 1949 with the adoption of the Basic Law, a strong written constitution. The occupying Western allies, particularly the United States government, exerted great influence over the shape of this constitution and of post-war West German society. The constitution puts firm emphasis on the rule of administrative law and regulation for the governance of social policy. It also devolves considerable power within the welfare state to the regional states (*Länder*) and local government. There is a continuous debate about the extent to which the Basic Law could meet socialist or other radical aspirations, but in interpretation so far it has certainly furthered a 'private capitalist philosophy with a certain social leaning' (Sontheimer, 1972: 34). Politically the dominant force in the FRG has been the Christian Democratic Party (CDU) with their more conservative Bavarian partners the Christian Social Union (CSU). They have led post-1949 federal governments, except for the period of Social Democratic Party (SPD) and Free Democrat Party (FDP) coalition between 1969 and 1982. All governing parties have embraced the idea of the Social Market Economy (see below) as an ideological shell.

The political economy of the FRG may be divided up into three chronological periods. Up to the mid 1960s rapid economic growth (the economic miracle) took place in a context of considerable austerity and deprivation for the mass of the population until the late 1950s. There was generally a marked absence of political conflict over social welfare issues, despite high levels of unemployment in the 1950s and the pressing needs of millions of incoming refugees from the East. Capital enjoyed 'the presence of a relatively technologically advanced production apparatus . . . [and] also the extraordinary weakness of the working class and its organisations after their devastation by fascism' (Hirsch, 1980: 116). Conservative CDU social policy reform in the 1950s won sufficient support from the demoralized working class to preserve their hegemony. The period from the mid 1960s to the mid 1970s saw a resurgence of industrial conflict and struggles over the welfare state, leading to the partial eclipse of a more conservative interpretation of the Social Market Economy. The SPD/FDP coalition deployed tripartite corporatism in response to growing pressures from the

organized working class. Welfare rights were extended, piecemeal progressive reform of the welfare state was implemented, Keynesian counter-
cyclical economic policies were adopted and real wages improved. In the
mid 1970s amidst stagflation, the SPD/FDP coalition abandoned elements
of their liberal Keynesianism and corporatism in favour of tougher fiscal
and monetary policies, continued by conservative governments since 1982.
Registered unemployment levels increased very quickly from 1973
onwards, remaining at around 10 per cent in the 1980s, while the growth in
real wages has faltered. This permanently high level of structural unemployment has been widely accepted apparently as necessary for controlling
inflation and restoring capital's profitability. Since 1975 public expenditure
on social welfare has been subject to increasingly effective limitations and
cuts, but the popularity of social welfare amongst both the middle class and
the working class has kept the system fairly intact. The past twenty years
has also seen the emergence of new social movements – greens, feminists,
gays, the peace movement for example – elements of which have sought
without spectacular success to reform social policy in radical directions.

Ideology and Welfare Expenditure

The Social Market Consensus

In Germany the concept of 'the welfare state' (*Wohlfahrtsstaat*) has a
rather pejorative connotation, implying a paternalistic dependence undermining individual freedom and initiative, not dissimilar to the meaning of
'welfare' in the US. However since the establishment of the modern
German state in 1871, there has always been a positive emphasis on social
policy or *Sozialpolitik*, from both conservatives and social democrats.
Sozialpolitik, an amalgam of social politics and social policy, implies a
general deployment of statecraft to ensure social cohesion and well-being.
In the Basic Law this is embodied in the concept of the social state
(*Sozialstaat*), whereby the state's general commitment to providing income
and employment security is complemented by an emphasis on the obligations of private associations or groups (above all employers and trade
unions), families and individuals to support themselves. There is no
question of any commitment to equalizing welfare outcomes, or even of an
unambiguous welfare safety net. As Zapf (1986: 132) points out, this may
sound 'like an abstract philosophical discourse, but these ideas still
materialize in the institutions and policies in West Germany, which are
governed by group-specific compulsory insurance systems' based firmly on
occupational status and income-related contribution principles. As social
partners in civil society according to the principles of the social state, the
employers and the trade unions have sole responsibility for wage and salary
determination. There have been no explicit government wages or prices
policies and no minimum wage legislation.

The notion of the Social Market Economy still best encapsulates the social policy ideology of the FRG. This concept emerged from the CDU in the late 1940s in Germany, to distinguish the legitimation of the new state from those that preceded it and that being imposed on the GDR. It represented a liberal capitalist reaction to fascist and Stalinist conceptions of an authoritarian state, both of which were distrustful and destructive of the institutions of civil society. Anti-Nazi and anti-communist sentiments, encouraged by the Western allies and by the creation of the GDR, were 'conducive to the condemnation of planning, nationalization and other policies seen as distinctly socialist' (Schmidt, 1989: 69). The Social Market Economy proposes a leading role for the market, that is private economic and social initiatives in civil society, with a subsidiary role for the state. In economic policy terms it signifies a compromise between Keynesianism and neo-liberalism or neo-classicism. Social and economic policy interventions must not interfere with market allocation processes, including the distribution of income and wealth, unless these interventions improve resource allocation, economic efficiency and individual incentives. One clear example is the autonomy of the central bank, the Bundesbank, which according to Schmidt (1989) and many others lies behind the FRG's relatively successful anti-inflation policies. The pursuit of monetary and fiscal orthodoxy has proceeded relatively unimpeded by political interference. The question of the extent to which social welfare measures contribute to economic efficiency by remedying market failures is however left open. The CDU's 1949 Düsseldorf Principles include 'a natural right to work', 'social insurance as the basis of general social security' and 'welfare provision for *proven* need from public funds outside social insurance' (my emphasis; quoted by Leaman, 1988: 53). The overwhelming emphasis however is on individual and family self-help bolstered social insurance with direct state welfare responsibilities only as a last, deterrent resort. The Social Market Economy ideology is not a set of policy prescriptions; it is simply a cloak which attempts to define the limits of state interventions in vague and ambiguous terms which can be adapted to circumstances by politicians. It is nevertheless a model of the capitalist welfare state which is distinct from, for example, Swedish Social Democracy or British Liberal Collectivism.

The social policy ideology in the FRG has been variously conceptualized. Rimlinger (1971) refers to a consensual combination of conservative 'social market' and social democratic 'socialist market' principles. Alber (1986) suggests that these are clearly discrepant conceptions of social policy, reflecting the distinction drawn by Titmuss (1974), Korpi (1983) and others between an 'institutional' and a 'residual' model of the welfare state. Hence according to Alber,

> the social policy efforts of the Social Democrats usually centre on the regulation of work conditions, on the promotion of full employment, and on social security, whereas the social policy of the bourgeois parties primarily seeks to strengthen the self-help potential of families and to promote a widespread capacity for

property formation. Thus all parties . . . seek to defend different models of the welfare state. (Alber, 1986: 104)

Alber claims that two sharp parliamentary party conflicts over pension reform in the late 1950s and over health insurance reform in the early 1960s substantiate his view. Since that time however it does appear that the Social Democrats when in power in coalition with the FDP have not deviated or have not been able to deviate radically from a Social Market model, which is neither socialist nor residual. This is illustrated by the period of SPD/FDP reform in the early 1970s which extended the social security system to many more citizens, but did not alter very significantly the distribution of income and wealth. The cost of these reforms also contributed to the subsequent fiscal crisis of the state and austerity measures which followed. As Schmidt (1978) suggests, the labour market reforms of the early 1970s which sought to improve the flexibility, mobility and training of workers had the effect of raising the price of labour power, with the contradictory and unintended outcome of increasing structural unemployment. By the mid 1970s as Schmidt (1978: 194) says, the SPD/FDP government 'preferred instead to put their trust in the problem-solving capacities of the market economy and in traditional circulation-regulating policies'. Given the conservative hegemony at federal government level, it still seems justified therefore to consider the Social Market model as hegemonic, particularly as it is explicitly advocated by moderate elements in the SPD.

Welfare Expenditure

It is well known that the FRG is a high spender on social welfare. On the OECD basis, in 1960 the FRG spent 20.4 per cent of GDP on 'real social expenditure' (Table A.1) which was the highest level amongst nineteen OECD countries. By 1981 the figure had risen to 29.2 per cent, putting the FRG fifth behind Belgium, Denmark, the Netherlands and Sweden. The FRG, unlike most other capitalist states, achieved its fastest growth in social welfare expenditures in the 1950s under the conservative federal administration. The average annual growth rate of real social expenditure in the period 1960–75 was below the OECD average, despite the presence of the SPD in government for most of this period. In the years 1975–81, the period of the so-called fiscal crisis of the state, the FRG had almost the lowest average annual growth rate in real social expenditure, only the Netherlands being lower. In relation to overall national resources (GDP), as measured by the real income elasticity of social expenditure (Table A.1), the FRG achieved the most severe welfare retrenchment of all OECD countries in the period 1975–81, when growth of real social expenditure was only 60 per cent of GDP growth. The FRG's Social Budget, which covers most of the welfare state, has declined as a percentage of GNP every year from 1981 to 1990 (Muller, 1989: 98). According to the OECD the major factors accounting for this are a fall in the average real value of pensions and a fall in the coverage of unemployment benefit (OECD, 1985b: Table 6c).

Income Maintenance Policies and Outcomes

Income Inequality and Poverty

Despite comparatively high levels of public spending on income maintenance benefits, cash benefits are much less significant as a source of personal income in the FRG than they are in Sweden, largely because income from self-employment is extraordinarily high in the FRG (Table A.2). In 1980 the percentage of average gross income taken by income tax was comparable to that in the US and the UK and very substantially lower than in Sweden, though employee social insurance contributions are much higher than in the other welfare states (Table A.2). Data on the distribution of disposable income shows that in the FRG in 1972/3 and 1980 the top fifth of the income distribution had the highest proportions of disposable income compared to the other welfare states examined in this book (Tables A.3 and A.4). The comparatively advantageous tax position of self-employed people appears to account for much of this exceptional feature. On the other hand the bottom fifth have a share of the income distribution near to the OECD average. Table A.6 suggests that the benefits system in the FRG in 1980 succeeded almost as well as the Swedish system in reducing income poverty, and performed much better in this respect than the systems in the UK and the US. Such an assessment is confirmed by recent comparative statistics on poverty in the European Community (EC, 1989). Defining poor households as those with less than 50 per cent of average disposable income, corrected for household size, the FRG was fourth best of the EC countries in 1985 with 7.4 per cent of households in poverty, covering 8.5 per cent of the population. All this data suggests that the welfare state in the FRG compensates the poor at an average or even better than average level, while the affluent are not greatly burdened with the costs of social transfers which are more of a burden on those with middle incomes, particularly through the high level of social insurance contributions. Using longitudinal data for the period 1960–80 Alber (1986) suggests that the growth of social expenditures has not led to progressive improvement in the distribution of disposable household income. Thus the welfare state succeeds in horizontal redistribution within occupational strata, predominantly from economically active to elderly people. Although the vertical redistribution is modest, it is of course vitally significant to the people at the lower levels of the income distribution. Hence in 1980 the bottom 20 per cent of the income distribution had only 0.2 per cent of income before redistribution, but 6.9 per cent after including transfers. Gini coefficients for the FRG also indicate a consistently more unequal distribution of disposable income adjusted for household size than most other advanced capitalist states over the post-war period, including even the US (Table A.5). The welfare state in the FRG is certainly redistributive at a basic level, but the gap between the most affluent and the most poor is above average, despite the high levels of social expenditure. The gap between the poor and those on middle incomes is probably narrower than the average for most capitalist welfare states. Furmaniak (1984) sees this as the result of successful trade union demands for higher wage increases for lower earners, at least in the 1960s and 1970s. Although only about 40 per cent of the labour force is unionized, the existence of single, industry-wide unions has

> led trade unions to seek a careful balance between different groups in the labour force and has restrained the ambitions of the strategically well placed . . . the fairly high degree of voluntary unionisation (there are no closed shops in Germany) has resulted in the adoption of union wage rates throughout much of the West German economy, including those sectors that are weakly unionised. (Furmaniak, 1984: 141–2)

Because pensions, unemployment and other social insurance benefits are closely earnings-related, the trade unions can thus be said to have had an extremely significant if indirect effect on the income maintenance system.

The view that the working class, broadly defined to include white collar workers, is becoming increasingly divided between a privileged majority and a marginalized underclass seems to have some application to the FRG. Schmidt (1989: 93), for example, refers to the winners in the welfare state being workers and their families within the primary labour market; pensioners with a full contribution record and above average pre-retirement incomes; and those with unearned income from private wealth. The losers are the households of the unemployed; people with intermittent and/or low income from work, often in the secondary (casual) labour market; pensioners and widows with poor contribution records; lone mothers; and the 'post-materialists' or drop-outs, including the homeless, variously estimated to number 500,000 to a million people. Schmidt estimates that the privileged constitute a 'substantial majority' of the electorate, with the underclass comprising perhaps as much as 35 per cent, but less likely to vote. The welfare state both disciplines and assists the underclass primarily through the social assistance system and the social insurance benefits system for the unemployed.

Old Age Pensions

Germany was the first major nation to introduce a statutory social insurance scheme for old age in 1889 under Bismarck. The coverage was initially limited to the organized working class and pensions were paid on a strictly contributory and earnings-related basis. This tradition is reflected in the present statutory scheme, a popular measure enacted by the CDU/CSU government in 1957. Given this long-established tradition of social insurance for old age, it is not surprising that private occupational and individual pensions account for only 11 per cent of total pensions expenditure in the FRG, and also that total pensions expenditure is highest in the FRG amongst the four states studied here (Tables A.7 and A.8). Compared to the UK and the US, elderly people in the FRG, as in Sweden, have to depend on paid employment for relatively little (11.9 per cent) of their income (Table A.9).

In the FRG the statutory pension is characterized as a substitute for wages indexed to wage inflation, and payments are firmly based on contribution records and on contributors' former earnings. There is no universal, non-contributory statutory pension. Hence according to the Federation of German Pensions Insurance Institutes (1988: 80) public pension entitlement 'is linked to the fulfilment of conditions laid down in insurance law, and neither the current income situation nor neediness aspects [of the pensioner] fall under this heading, and neither should they either'. Thus although it is a public pension scheme, it is governed by actuarial principles associated more with the private sector in many other countries. As a result the pensioners are extremely stratified and there are many gaps in coverage. For example the average pension for white collar workers has fluctuated at between 65 and 75 per cent of average net white collar earnings, while for blue collar workers the average pension has fluctuated around 45 to 55 per cent of average net blue collar earnings. Data for 1980 suggests that 9.3 per cent of elderly families in the FRG were poor, which compares favourably with the situations in the US and UK, but compares adversely with Sweden (Table A.6). Since the mid 1970s there have been a number of restrictive changes to pension entitlement and payments, so that by 1984 according to Alber (1986: 120) 'the standard pension was 15 per cent lower than it would have been on the basis of the original pension formula.' Alber (1986: 62) suggests that 'nearly one half of all pensions barely exceed the social assistance poverty line' and 72 per cent of female pensions were close to the social assistance level in 1982. However during the 1980s as more retired people have qualified for a full earnings-related pension, the proportion of elderly households actually claiming social assistance has declined to less than 2 per cent. It is still true that, as Alber (1986: 64) concludes, 'the fact that these schemes aim at income maintenance, but do not even effectively prevent poverty among beneficiaries, must be considered a significant failure.' Thus although old age insurance is the direct responsibility of the welfare state in the FRG with a high level of expenditure, it appears to reflect and maintain class and gender inequalities comparatively explicitly.

Social Assistance

The poverty line is defined according to the federally established cash value of a basket of goods considered sufficient to live a dignified life. Households with incomes at or below this poverty line are entitled to means-tested social assistance (*Sozialhilfe*). The poverty line has been kept consistently at the modest level of around 20 per cent of average net earnings since it was established in 1957 (Alber, 1986: Graph 35). The purchasing power of social assistance benefit fell by 6 per cent between 1977 and 1983 (Alber, 1986: 121). Hence it would appear that social assistance payments are set at levels which do not threaten work incentive. In the balance between the 'social' and the 'market' in this aspect of the Social Market Economy, the requirements of the labour market predominate.

In 1970 around 0.75 million adults were dependent for their regular income on social assistance, mostly elderly women and lone mothers. By 1980 the numbers had doubled to 1.4 million and by 1987 had reached 2.4 million. These large increases are accounted for by the growth of long-term unemployment, lone motherhood and perhaps also by increasing claims from the previously hidden poor. In 1987 only 28 per cent of the heads of households dependent on social assistance were over the age of fifty, yet half of the recipients were single heads of households. This may suggest that more 'post-materialists' are claiming social assistance. From being a rather peripheral aspect of the West German welfare state in its first two decades, social assistance now functions increasingly as a front-line institution dealing with the new poor, though in 1988 it only accounted for 4.6 per cent of the benefits expenditure of the Social Budget. Alber (1986: 55) suggests that, over and above the claimants of social assistance, 'another group of about the same size lives below the official poverty line, but does not claim assistance benefits.' These are the hidden poor, whose exact numbers are unknown but have probably grown in the 1980s with the increase in unemployment. The low paid are generally not eligible for social assistance. In 1988 31 per cent of the registered unemployed were not entitled to unemployment benefits, and many of them claimed social assistance or joined the ranks of the hidden poor.

The low take-up of social assistance is explained by Leibfried (1979) as the result of the filtration of welfare rights by administrative and social devices. The claimant is called an 'applicant', a term redolent of applying for poor relief. The applicant is 'not seen as a client and especially not as someone who need be taken seriously as a particular person, whose share in a social problem of *ours* is at stake' (Leibfried, 1979: 176). There are therefore various administrative deterrents which claimants face, reflecting their less than deserving status – lengthy written application forms, pressure on those of working age to find paid employment, strong liable relative stipulations, threats of prosecution for false statements and so on. The cohabitation rule applies when a couple are living together with joint finances, whether they have a sexual relationship or not. Benefit levels and eligibility rules are prescribed by federal law, but 'within these legislated guidelines . . . the local Social Welfare Offices have considerable freedom to award benefits according to the individual circumstances' (Whittle, 1977: 26). The social assistance scheme is administered by the local authorities who provide 80 per cent of the finance, the other 20 per cent coming from the regional states, the *Länder*. Thus 'social assistance is closely bound up with local politics . . . the district council can decide on the way discretion should be exercised' (Whittle, 1977: 35). In practice however it appears that the administration of the scheme is fairly uniform across the country, generating little significant local political or community conflict. During the 1980s the federal government regularly succeeded in preventing local authorities indexing social assistance to prices (Alber, 1986: 121). Although there is a two tier appeal mechanism for the applicant, in reality the administrative and legal barriers to challenging the system seem to be very substantial. Claimants in the FRG appear to have very few legal and pressure group resources to call on in support of challenges to the system. A fully fledged welfare rights movement, comparable to those in the US or Britain, does not exist. The politics of poverty were submerged in the post-war years by the atmosphere of the Cold War, the social dislocation following defeat and partition, and the political weakness of the trade unions and the left. As Lawson (1980: 216) explains, 'the poor in Germany would seem to have been under more pressure than in Britain and a number of other countries to keep silent about their poverty and not claim assistance.' The stigma of claiming means-tested assistance, a general lack of confidence amongst claimants and little advocacy on their behalf remain strong features of the German system, perhaps as much as in the US and certainly more so than in Britain and Sweden.

Unemployment and Labour Market Policies

The immediate post-war history of unemployment in Germany was quite different from that in other capitalist welfare states. Registered unemployment in 1950 stood at 10.4 per cent, which remains a post-war record, and the level did not come down to 'full employment' levels below 2 per cent until the early 1960s. Unlike Britain and the US, for example, in the 1950s the FRG did not experience 'full employment'. The 1960s and 1970s, however, witnessed a strong demand for labour and the recruitment of women and migrant workers. On the OECD basis unemployment was extremely low in the FRG until the recession of the early 1970s, much lower even than in Sweden up to that point. Since then the unemployment rate in the FRG has moved towards the OECD average, though never exceeding it, in contrast with the US and the UK (Table A.10).

Fluctuations in registered unemployment in the 1960s and 1970s were commonly considered to be cyclical, though after the 1973 recession the level remained around 4 per cent for the rest of the decade. The figure was kept down by the departure of over half a million guestworkers in the mid 1970s. The more severe 1981 recession raised the level for the rest of the 1980s to between 8 and 10 per cent. Women and 'foreign' workers have borne more of the burden of registered unemployment than German men. In 1979 the rate of registered unemployment amongst women was over double that for men and had increased much more sharply over the decade. In the 1980s the growth of unemployment has affected men to a greater extent than in the 1970s, so that according to an April 1988 minicensus (*Statistisches Jahrbuch*, 1989: Table 6.3) 9.9 per cent of women were unemployed but seeking employment compared to 6.3 per cent of men. The same census revealed that 13.0 per cent of foreigners were unemployed but seeking paid employment, compared to 7.4 per cent of Germans, and also that 17.5 per cent of foreign women were unemployed and seeking paid employment. Clearly unemployment continues to affect women differentially, and ethnic minority women in particular. In 1981 the government estimated that what they called the 'silent reserve' of unemployed people constituted another 4 per cent of the economically active. Critical analysts would suggest that even this is an underestimate of the level of unemployment when one includes the 'dormant labour force'. This encompasses early retirees, women at home, 'post-materialists', people working in the informal economy and so on, many of whom government statisticians do not number amongst the 'silent reserve'. Official youth unemployment has been at much the same level as the general average, since young people are mostly catered for by employment training schemes, by further/higher education and by national service. On the right, it has been argued that the official figures are an overestimate. Hallett (1985: 185) reports that 'the General Secretary of the CDU recently suggested that the unemployment figures should be revised, so as to include only "breadwinners" – and not wives, young people etc. who could be supported by their families . . . The suggestion did not get a good press and was hastily disowned by other CDU leaders.' With the renewed influx of refugees from the East and the slowdown of the world economy in the late 1980s and early 1990s the prospects for an improvement in the unemployment situation seem remote.

The benefits system in the FRG divides the registered unemployed into several groups of different status and therefore of different income from the welfare state. The most privileged are the short-term unemployed with a full contribution record, who receive 68 per cent of their previous net, take-home pay for up to a year, called Arbeitslosengeld. There are obvious parallels here with the old age pension system; benefits are strictly earnings- and contribution-related in accordance with the Social Market philosophy which reinforces material and status inequalities within the labour force along class, intra-class, gender and racial lines. Having said that, compared to most other welfare states, the scheme is generous to workers in the primary labour force. It was first instituted in 1927 as the jewel in the crown of Weimar corporatism, but in its present form it was introduced in 1969 and stands as one of the foremost achievements of the SPD/FDP coalition. Since 1975 however federal governments have regularly tightened eligibility and contribution conditions in pursuit of public expenditure restraint. Around 40 per cent of the registered unemployed received Arbeitslosengeld in the mid/late 1980s compared to around 65 per cent in the 1960s and mid 1970s (Table A.11). For those not eligible for the latter, there is Arbeitslosenhilfe, a means-tested insurance benefit giving

58 per cent of former net pay. The means test however 'is quite severe and limits dramatically the numbers of women and young people who are eligible' (Furmaniak, 1984: 148). Between 20 and 25 per cent of the registered unemployed were dependent on Arbeitslosenhilfe in the 1980s. The third group of the registered unemployed are those dependent on the means-tested social assistance described above, with flat-rate benefit levels far below those of the other schemes. The official statistics only allow an estimate of between 10 and 20 per cent of the registered unemployed in the 1980s as dependent on social assistance. This apparently leaves 15 to 25 per cent of the registered unemployed without any social security benefits from the welfare state. This group will include many married women, people in their teens and twenties dependent on their families, some 'foreigners' and some 'post-materialists', groups who are also predominant among the unregistered unemployed.

Of course besides the benefits system there is a wide range of other measures which the welfare state deploys to assist and regulate the unemployed or potentially unemployed – grants and subsidies to employers for training, allowances for trainees, a job creation programme, subsidies for short-time working, early retirement and so on. With the exception of youth training, the conservative governments since 1982 have cut back on many of these schemes, preferring to rely on fiscal and monetary austerity policies to counter inflation and unemployment, without great success in the case of the latter. Perhaps the most significant response of the trade union movement to the development of structural unemployment since the mid 1970s has been the long struggle for a shorter working week, an issue which the labour movement in the FRG in contrast with most others has taken up tenaciously. The issue emerged out of serious disputes about new technology and job security starting in 1978 in the steel and printing industries. Strikes and industrial action around the demand for a 35 hour working week have persisted throughout the 1980s, with a partial victory in 1984 when the engineering employers accepted a 38.5 hour week without loss of pay. This was however implemented in ways which had little effect on overall employment levels. In return as it were the employers 'persuaded the government . . . to prevent the payment of unemployment benefit to workers indirectly laid off during disputes who later benefited from strike settlements' (Derbyshire, 1987: 113). Engineering workers struck again for the 35 hour week in the summer of 1990. The popular struggle against unemployment therefore continues to be fought on a number of fronts, in which benefits policies play an integral role.

Women, the Labour Market and Income Maintenance

We have already seen that women have a distinctly inferior position in the social security system of the FRG, getting less benefit from the privileged social insurance schemes and being more dependent on the pauperizing social assistance scheme. Women's entitlement to the earnings-related social insurance benefits for old age and unemployment is limited by strict eligibility and contribution rules which discriminate against them, because their periods of paid employment are often low-paid and/or interrupted or limited by unpaid caring work. The social insurance system since its inception in the 1880s has been built upon the assumption that the contributor is a man earning a 'family wage' sufficient to support dependants, and that benefits should therefore firmly reflect the woman's dependent status within the household. The pension payment, being like a wage, is the same for married and single people. The widow's pension is 60 per cent of the contributor's pension. Since 1972 housewives have been able to contribute voluntarily to the state pension scheme, but dependants' benefits from the scheme are still fairly meagre. In their own right retired women workers receive on average only about 30 per cent of their previous net pay from the pension system, while men receive about 50 per cent. Most claimants of social assistance are either poor elderly women or mothers (divorced, separated or single) who have no maintenance from a former partner. Less than a third of divorcees are entitled to maintenance. Under pressure from the women's movement and the EC, as from 1986, the first year after a child is born is considered as insured time for the mother in the statutory old age pension scheme. This is of course a very limited and belated recognition of women's unequal position (see below for details of maternity leave and maternity pay). It remains the case that women have to have 35 years of contributions to qualify for the state pension in full, with no reduction in qualifying time to take account of child care (Federation of German Pensions Insurance Institutes, 1988).

The inferior status of women in the FRG's social security system is in considerable measure a reflection of their position in the paid employment structure, which is fairly typical of advanced capitalist economies. Hence there are marked vertical and horizontal divisions of labour between men and women in paid employment, with women's average earnings at around 70 per cent of men's. Despite equal rights legislation in the 1970s these features have remained stubbornly resistant to significant change. There are also some special features of the situation in the FRG. The growth in the female share of the labour force over the post-war period has been extremely modest, rising from around 35 per cent in 1950 to around 40 per cent in the late 1980s. Thus from a situation in the early 1950s when the FRG had almost the highest labour force representation of women, today the FRG has one of the lower levels in the West (Tables A.12 and A.13). In 1950 about a third of paid women workers were described as 'assistants in family-run concerns' especially in agriculture (Haug, 1986: 72). Today female paid workers are of course largely independent wage and salary earners. Particularly for working class women who cannot afford paid child care, it is still extremely difficult to combine full-time paid employment with motherhood. The school day finishes at 1 p.m., shops close at 6.30 p.m. and there is little out-of-school care available. Although the growth of part-time paid employment of women has accelerated rapidly in the last decade, the proportion of part-time women workers has historically been comparatively low. This is changing as employers realize that they can often avoid the heavy social insurance contributions by substituting women part-time workers. In 1985 a new employment law came into effect permitting temporary employment contracts which undermine employment protection for pregnant women and curtail the social insurance rights of such workers. According to the Ministry of Labour this will allow employers to call up workers only when work is available, thereby contributing to employment flexibility and economic efficiency. As Vogelheim (1988: 115) says, 'this law will push women into unprotected and marginalized relationships to the labour market.' In April 1988 18.9 per cent of women in paid employment were working under twenty-one hours per week (*Statistisches Jahrbuch*, 1989: Table 6.3). A third feature is that women in the FRG have been particularly hard hit by unemployment in the last two decades. On the OECD basis, male and female unemployment rates were very similar up to the 1970s recession, but since then the unemployment rate for women has been significantly higher than for men, much more so than in the US and Sweden (Table A.14). By the late 1980s there were a million women registered unemployed, with another 800,000 in the 'silent reserve', that is 'women who had given up registering for state unemployment benefits because they had either lost their rights to benefits or did not think the effort worthwhile, since the chance of finding work was so remote' (Vogelheim, 1988: 108). Much of the female unemployment since the mid 1970s has resulted from job cuts in the welfare state itself. The continual and increasing restraint in public expenditure has led to freezes on recruitment in teaching, health care and social services which 'cut off one of the few areas of employment possibilities and promise for both educated and less-skilled women workers' (Erler, 1988: 234).

It would therefore seem that women in the FRG have fulfilled the role of a labour reserve, to a considerable extent moving into and out of paid employment according to the demand for their labour power. However, recently there is more evidence of women being deployed as cheaper, more flexible substitutes for men in the labour force. As we have already suggested, there has been a long-established dual labour market in the FRG, made up of a primary, privileged section of predominantly male blue collar and white collar workers, and a secondary, less privileged sector of both blue and white collar workers, who are increasingly female. These processes structure the patriarchal form of the social security system.

Ethnic Minorities and the Welfare State

Migration

The position of ethnic minority groups in the FRG has much in common with other capitalist welfare states, but it is also quite distinctive in a number of ways. The post-war pattern of immigration has not been shaped directly by colonialism, unlike the processes in Britain and France. During the immediate post-war years, quite unlike any other state, the FRG received about fourteen million refugees, almost all ethnic Germans, from Eastern Europe. By the late 1950s shortages of unskilled labour led the federal government to promote the recruitment of single male workers from Southern Europe, who became known as *Gastarbeiter* or guest-workers. The Federal Labour Office established recruitment agencies in Italy, Spain, Greece, Morocco, Turkey, Yugoslavia and Portugal, and also concluded bilateral recruitment agreements with these countries' govern-ments. The term 'guestworker' suggested, intentionally, that they were recruited on a temporary basis. Indeed the government's stated policy was that they should be rotated on a three year 'tour of duty'. In recessions in the mid 1960s, early 1970s and early 1980s many hundreds of thousands of guestworkers returned home, often with financial encouragement from the federal government. In 1973, active recruitment of guestworkers was ended and tough immigration controls were introduced in a major policy U-turn. This was prompted by a number of factors including increasing industrial militancy amongst the guestworkers, rising unemployment and falling labour demand, the expansion of the EC giving EC guestworkers easier access, growing racist feeling, and concern about the costs of the increasing use of the welfare state by guestworkers. Partly in response to the firm immigration control after 1973, many of the already established guestworkers brought over their wives and children and have settled permanently, if never too securely, into German society. It is a clear paradox that in the FRG as elsewhere, the tightening of immigration control increased the level of permanent settlement. Federal governments have tried many measures to discourage permanent settlement including financial inducements to leave and at one point withdrawal of child benefit, and the reality of permanent settlement is still not accepted. Forced repatriation is not on mainstream party political agendas, not least for fear of the international outcry and the economic dislocation this would undoubtedly cause. In the late 1980s the number of 'ethnic German' refugees from Eastern Europe rose sharply again in response to events in the East, which, with the absorption of the GDR into the FRG in 1990, is likely to have adverse, long-term implications for the former guestworkers, as suggested by Räthzel (1991).

The Status of Ethnic Minorities

With the shift to permanent settlement and immigration control since 1973, the term 'guestworker' has been replaced in popular discourse with the term 'foreigners' (*Ausländer*). This is a

> seemingly neutral term [which] is becoming pejorative, just as the word 'immigrant' did in Britain two decades ago . . . the legal, socioeconomic and cultural status of 'foreigner' is the distinguishing mark of the minorities in West Germany, just as being black is the clearest sign of minority status in Britain. (Castles, 1984: 98–9)

In practice the term 'foreigner' is not applied in normal discourse to white people from Northern Europe or North America; it refers to the former guestworkers from Southern Europe, their families and their descendants, who are a racialized group in the FRG. In the 1980s the number of 'foreigners' thus defined has remained quite stable at about 4.5 million, around 7.5 per cent of the total population. The largest, most culturally distinct and most racialized ethnic group are the 1.5 million people of Turkish origin. Most foreigners live in ethnically segregated inner areas of the big cities in privately rented tenement flats. There is also a hidden group of foreigners without work permits, illegally employed often on subcontracts by large corporations. They are especially vulnerable to exploitation and brutality because of their status. This was revealed in the work of Gunther Wallraff (1988), who disguised himself as a Turkish worker and experienced at first hand highly dangerous and exploitative working conditions, and extremely overt racism from German bosses and workers. It was all recorded by a secret video camera. As Sivanandan has written:

> The racism that defines [the Turk] as inferior, fit for only dirty jobs and disposable, and locks him permanently into an underclass, is also that which hides from the public gaze the murkier doings of industry. And contracting out the shit work allows management itself to avert its face from its own seamy activities. That also saves it from the legal consequences of employing unregistered, uninsured workers and/or transgressing safety regulations – for these are the responsibility of the firm that hires out the labour. But since that labour is alien, foreign and therefore rightless, the law does not want to know. Nor does the government, which wants the work – cheap, unorganised, invisible – but not the workers . . . A whole system of exploitation is thus erected on the back of the foreign worker, but racism keeps it from the light of day. (Sivanandan, 1988: xiii)

The use of 'illegal' migrant workers as highly exploitable cheap labour is of course common in many advanced capitalist economies, including Britain and the US.

Despite the reality of permanent settlement in the last two decades, state policy continues to treat these minorities in ways which reflect their status not only as foreigners but as an underclass. The fundamental policy principle has been that the FRG 'is not nor should ever become a "country of immigration" ' (Edye, 1987: 13). This was emphatically restated in a report commissioned by the SPD/FDP coalition in 1977, which said that it was 'necessary to restrict the employment of foreigners and to maintain an awareness of the possibility of returning home' (Edye, 1987: 35). Thus the legal and policy status of foreigners is very distinct at a formal level and extremely ambiguous at a day-to-day level. The Foreigners Law of 1965 denied them the right to vote, although this has been conceded by some local authorities for local elections in the 1980s. The 1965 law states clearly that:

> Foreigners enjoy all basic rights, except the basic rights of freedom of assembly, freedom of association, freedom of movement, and free choice of occupation,

place of work and place of education, and protection from extradition abroad. (Castles, 1984: 77)

Legislation in 1969 prescribed that German citizens must always be given preference over a foreigner when a job vacancy is filled. In effect this legislation, refined by several other subsequent measures and enforced by specialist local foreigner departments and police forces, has established an unusually explicit form of institutional racism. It bestows the privilege of residence in the FRG, which can be rescinded in the event of unemployment, differences with an employer, brushes with the law and so on, so that 'deportation is a permanent Damocles' sword' (Castles, 1984: 77). A tiny proportion of foreigners have become naturalized citizens of the FRG, the main reason being the government's opposition to dual nationality. The children of foreigners remain foreigners. The barriers to naturalization and citizenship are much higher in the FRG than in other European countries. It follows from this that the FRG has no effective legislation on even the most direct forms of racial discrimination, as proscribed by the US Civil Rights Acts or the Race Relations Acts in Britain. According to Ardagh (1987: 256), 'small ads for job vacancies or flats to let often stipulate "Nur für Deutsche" ("Germans only") or "Nur Europäer" ("Europeans only"); many pubs refuse *Gastarbeiter* and one in Frankfurt even had a notice up, "Kein Zutritt für Hunde und Türken" ("No entry for dogs and Turks").'

The ethnic minorities have thus enjoyed few civil and welfare rights in law, but since the early 1970s they have received some of the benefits and services of the welfare state, including unemployment benefit and social assistance. The proportion of social assistance claimants from the 'foreign' communities has risen in recent years, from 9.1 per cent in 1984 to 14.2 per cent in 1987. In part this is a result of pressure from the ethnic minority communities, making the point that they have always been net contributors to the welfare state through social insurance contributions and taxation over the past two or three decades. There are two obvious reasons for the relatively low level of claims by the 'foreign' community in the past at least. First, before the settlement of dependants since the early 1970s, single guestworkers made very few demands on the welfare state. Second, the number of ethnic minority elderly people is very small, when compared to the number of German state pensioners. The ethnic minorities are therefore net contributors to rather than net beneficiaries of the social security system. There are few if any official statistics which document ethnic minority welfare needs and the effectiveness of the welfare state in meeting them. Although unemployment has differentially affected the ethnic minorities very clearly over the past two decades (see above), in the decade 1978–88 the registered unemployment rate for foreigners rose relatively modestly from 10.4 per cent to 12.0 per cent, while doubling from 4.3 per cent to 8.7 per cent for the population as a whole. It is impossible to quantify the position of ethnic minorities as a welfare underclass in the FRG, but it is readily apparent that they do occupy such a status in terms of income, housing, education, health care and so on, as suggested by Castles (1984) and Ardagh (1987) for example.

The present position of the ethnic minorities has not of course gone unquestioned in German politics. With the sharp increase in unemployment in the early 1980s local citizens' action groups began to campaign for 'Ausländer raus' ('foreigners out') (Derbyshire, 1987: 95). The Republican Party, formed in 1984 as a breakaway from the CSU advocating forced repatriation, has scored significant successes in local and regional elections in the late 1980s. Racial attacks and harassment of ethnic minorities have also increased in the 1980s. Since the end of the guestworker system in the early 1970s, liberals have advocated integrationist or multiculturalist policies. The most important example of this at federal government level was the Kühn report of 1979, commissioned by the SPD/FDP coalition. The report recognized the reality of permanent settlement and advocated giving foreigners a more secure legal standing. Specific proposals included the right to employment and to naturalization for foreigners' children, and the right to vote in local elections after ten years' residence. The Kühn report reflected political pressure exerted by foreigners through the trade union movement and their own community political organizations. Foreigners form about 10 per cent of trade union membership; around 50 per cent of Turkish workers are unionized. The biggest trade union, the engineering workers of IG Metall, supported the Kühn report, but the trade union federation, the DGB, did not. The SPD/FDP government did not implement any of Kühn's proposals. The government's support of the status quo was indicated by the introduction of tougher immigration rules in 1981. The election of the conservative federal government in 1982 prompted further rule changes which have curtailed foreigners' welfare rights and the possibilities for family reunification. However a government proposal in 1984 to reduce from sixteen to six the maximum age at which children abroad can join their families in the FRG was successfully opposed by a broad coalition of ethnic minority organizations, the churches, liberals and anti-racists. Under these latter pressures, regional and local government and some progressive employers have invested substantially in education, welfare, housing and health care projects for the ethnic minority communities, as described by Ardagh (1987).

In 1990 a new double-edged Immigration Law was passed. On the positive side it is hoped that it will improve the legal right of abode for long-settled foreigners, giving easier access to close relatives and to achieving naturalization. Dual citizenship, however, remains impossible. The new legislation also gives the authorities further repressive powers, for example to eject 'undesirables', including AIDS victims, to establish a computerized register of foreigners and to limit the right of abode for separated and divorced foreign women. Under the new law, according to Räthzel (1991: 43), foreign workers, except for a very small minority [EC citizens], can be treated even more absolutely as disposable units of labour; they can be repatriated or 'rotated' at will – a demand hitherto voiced in public only by the extremist right-wing Republican Party.

The Minister of the Interior commented that 'the main aim is to take steps to ensure that hostility to foreigners is not allowed to grow . . . [but] Third World problems cannot be solved by unrestricted access' (*The Guardian*, April 13th 1990: 15). Sadly of course the hostility to ethnic minorities has very little to do with their legal status, nor was the recruitment of foreign labour anything to do with solving Third World problems.

To conclude therefore, racialized ethnic minorities in the FRG, recruited by the state as guestworkers, have now settled permanently. They have a more insecure and inferior status within the labour market and within the welfare state than in any of the other states examined in this book. This is enforced by comparatively explicit racist immigration laws and institutional racism. These processes are stoutly resisted by the ethnic minority communities supported by many German liberals and anti-racists.

Women and Family Policies

Ideology

The ideology of the Social Market Economy has clearly shaped post-war state policies towards the roles of women and the family, emphasizing traditional, patriarchal values which have been strongly contested throughout the post-war period particularly by women themselves. The Basic Law of 1949 itself reflected perhaps the most fundamental contradiction between, on the one hand, its proclamation of equal rights for women and, on the other hand, its implicit support for a conventional private, patriarchal family form with separate spheres for men and women. Most feminists and their supporters would see these two principles as opposites. Article 3 of the Basic Law stated that men and women have equal rights and 'prohibited any preferences or detriment on grounds of gender' (Gebhardt-Benische, 1986: 27). This clause was the result of persistent lobbying by women's organizations in the 1945–9 period, and was a significant improvement on the Weimar constitution. Another article of the Basic Law states that 'marriage and the family are under the particular protection of the state order.' In the post-war years this was widely interpreted as meaning the reconstruction of the two parent family as the cornerstone of civil society, a private institution free from direct state intervention. The 1950s saw quite intense intellectual and political debate over how the federal government should implement such policy principles. The conservative parties, the CDU and CSU, considered the patriarchal family as a 'natural order, ordained by God' which should be supported by a male breadwinner's wage sufficient to maintain a wife and two children. The conservatives suggested that employers should contribute to a special insurance fund to provide support to families with more than two children, but this was not adopted. Direct state involvement, even in the form of child benefits, was considered to be antithetical to the Social Market Economy and anyway discredited by the family policies of the Nazis. This conservative interpretation of family policy had significant consequences for lone mothers, who in the late 1940s comprised about one-third of parents as a result of the war. The particular and pressing needs of lone mothers have never really been explicitly recognized in the welfare state in the FRG. Hence the benefits system only succeeds in halving the numbers of lone parent families in poverty, a performance comparable to that in the UK (Table A.6). This is also borne out by data on the net income of lone parent families as a proportion of that of two parent families, which is 78 per cent in the FRG, comparable with the UK, much lower than Sweden and much higher than the US (Table A.18). Nevertheless a much lower proportion of lone parent families are in poverty in the FRG compared to the UK and the US (Table A.6), although many lone mothers are dependent on social assistance. Possibly in part because of the deterrent effects of the welfare system, the level of lone motherhood in the FRG is lower than in the UK and much lower than in Sweden and the US (Table A.16).

A more liberal view of family policy was taken by women's organizations and the left in the post-war years, who pressed for universal child benefits and withdrawal of the highly regressive child tax allowances, which remained as a legacy of the Nazi period. In 1954 the conservative government conceded a very modest child benefit for wage earners with three or more children, excluding the majority of families with only one or two children and/or with parent(s) not in paid employment. It was not until 1975 that the SPD/FDP coalition abolished the child tax allowances and introduced a universal child benefit on a scale which rises with the number of children. Child benefit is not indexed to inflation, and for the first child has not been raised from the DM50 per month set in 1975. For the second child the payment is DM100 and for the third DM220, reflecting more than a vestige of pronatalism. In 1983 the incoming conservative government introduced a means test for child benefit, in effect reducing it by one-third for households on middle incomes and above (Adams, 1989). The real value of child benefit has been eroded steadily by non-indexation in the 1980s.

Until at least the emergence of the women's movement in the early 1970s, the SPD and the trade unions endorsed most of the conservative positions on the family, in particular the family wage and motherhood as a full-time, unpaid activity. The SPD's most significant post-war policy statement, the Bad Godesberg programme of 1959, endorsed the right of women 'to be housewife and mother, [which] is not only a woman's natural obligation but of great social significance' (quoted by Moeller, 1989: 155). The new women's movement of the 1970s and 1980s has attacked this party policy orthodoxy with great vigour, as described for example by Haug (1986). However, as Hoskyns (1988: 46) concludes, the main emphasis in the German feminist movement has been on creating the radical alternative and establishing the difference of women. There has been much less emphasis on operating through the institutions and taking on the state apparatus. When this has been attempted, as in the trade unions and in the SPD, the resistance of the patriarchal core has been extremely strong.

Hence the depoliticization of social policy, characteristic of the post-war reaction to Nazism, and the popular antipathy to state 'intervention' in family life, has helped to sustain patriarchal policies and welfare practices, which are seemingly more deeply entrenched in German social policy compared with the other states examined in this book.

Abortion

A foremost target for the new women's movement was the long-established restrictive abortion law, known as Paragraph 218 of the penal code, which criminalized virtually all induced terminations. Middle class women had long been able to go abroad or get access to a safe, illegal abortion, but poorer women in particular suffered from the lack of safe and inexpensive procedures. One of the central demands of feminists was that social health insurance should cover the costs of legal abortions, which has now been achieved. Early attempts at liberalization of the law had foundered on the opposition of the Catholic Church in the main. Persistent demonstrations and lobbying by women between 1971 and 1973 finally put abortion law reform on the federal parliamentary agenda. The SPD/FDP MPs were split into two camps, one supporting abortion on demand and the other supporting the doctor's right to decide with sociomedical indications. The conservative CDU/CSU opposition were split between those supporting medical and ethical grounds, and those supporting only strictly medical grounds, where the life of the mother was threatened. The SPD/FDP Bill supporting abortion on demand in the first three months of pregnancy eventually passed through the lower house of parliament in April 1974 with a small majority but the conservatives succeeded in having the new law suspended by the Supreme Court. Eventually in February 1976 a new abortion law was implemented which permitted abortion in the first three months of pregnancy on medical, ethical and/or social grounds, adjudicated by a panel of doctors and counsellors. Abortion is also legal up to the twenty-second week of pregnancy in circumstances where 'according to medical findings, the life or physical/mental health of the woman or the health of the foetus is endangered' (Morgan, 1984: 249). Abortion on demand was therefore firmly defeated. A woman seeking a legal abortion has to explain her reasons to a counsellor, the purpose of the interview being 'to encourage the woman to carry the baby to term' according to Keiner (1986: 444). If she still wants an abortion after this interview, she has to see a doctor who must give a medical indication of the grounds for the termination. The most common legal grounds are the 'social indications' where 'the social situation of the woman and her family is such that bearing the child might lead to grave conflicts or burdens' (Keiner, 1986:

444). Obviously the legislation gives wide discretionary power to doctors, which according to Ardagh (1987: 170) 'is being applied varyingly from *Land* to *Land*. In most parts of north Germany, abortion is now fairly easy to obtain. But in the rural Catholic areas of the south, not only do the medical panels tend to be stricter, but a great many doctors and hospitals refuse on conscience grounds to perform the operation'. In other words the practical obstacles to obtaining a legal termination have a considerable deterrent effect in some parts of the FRG. This may explain the fact that the annual number of abortions among women of childbearing age is markedly lower in the FRG than in Sweden, Britain and the US. It has been estimated that as many as 200,000 West German women obtain abortions abroad each year (Morgan, 1984: 249). The anti-abortion movement has achieved more influence since the return of the conservative government in 1982, proposing a Bill to outlaw the 'social indications' for abortion, which has so far been set aside by the government. The present provision has had to be defended against anti-abortion pickets and attacks on clinics. The pro-choice movement has sought the abolition of compulsory counselling, but according to Keiner (1986: 456) 'the majority of women seem to have adjusted to the law as it stands.' The ideology of the Social Market Economy, emphasizing as it does the privacy of the family and the autonomy of the individual, is unable to countenance a woman's right to control her own fertility.

Abortion has been one of the most controversial issues arising out of the unification of Germany in October 1990. In East Germany, where 90 per cent of women had paid employment, free abortion on demand during the first twelve weeks of pregnancy has been legal since 1972. In June 1990 a large demonstration in Bonn by women from East and West demanded the extension of the liberal East German law to the West rather than the extension of the restrictive West German law to the East. However the Roman Catholic Church holds a powerful position in the West, which will block the former scenario. Under the unification treaty, a two year transition period has been declared, which allows both halves of the country to keep their old laws on abortion. A further period of struggle over abortion rights is therefore in progress.

Parental Leave and Day Care

Statutory paid maternity leave has remained unaltered since the 1960s, despite the rise of the women's movement and the growing EC pressure for effective equal rights measures. It gives women the right to 100 per cent of their earnings for six weeks before the birth and eight weeks after the birth. In 1979, in response to EC and women's pressure, an additional four months of maternity leave supported by an earnings-related benefit was introduced with the right to return to the job guaranteed. According to Hesse (1984: 77) in the early 1980s 95 per cent of those entitled took up these rights, though only half of them returned to paid employment at the end of their leave. By the mid 1980s the conservative federal government found itself under several contrasting pressures – to extend and improve maternity leave, to encourage paternity leave, and to encourage women to stay at home or take part-time paid employment. The result was the 1987 Parental Allowances Law under which

> either parent may take eighteen months parental leave. This actually consists of a period of leave for parents who were previously employed, and a cash allowance for all parents who are not employed for more than eighteen hours a week . . . During the first six months, all parents receive the same benefits – DM600 a month. (Moss, 1990: 14)

After six months, the payment is means-tested, and only about 40 per cent of families continue to get the full allowance. Women comprise 98.5 per cent of those who claim the cash allowance. Hence, despite the formal possibility for paternity leave, women take up the great majority of the leave, not least because households would generally lose more income if fathers took leave. The conventional gendered division of labour in the family is not threatened. Additionally this law is part of a package of measures (see above) to use mothers as a source of cheap, flexible and unprotected part-time labour power. It also appeals to the pronatalist lobby, concerned that during the 1980s the birth rate in the FRG was the lowest in Europe. Hence Vogelheim (1988: 116) concludes that 'the Parental Allowances Law is less a policy to improve women's or families' situations and more a population policy and effort to sanitize labor market statistics at women's expense.'

Most women with children under five (61 per cent in 1985) are not in the labour force (Table A.15) which is perhaps a reflection of the lack of day care, the high level of female unemployment and the continuing strength of the ideology of domesticity. There is very little out-of-home day care for pre-school children which caters for the needs of full-time dual earner households. Only 3 per cent of the under threes are in publicly funded nurseries, of whom between 30 and 40 per cent are children from ethnic minorities. Of children aged three to five 74 per cent attend kindergarten, most of which are run by the churches with public funding support (Moss, 1988). Ethnic minority attendance at kindergarten is lower than the average for the population as a whole, indicating some inaccessibility or inappropriateness for inner city dwellers. Very few kindergarten places offer full-time care. Provision of nurseries and kindergarten is very uneven across the FRG, with very little provision in rural areas. There are very few employer-provided day care facilities. There is no tax relief on child care costs for parents. There are only 15,000 places with registered child-minders. Obviously a large number of pre-school children with parents in paid employment are being cared for informally by relatives, childminders, friends, neighbours, nannies and so on. The scale, nature and adequacy of this provision is largely unknown.

The federal government takes no direct responsibility for day care. A small experimental day care programme initiated by the government in the early 1970s met such public hostility that 'it appears to be highly improbable that a formal family day care program ever will be institutionalized on a broader scale in the FRG' (Neidhardt, 1978: 235). Socialized child care is very much associated with the state collectivism of the GDR. Nevertheless the public funding of nurseries and kindergarten by the *Länder* and the local authorities increased substantially during the 1970s. Since then, however, cuts in funding have adversely affected the existing provisions, resulting in bigger adult/child ratios, and deteriorating working conditions and less preparation time for staff, with more use of unqualified staff and short-term contracts (Moss, 1988). Public policy on day care in the FRG therefore seems to have been fairly consistent, if implicit. It suggests that mothers of pre-school children should stay at home as their full-time, unpaid carers, reflecting the conventional male breadwinner 'family-wage' view. Subsidized kindergarten are overwhelmingly part-time, which deliberately discourages mothers from having paid employment. Parents who deviate from the conventional model are largely at the mercy of unsubsidized and unregulated forms of private care.

The unpaid caring work of women in the FRG extends also, of course, to the care of the infirm elderly and the chronically ill, of whom over 80 per cent are cared for by their daughters or daughters-in-law. With the increasing numbers of these dependants, 'the "sandwich" phenomenon – women who are still responsible for children of their own and already responsible for their mothers or even grandmothers – is increasing rapidly' (Erler, 1988: 236). This has prompted renewed discussion on the possibilities of a new 'welfare mix' involving partnership between the caring roles of women (and men) in the family and the community care roles of private and public welfare agencies. As Erler (1988) indicates, to be successful this must involve reappraising traditional family values, gender roles and even rigid definitions of full employment.

In conclusion therefore, family policy in the FRG has been shaped by strong anti-collectivist sentiment derived more from the 'market' than the 'social' element of the Social Market Economy. This embraces traditional notions of separate gender roles in the family, women's economic dependence on men, and the privacy of the family, with a residual state interest in pronatalism. During the last two decades, the women's movement has succeeded in weakening some elements of this formidable ideology, particularly in the area of abortion policy, but the struggle to transform the patriarchal welfare state continues.

The Health Care System

Finance and Administration

There is no national health service in the FRG; essentially the system is financed and organized on the social insurance basis established by Bismarck in the 1880s, modernized to accord with Social Market Economy principles. Thus the health insurance funds, the medical profession and the health technology industries remain relatively autonomous from the state. Yet over 90 per cent of the population today is covered by social insurance for sickness benefits and health care, predominantly financed by earnings-related fifty/fifty employer and employee contributions. The majority of the rest are covered by private insurance, mostly taken up by high-salary earners who opt out of the state scheme to avoid high contributions. Services are largely free at the point of consumption, with doctors and hospitals reimbursed by the insurance funds. Total health care expenditure (public and private) rose steadily from 4.7 per cent of GDP in 1960 to 8.1 per cent of GDP in 1984 (Table A.20). Health care expenditure in the FRG as a proportion of GDP has stayed just above the OECD average throughout the post-war period (Table A.20), in sharp contrast with the other states examined here. On a 'real' basis, the growth of total health care expenditure has never been much in excess of GDP growth in the FRG in the past three decades, unlike most OECD states (Table A.22). In other words the growth in health care spending has been much more in line with the growth of national economic resources. This suggests that the decentralized and depoliticized, predominantly non-profit system in the FRG may of itself contribute to cost containment.

In 1960 67.5 per cent of health care expenditure was 'public' (predominantly from the sickness insurance funds) rising to 78.2 per cent in 1984 (Table A.19). The public–private mix has also remained close to the OECD average, again in contrast with the health care systems of Sweden, the US and Britain (Table A.19). 'Private' expenditure includes prescription and other charges in the public sector, private health insurance and charitable, church, corporate and other private funding. Hospital beds are predominantly provided by the local or regional authorities, supplemented by a substantial number of church and other non-profit making hospitals. The number of for-profit hospital beds is around 10 per cent of the total, but has risen disproportionately since the mid 1970s. Doctors operate on a fee-for-service, private contractor basis except for public sector hospital doctors who are salaried. Ardagh (1987: 198) argues that the German system is fairer than the British NHS because health care finance is related to earnings, while everyone gets the same service. However the latter is only true in the most basic sense of service availability rather than need-related access. This assertion also fails to acknowledge that the British NHS is largely funded by taxation, which is also earnings-related. In contrast to Ardagh, Deppe (1989: 1161) argues that in the West German system employers pass on their contribution burden in higher prices, while the real burden of health care costs is carried by workers through their contributions.

With the emergence of the fiscal crisis of the state in the mid 1970s, federal governments have sought to limit public expenditure on health care, but the relatively autonomous nature of the system has not facilitated this. For many years, direct public finance of the health care system has provided only about 14 per cent of the total expenditure. Legislation in 1972 shifted the financial burden of new hospital investment further away from direct taxation to the indirect form of the social insurance funds, leading to a sharp increase in health insurance contributions. Statutory health insurance premiums as a percentage of average wages rose from 4.1 per cent to 6.3 per cent in 1987 (Steele, 1988). To deal with this lack of central control, in 1977 the federal government passed the Health Cost Containment Law, which established a federal health finance and budget commission, called 'Concerted Action'. However this body had no executive powers to impose cost containment and in this respect it seems largely to have failed. In the 1980s federal governments, both SPD/FDP and CDU/FDP, resorted to legislation, which introduced patient charges 'for hospital care and cures, higher charges for medicines, schemes for non-reimbursable medicines, and contributions by pensioners to health insurance' (Murswieck, 1985: 101). Direct payments by patients within the statutory health insurance system more than doubled between 1977 and 1984. Through the Concerted Action machinery there has been increasingly effective federal government pressure in recent years on the local and regional authorities to privatize elements of the hospital service and to impose a 'monetary cost–profit rationality' on the hospitals. There are certainly some examples of apparent waste of resources in the system. The insurance funds employ over 70,000 people, mostly billing hospitals and doctors, and tracking down contributors, an administrative feature of all insurance-based systems of course. Since the hospitals are reimbursed on a fixed daily fee for patients regardless of their treatment, there is an incentive to keep patients in hospital. The average length of hospital stays in the FRG is the longest in Europe. Out-patient facilities on the other hand are underdeveloped. Pharmaceutical prices are about 70 per cent above the EC average with little resort to cheaper, generic substitutes. In 1987, for the first time, the federal government sought to make the insurance funds liable only for the costs of generic drugs and to establish a limited list of inexpensive items available to patients through the funds such as contact lenses, hearing aids, wheelchairs etc. (Steele, 1988). Deppe (1989: 1164) describes the restructuring of the health system since the mid 1970s as 'aiming at an intensification of selection and filtering mechanisms [which] will lead to a deepening of social differences between employee groups'. The decentralized and relatively autonomous structure of health care finance and administration in the FRG inevitably means that the system is not quite as uniform or egalitarian as it might seem. Federal laws establish which occupational or social groups a statutory health insurance fund may cater for, the management structure of the funds and minimum levels of contribution and benefits, but within these parameters, the 1182 (as of 1987) different funds can determine actual contribution and benefit levels. Funds are organized on both a geographical (local/regional) basis and on an occupational basis. Variations in the membership's mean income levels, age and gender structures, the distribution and cost of medical facilities, different occupational health and safety risks, coverage for dependants and so on shape the income and expenditure of the different funds. The funds for white collar workers offer better services for higher premiums, for example offering higher fees to doctors, thereby in theory attracting better practitioners. The funds to some extent compete with each other in providing non-statutory extras such as coverage for recuperation, health checks, cures etc. The policies of the funds are therefore by no means uniform. This applies too 'to the recognition of new medical techniques or treatments, to the exclusion of medicines of doubtful value and to efforts at controlling hospital and medical costs' (Rosenberg and Ruban, 1986: 273). In the 1970s these differences between the funds, particularly the regional funds which cover about half the population, were diminishing under pressure from federal government regulation, but the thrust of deregulation and privatization in the 1980s and 1990s may be reversing this.

Power Struggles in the Health System

The administration of the statutory health insurance funds is remarkably bureaucratic and depoliticized. Under Bismarck's original scheme, employees had two-thirds of the representation and employers one-third. Before 1933, the funds were therefore a local power base for the trade unions and white collar organizations. In the 1920s there were some intense class conflicts between medical professionals and left-controlled insurance funds over reimbursement of doctors and quality of service. In the FRG however, worker representation was reduced to 50 per cent and these bodies became rather distant from party political and industrial conflict, and from the communities they serve, so that 'there are no real organized counter-powers on behalf of the insured and the consumers' (Murswieck, 1985: 102).

   This is not to suggest however that working class pressure, mediated through the political parties and the labour movement, has not contributed directly to shaping the health care system in the FRG. The foremost example of such pressure being successfully applied was the abortive health reform of the late 1950s. The conservative federal government, following the Social Market Economy ideology, attempted to introduce 'cost-sharing' to reduce the allegedly excessive number of trivial cases burdening the insurance funds and the health care system. Means-tested fees for ambulatory visits to doctors were proposed, as well as an effective lowering of the income ceiling for compulsory social insurance, to encourage the private health insurance industry. There ensued a bitter and lengthy public debate, as the proposals were vigorously opposed by the trade unions, the SPD and the health insurance funds, as described by Stone (1980) and Safran (1967). The proposals directly threatened one of the bureaucratic citadels of revisionist social democratic power in Germany, the health insurance funds established since the 1880s. Eventually this opposition proved successful, thereby delineating the limits of health care privatization in the Social Market Economy up to the present at least.

A second important example of social democratic influence was the extension of both health insurance coverage and the minimum range of services offered by the funds. Alongside the improvement of social security coverage, this was the foremost social policy achievement of the SPD/FDP federal government in the late 1960s and early 1970s. Many students, farmers and disabled people were brought into the system for the first time, where necessary their contributions being paid from public funds. Birth control, abortion, sterilization and cancer-screening services for example became compulsory elements of the health funds' package. One glaring gap in the social health insurance scheme is that it only covers for a certain amount of medical care, leaving the chronically sick in a very vulnerable position. Hospitals are keen to discharge the chronically sick who have no private resources, since they are not reimbursed for their care, with the result that there are 'many patients living in poorly-supplied old people's homes' (Steele, 1988) financed by a mix of charity, social assistance and local authority funds.

Aside from these various federal government interventions and the funds' limited room for manoeuvre as described above, real power in the West German health system is bestowed upon the medical profession, particularly in the shape of the Health Insurance Physicians' Associations (KVs). The KVs have overwhelming day-to-day influence over the quality and distribution of health care services. They also have a strong monopoly bargaining situation in negotiating fees with the funds. Hence for GPs, dentists and specialists outside the public hospitals,

> so generous is the scale of fees that a good doctor can always earn a lot of money . . . these 'Götter in Weiss' (gods in white) are among the wealthiest members of the post-war German plutocracy . . . in the early 1980s a campaign by the media cast a spotlight on the huge incomes being amassed by surgeons and other specialists, who for relatively little work were able to charge their insurance agencies extravagant sums for the use of their modern equipment. Under this pressure, the medical profession finally agreed to accept some cutbacks in their scale of consultancy fees. Even so, they still do very nicely. (Ardagh, 1987: 198–9)

According to Pflanz (1971) however, the insurance funds exert quite a significant degree of day-to-day control over doctors' expenditure and patients' demands. Many insurance fund officials believe that 'insured persons tend to crave more benefits than they are entitled to receive' while 'discontent with the surveillance [by fund officials] over economical behaviour is high among the doctors' (Pflanz, 1971: 320). As the administrators of health finance, the insurance fund officials try to contain the demands of doctors and patients, rather unsuccessfully perhaps in view of the health care cost explosion of the last two decades.

Health Status and Health Inequalities

Use of a composite of seventeen age- and sex-specific mortality rates for 1975 as an index of national health status (Table A.23) suggested that the FRG ranked bottom in a group of ten advanced capitalist states, including Sweden, the US and the UK. The infant mortality rate in the 1980s has remained around the OECD average. These figures are perhaps a little surprising in view of the FRG's higher than average GNP per capita, if one accepts the view that the health status of the population is closely related to the general affluence of a society. Infant mortality rates are higher in the cities than in the countryside even though the cities have better health care provision. This suggests that higher infant mortality may be associated with urban poverty. Indeed the comparatively inferior overall health status of the population of the FRG may reflect the degree of hidden poverty in the FRG, as discussed above. This is confirmed by surveys cited by Siegrist (1989: 357) showing that 'poor people (i.e. those with an income up to 60 per cent of mean income per capita) visit physicians less frequently than wealthier people', particularly for screening and preventive services including ante-natal care. To a less marked extent this is also true for blue collar families in general. There is therefore evidence of class differences in the effective utilization of health care services not so much in acute crises, but in preventive measures and early diagnosis. Inevitably this must have a knock-on effect on mortality and morbidity. Siegrist suggests that class difference in attitudes and lack of awareness on the part of working class consumers are the problems, but this perhaps implicitly blames the victims. A class biased subculture within the health care system which favours the middle class seems to be in evidence. Despite the near universality of health insurance and the accessibility of health services, some consumers are more equal than others. Unfortunately there is no national epidemiological data on inequalities in health status or on access to and use of health care services in the FRG. Siegrist (1989: 361) explains that the discipline of epidemiology was destroyed during the Nazi period, and has a weak position in medical science. Both public health services and occupational health services seem to have a marginal position and low status within the health care system in the FRG, where 'first priority is given to somatically oriented treatment by the physician' and there is 'a virtual absence of research, training and practice in industrial and social medicine' (Rosenberg and Ruban, 1986: 258). In this respect also, the health care system seems to faithfully reflect the Social Market Economy ideology, with the emphasis on the doctor as entrepreneur, high-technology scientific medicine and individual consumer responsibility for preventive measures. Although quantitative data is very scanty, it seems likely that the health care system in the FRG contributes fairly directly to the reproduction of the class, gender and racial inequalities and oppression associated with modern capitalism.

Conclusion

By comparison with Britain and the US, the welfare state in the FRG seems to be extraordinarily depoliticized. The formulation and implementation of social policy is marked by an apparent lack of serious social and political conflict. In the policy areas examined here, policy formulation and execution is left largely in bureaucratic and professional hands, administratively decentralized or privatized but regulated by federal laws. This structure has created some obstacles to the efforts of federal governments to restrain welfare expenditures since the mid 1970s. The welfare state in the FRG is formally enshrined in public laws and collectivist policies. However welfare consumers are highly stratified and individuated along occupational, gender and racial lines. There is little collective representation of consumers or potential beneficiaries outside, of course, the major political parties and the trade unions. Welfare pressure and interest groups are largely absent. The 'producers' of social welfare are in many ways 'private' institutions. The social security system is based on actuarial, contributory principles which are similar to those adopted by commercial private insurance companies. The same may also be said of the health insurance funds. The health care system as a whole is only nominally 'public' in nature. Half of the hospitals and most of the doctors are in the private sectors, much of it for profit. Family policies emphasize the primacy of the family, and women's unpaid caring work as private welfare. The great bulk of the personal social services are provided by the Roman Catholic and the Protestant Churches, regulated by the local authorities (Brauns and Kramer, 1989: 132). In this sense, the welfare state in the FRG is market-driven in line with the Social Market Economy ideology, supporting and reinforcing fundamental inequalities and oppression, while at the same time offering assistance, to some extent as a form of control, to many of those in greatest need.

Of course there is political conflict over social policy in the FRG but it is relatively concealed at a local level and within the bureaucracies, compared to Britain and the US. Struggles over pensions and health insurance reform in the 1950s and 1960s were in many senses encounters between the labour movement and the state. In more recent years successful lobbying against cuts in the welfare state has come from workers and middle class professionals, particularly those employed in the welfare state itself. Over the past two decades, welfare politics has also been transformed by the emergence of the new social movements – feminism, environmentalism, the peace movement, squatting, the gay and lesbian movement, ethnic minority and anti-racist organizations and so on. The central influence of the women's movement on family policy, particularly abortion reform, was noted above. Similarly the ethnic minority organizations have struggled with some success to become enfranchised in the welfare state and to challenge its institutional racism. Beyond this, the influence of the new social movements, often under the umbrella of the Greens, has been

confined largely to local, single issue campaigns, which have not as yet
shifted national policies in the fields examined here. Nevertheless the
Greens and the new social movements

> with their readiness to demonstrate, protest, and employ direct action, as well as
> to operate directly in neighbourhoods, inner cities, polluted areas, immigrant
> ghettos and the like . . . have demonstrated an ability to enter into the extra-
> parliamentary realm which has hitherto been practically a monopoly of the Right
> with its presence in the churches, schools, clubs, mass media and other ostensibly
> 'non-political' areas of social life. (Graf, 1986: 132)

Two principles emerging from the new social movements have radical
implications for the welfare state – debureaucratization and self-help, self-
organization or empowerment. Such principles appeal as much to free-
market conservatives as to libertarians of the centre and the left. As
Grunow (1986) suggests, to some extent these groups form an unholy
alliance around these principles, representing a reaction to state collectivism, yet distinct from the Social Market Economy. It is unclear whether the
Greens, essentially a left of centre movement, and the Social Democrats
can coalesce around redistributive yet anti-bureaucratic social policies,
which would be sufficiently popular with their heterogeneous constituen-
cies – the labour movement and the liberal middle class on the one hand,
and the 'post-materialists', feminists etc. on the other hand. The Social
Democrats' implicit corporatism tends to exclude ethnic minorities,
women, old people and young people and does 'nothing to reduce racism,
sexism and anti-welfarism amongst the subordinate classes' (Graf, 1986:
118). The Greens have to develop a coherent, alternative conception of the
welfare state upon which to build a mass base. On the New Right, beyond
the supporters of the status quo and the Social Market Economy, there are
equally important and contrasting shades of opinion on the future of the
welfare state. On the one hand there are free-market neo-liberals advocating large-scale privatization of utilities and the welfare state. On the other
hand there are conservatives who emphasize authoritarian strengthening of
the welfare state as a means of social control, implying a state inspired
offensive against welfare dependency, particularly amongst ethnic minorities and lone mothers, and against the anti-capitalist attitudes of the new
social movements.

The social policy implications of the expansion of the FRG by the
absorption of the *Länder* of East Germany in October 1990 are, of course,
enormous. Essentially the social and economic policies of the Social
Market Economy are being extended to the East, and the Stalinist welfare
state in the East is being dismantled. The process of economic restructuring is creating sudden and massive unemployment on top of the social
deprivations already experienced by the East German people. The future
for women's paid employment and the nursery provision in the East looks
very insecure in the context of West German family policy. The East/West
stratification of the working class will become institutionalized into the
welfare state. Whether or not, in the long term, federal social and

economic policies succeed in mitigating or otherwise successfully managing that stratification is an open question looming large over European social policy.

The Federal Republic of Germany is then a particular model of the modern capitalist welfare state, which is in many ways distinct from the others examined here. It claims legitimacy by its appearance of combining market and individual freedoms with social justice. We have suggested that in its actual functioning, it is primarily shaped by market forces, thereby maintaining substantial class, intra-class, gender and racial inequalities and oppression. The ideology and the welfare system it has produced have proved very resilient and adaptable, thus far withstanding the fiscal crisis of the state and the rise of the new social movements and the New Right.

4

The United States: the Welfare State in the Corporate Market Economy

The United States (US) has often been stereotyped as a 'welfare laggard' with a residual or underdeveloped welfare state compared to many Western European states. To the extent that the idea of the welfare state is often popularly associated with the Social Democratic, Social Market and Liberal Collectivist achievements of the post-war period in Western Europe, then the US might not be considered to be a welfare state at all, because of gaps in programme coverage and the emphasis on private welfare initiatives. Of course there are elements of truth in such stereotypes, but there is no question that the US has a welfare state, with prominent involvement of public finance, law and agencies in the provision of welfare services and benefits. The form of the US welfare state is of course unique in many facets and certainly presents a distinct contrast with the West European welfare states we have examined so far. Up to the 1980s, supporters of West European welfare state collectivism on both sides of the Atlantic saw the US welfare state developing to catch up with Western Europe. It is very important to discard such notions which portray the US welfare state as embryonically European. The fact is that the US welfare state since the 1930s has been a viable, working model of the welfare state under capitalism which ranks alongside the European models in status and significance. Indeed with the rise of the New Right in Europe, described as neo-conservatism in the US, elements of the US welfare tradition are being advocated and adopted by conservative European governments, most notably by the recent Conservative governments in Britain. It is possible that we might see the Americanization of the European welfare states in the future.

The modern welfare state in the US developed in two short bursts of popular pressure and social reform – the New Deal of the 1930s, and the rapid expansion of social programmes in the Great Society era of the 1960s. The New Deal was prompted by the deep crisis of free-market capitalism, and the political agitation of many of its victims – farmers, capitalists, unemployed people and elderly people in particular. The New Deal inaugurated federally sponsored social insurance and social assistance schemes, industrial relations machinery and support for business, farmers and homeowners. The main beneficiaries of the New Deal were the middle class, the farmers and the organized, predominantly white urban working class. The Great Society programmes substantially extended public involvement in most areas of welfare. They were prompted by the redis-covery of poverty and unmet welfare needs in the affluent society, pushed forward above all by the black civil rights movement, and also by the women's movement and the wider welfare rights movement. Arguments continue to rage about whether and to what extent the Great Society programmes succeeded in mitigating poverty and racial and gender inequalities. Since the late 1960s there has been a so-called backlash against the welfare state, whose impact has been significant but patchy. The recessions of the mid 1970s and early 1980s sharply increased registered unemployment, which has fallen significantly since then. During the 1980s the Reagan administration succeeded in retrenching many of the anti-poverty programmes while maintaining the programmes which benefit the majority, particularly elderly people. During the recent recessions, real incomes have actually fallen in the US, but household incomes have been sustained by the increased participation of women in the paid labour force.

The most distinctive features of the welfare state in the US are the enormous local diversity in policies and practices, the accompanying absence of a coherent national social policy consensus, a sharp division between social insurance for those considered deserving and punitive means-tested programmes for poor people, and the integral role of private charitable and commercial interests within the welfare state. This distinct-iveness is derived from the particular characteristics of the state apparatus, the class structure and corporate capital in the US. The domestic state apparatus is characterized by anti-federalism, decentralization of power, the absence of a powerful domestic civil service, and the separation of powers at all levels of government between executive, legislature and judiciary (Amenta and Skocpol, 1989). The absence of a strong central state apparatus is explained in part by the early achievement of white male suffrage by the 1830s. In Western Europe throughout the nineteenth century male suffrage was the main focus of working class political struggle against the state. In the US the central state has never had to develop the capacity to confront and respond to the demands of a politically and nationally unified working class. The working class in the US has also been particularly divided by racism, by successive waves of migration from different parts of the world and by religion. The labour movement has never been able to unite the working class, and the influence of socialism and social democracy have usually been eclipsed by the ideology of 'business unionism', which entirely accepts the capitalist system and aims to get the best possible deal out of employers by collective bargaining. Nevertheless the labour movement was a keen advocate of the New Deal social insurance schemes, which it still defends strongly. The meagre influence of social democracy and socialism in the US during the construc-tion of the modern welfare state left an ideological vacuum. In part the vacuum has been filled by the 'liberalism' of the industrial and financial corporations (corporate capital) which dominate the economy. Since the late nineteenth century they have involved themselves in many aspects of welfare – the management, sponsorship and funding of health care, educational and other welfare institutions, the provision of occupational welfare benefits and services to employees (welfare capitalism) and welfare philanthropy. The early years of this century in the US witnessed the development of a corporate hegemony within the liberal state (Weinstein, 1968). The major financial and industrial corporations in the US have serviced and shaped the welfare state in the US to an extent quite unknown in Western Europe.

Ideology and Welfare Expenditure

Voluntarism and Liberalism: an Awkward Social Policy Consensus

There is no single term which adequately describes the social policy consensus in the US, because the *idea* of the welfare state is much less securely established than in Western Europe. Yet a kind of social policy consensus has existed since the 1930s, formed out of a pragmatic and flexible combination of voluntarism and liberalism. Voluntarism encapsulates two principles. First, the individual and the patriarchal family should be almost entirely responsible for their own welfare, with if appropriate the support of private agencies such as charities, churches, employers and unions. Second, the role of public welfare interventions should be to restore the individual and the family to self-sufficiency and to deter dependence on public support. Conservatives differ in their emphasis on these two principles; neo-conservative, free-market conservatives emphasize the first, authoritarian conservatives the second. This Victorian interpretation of the Protestant ethic remains hegemonic in the US, which has not been the case in much of Western Europe since the war. Voluntarism implies that social policies which undermine these principles are 'un-American' or even 'communist'. Thus there is continued and heavy stigmatization of the substantial number of people who are dependent on welfare benefits and services targeted at the poor. However voluntarism has been tempered and blunted throughout US history by 'liberalism' which has a particular meaning in the US. Liberalism accepts the necessity of positive, social policy interventions to meet social needs, which are pushed forward by pressure and interest groups of many kinds, including those of the poor and oppressed, the middle classes, the women's movement, the labour movement, the business corporations and so on. Liberalism implies a pragmatic, welfare collectivism without explicit left–right bias, but symbolized in concepts like 'the New Deal' and 'the Great Society' associated with Democratic presidents, while the Reagan presidency was explicitly hostile to liberalism.

Another peculiar and important aspect of public policy in the US is the apparent lack of explicit interaction between social and economic policy. During the New Deal in the 1930s 'social Keynesians' advocating high levels of federal government spending as a counter-cyclical device to ensure 'full' employment seemed to have prevailed. However, after the war, what has aptly been described as 'commercial Keynesianism' predominated which 'stressed the fine-tuning of fiscal and monetary adjustments within relatively limited parameters of government action and domestic social spending' (Skocpol, 1987: 43). Hence the Great Society programmes for example were not specifically linked to notions of Keynesian labour market or expansionary economic policies. With faltering economic growth and stagflation in the mid 1970s, commercial Keynesianism was adapted fairly easily to monetarist and supply-side arguments in favour of higher unemployment, tax cuts and cuts in the welfare state. Certainly since the mid 1970s social policy has been driven more explicitly by the new economic policies.

The combination of voluntarism and liberalism is reflected in an extremely significant dualism in US social policy between programmes which are universally provided and those which are targeted at poor people. Of course this dualism, reflecting notions of the deserving and undeserving, historically has shaped all welfare states, but it remains of central significance in the US. Glazer (1986: 43) refers to two systems, Welfare I and Welfare II; Weir *et al.* (1988: 422) refer to social programmes 'bifurcated into two tiers'. Welfare I or the upper tier consists of the social insurance based programmes and the public education system, while Welfare II or the lower tier consists of means-tested benefits and other non-contributory programmes directed specifically at poor people. During the 1980s the upper tier has come under far less political pressure for cuts than the lower tier. O'Connor (1973: 138) has theorized the bifurcation by describing the function of social insurance as being 'to create a sense of economic security within the ranks of employed workers . . . and thereby raise morale and reinforce discipline . . . Social insurance is not primarily insurance for workers, but a kind of insurance for capitalists and corporations.' Social insurance is generally therefore strongly supported by organized labour and business corporations, and is a form of 'social capital'. The function of means-tested assistance is to 'pacify and control the surplus population' (O'Connor, 1973: 7) as a 'social expense', which is merely an unproductive burden on capital and the state, rather than being indirectly productive like social capital. The lower tier is therefore much more politically vulnerable, unless sustained by continuous agitation by poor people. This dualism in the US welfare state presents a sharp contrast with much of Western Europe, where social capital has, as it were, embraced social expenses. The bifurcation is reflected in the phrases used to describe the two elements in the income maintenance system, both inaugurated with the 1935 Social Security Act. 'Social security' in the US is used to describe social insurance programmes for retirement, widowhood and disability. The notion of social security is popular and the term has a positive aura. 'Welfare' on the other hand is used to describe the means-tested assistance for poor people, which often carries with it eligibility for other services including health care, food stamps, day care and training. 'Welfare' claimants are heavily stigmatized and the term has a strongly negative aura. The obviously close association of the terms 'welfare' and 'welfare state' help to give the latter its negative connotations in the US, reflecting the continuing strength of voluntarism.

Welfare Expenditure

In terms of social welfare expenditure as a proportion of GDP, the US has remained consistently below the OECD average, and well below the levels for the FRG, Sweden and the UK (Table A.1). Yet in the period from 1960 to 1975, roughly the peak years of the Great Society programmes, the welfare state in the US expanded more rapidly in relation to GDP growth than in the other three states, and much more than the OECD average. In other words during that period there really was a 'welfare state explosion' in the US. However, during the years 1975 to 1981 the situation changed dramatically as the growth of social welfare expenditure fell behind GDP growth (Table A.1). Although precise OECD figures are not available, there is no question that since 1981, social welfare expenditure has fallen further behind GDP growth.

The extent to which the income maintenance system removes people from dependence on the labour market in old age, sickness and unemployment has been assessed by Esping-Andersen (1990) using his de-commodification index (Table 1.1). On this scale for the year 1980, the US had the second lowest level of welfare de-commodification amongst eighteen capitalist states. In other words the people of the US are comparatively unprotected from the vagaries of market forces in meeting these three basic needs. This is reflected in the high levels of private spending on welfare which amounted to 7.5 per cent of GNP in 1973, which was about 30 per cent of the total expenditure on welfare (Higgins, 1981: 137). Much of this private expenditure consists of private philanthropy devoted to welfare causes, which is administered on a scale quite unprecedented anywhere else. In 1985 private philanthropy in the US was equivalent to 2 per cent of GNP or $80 billion, 82 per cent of it coming from individuals and only 5 per cent each from foundations and corporations respectively. About half of this money was allocated for religious purposes, of which an unknown proportion was dedicated to welfare activity. The great bulk of the rest of private philanthropic contributions was dedicated to health care, education and social services, amounting to over $30 billion in 1985 (US Bureau of the Census, 1987: Table 630). Private, voluntary agencies organized by ethnic, religious and community groups play a dominant role in the personal social services. They are usually closely interrelated with the public authorities, but their robust survival 'prevents uniformity on nationwide (or in many cases, citywide or statewide) basis, and it also provides a means of disengagement for an administration that wishes to reduce the government's role in providing social services' (Glazer, 1986: 54). Thus examining public policy and spending on social welfare in the US gives only a partial view of the ways in which basic welfare needs are met or not met. Wherever possible, it is necessary to examine the role of the various private sectors.

Income Maintenance Policies and Outcomes

Income Inequality and Poverty

As one might expect in view of the modest de-commodification discussed above, cash benefits contribute comparatively little (8.0 per cent) to average gross incomes in the US (Table A.2). In other words, people are overwhelmingly dependent on 'market incomes' from employment, property and private pensions. This is a considerable contrast with the West European welfare states, particularly Sweden. Data on the distribution of income in 1972/3 and 1980 (Tables A.3 and A.4) shows, not surprisingly, that the gap between the rich and the poor is widest in the US amongst the welfare states studied here. The bottom 20 per cent of the distribution have by far the smallest proportion of disposable income. Nevertheless, surprisingly perhaps the top 20 per cent and the top 10 per cent of the distribution are not as relatively affluent as in the FRG. The Gini coefficient for distribution of disposable income, adjusted for household size, shows the US to have a far more unequal distribution than Sweden and the UK in 1972/3 and 1980, though not in fact as unequal as that for the FRG. However, income taxation and social security transfers achieved a greater fall in the Gini coefficient for the US than for Sweden, and a much bigger fall than that in the UK and the FRG (Table A.5). In other words, without the taxation and social security systems, the distribution of incomes in the US would be considerably more unequal. All this data suggests that it is the gap between poor and low-paid people, and those with middle incomes and above, which is comparatively wider in the US. It is widely agreed that Reagan's 1981 and 1982 tax cuts brought about a substantial upward redistribution of income, benefiting the top 10 per cent in particular (Edsall, 1984; Miller and Jenkins, 1987; Ruggles and O'Higgins, 1987).

Comparative data suggests that the US had a level of post-transfer poverty in 1980 almost double that of the UK, and around three times that in Sweden and the FRG (Table A.6). Almost uniquely amongst welfare states, the US has developed a national definition of poverty. Every year since 1964, the start of the War on Poverty, the federal Social Security Administration establishes the cash income required by households of different sizes to achieve a minimum level of nutrition, housing, clothing and health care. This is the official poverty line, and it includes income from social insurance and assistance benefits but not benefits 'in kind' such as food stamps. Inevitably it has its inadequacies, and it is criticized for being too crude, too generous or too mean (DiNitto and Dye, 1983:

Table 4.1   *Percentages of families below and just above the poverty line in the US*

	All families	White	Black	Hispanic	Lone mother
Below the poverty line					
1960	18.5	15.2	48.1	N/A	N/A
1970	9.7	7.7	27.9	N/A	32.7
1980	9.2	6.9	27.8	20.3	30.4
1986	11.4	9.1	28.7	25.5	34.0
Within 125 per cent of the poverty line					
1986	15.3	12.7	35.8	N/A	40.8

Source: US Bureau of the Census, 1987: Tables 746, 749

Chapter 3), but it remains widely accepted and quoted. In 1985 14 per cent of the population lived in households with incomes below the poverty line and a further 4.7 per cent within 125 per cent of the poverty line. The percentage of people in poverty varies very significantly from state to state. In the mid 1980s New Hampshire had the lowest proportion at 5.6 per cent and Mississippi the highest at 25.6 per cent. Table 4.1 suggests that the reforms of the 1960s halved the total poverty rate, but in the 1980s the poverty rate climbed again, particularly in the recession of the early 1980s. The reduction in poverty amongst white people has been much greater proportionately than amongst black people, while poverty amongst people of Spanish origin and amongst lone mothers has increased significantly during the 1980s. Black families remain over three times more likely to be in poverty than white families, a ratio which has not changed since the 1950s.

Old Age Pensions

Total public and private expenditure on pensions as a proportion of GDP in the US in 1980 was below the OECD average, and far below the proportions in the other welfare states examined here (Table A.7). This is an interesting contrast with health care spending where the reverse is the case, possibly reflecting a relatively unaggressive private pensions industry. Elderly people in the US are particularly dependent on paid employment, which contributes 26.8 per cent of elderly households' income, a very much higher proportion than in the FRG and Sweden (Table A.9). Perhaps surprisingly in view of the generally predominant influence of voluntarism and the extent of private welfare in the US, the provision of old age pensions is dominated by the public sector. In 1980 79 per cent of pensions expenditure occurred in the public sector mostly from the social insurance funds, supplemented by special funds for war veterans and some public employees (Table A.8). While the proportion of occupational pensions in the mix is higher than in most other capitalist states, they only accounted for 17 per cent of spending in 1980. The origins of this situation lie in the inter-war years. The first three decades of the twentieth century were the golden years of welfare capitalism, that is the provision of occupationally based welfare benefits and services. According to Brandes (1976: 105), 'pension plans were enlisted in the struggle against unions' by employers, and probably over three million workers were covered by the late 1920s. This was, however, only a small, elite section of the workforce and both employers' and workers' enthusiasm for such schemes declined. They did not undermine unionism and workers resented the attempts by employers to use pensions as a means of disciplinary control (Lubove, 1968: 131). In the 1980s, according to Wilson (1987: 44),

> about 50 per cent of workers are building up occupational pension rights and about one in three of the retired population are actually drawing occupational pensions . . . Coverage, however, is far from even and it is the lower-paid, unskilled manual workers, women workers and employees in non-unionized occupations who are without this additional protection.

In the recent recessions a number of company pension schemes have got into difficulties or even been wound up; tighter federal government regulation was introduced in the 1970s.

There were many attempts by individual states to introduce social insurance pensions in the first three decades of this century, which were largely thwarted by business opposition to the payroll taxes required to finance them. Then in the early 1930s, amidst the mass destitution of the depression, populist movements for radical redistribution of income and assistance to elderly, unemployed and poor people emerged. Amongst these was the Townsend Movement demanding a flat-rate, universal public pension which was the first mass movement of old people in history, at its peak in the mid 1930s claiming several million active supporters. The movement 'unleashed a new force in American politics: the old people' (Leuchtenburg, 1963: 106) which remains of great significance in contemporary interest-group politics and lobbying. Although the Townsend Plan was not adopted, the Social Security Act 1935, one of the centrepieces of the New Deal, implemented statutory insurance for old age, supplemented by means-tested assistance for elderly poor people. Since 1935 social insurance has been extended gradually to cover survivors (widows and their children), people with disability, and hospital expenses of the elderly. The scheme, known as OASDHI (Old Age, Survivors, Disability and Health Insurance), is the cornerstone of the welfare state in the US and is popularly known as 'social security'. The earnings-related benefits are financed by fifty/fifty employer/employee earnings-related contributions, which in 1988 amounted to a payroll tax of 15.2 per cent. Benefits are mildly weighted towards lower earners. Eligibility conditions are neither very strict nor very generous. Benefits have been indexed to the cost of living since 1974. The social insurance funds are not subsidized from taxation and since the mid 1970s the social security system has frequently been described as being in financial crisis because, with the increasing numbers of elderly people eligible for OASDHI, the old age and survivors insurance fund has been in deficit. The crisis culminated in 1982/3 with a sharp power struggle within the Washington political and bureaucratic establishment between neo-conservatives and traditional liberals (Light, 1985). The outcome in the shape of the 1983 social security amendments was that cost-of-living adjustments were delayed, payroll taxes were planned to increase again, benefits to higher-income groups became taxable, social security coverage was made mandatory to increase contribution income, and, in the long term, raising of the retirement age from sixty-five was envisaged. The liberals seemed to have largely succeeded in defending the New Deal in this instance, without achieving very much for women and lower-income groups. Although neo-conservatives continue to seek cutbacks in eligibility and indexation, popular support for OASDHI has made this very difficult.

Officially (which is likely to be overoptimistic) over 90 per cent of the population over sixty-five were receiving OASDHI benefits in the 1980s, and it was their major source of income in most cases. OASDHI coverage is by no means universal; in 1985 91 per cent of wage and salary earners were covered, but this was only 85 per cent of the *total* labour force (US Bureau of the Census, 1987: Table 582). Since OASDHI pensions are earnings-related there are considerable variations across the country in the average monthly benefits paid, reflecting differences in earnings and contribution records. In 1985 the highest average monthly payment to retired workers was in Connecticut at $525, and the lowest was in Mississippi at $403, the average for the whole country being $479 (Duensing, 1988: Table 6-11). The level of replacement of lifetime earnings from OASDHI was officially estimated in 1983 as 50 per cent for the low paid, 40 per cent for those on average earnings and 23 per cent for high earners (Wilson, 1987: 45). Nevertheless, as Aschenbaum (1986: 124) says, 'OASDHI's methods of determining eligibility . . . militate against the interests of those whose employment and earnings histories differ from those of "average" white males.'

For women, social security is more beneficial to married women who are not in paid employment, because their benefits are related to their husbands' contribution records. The system remains based on a traditional 'family-wage' model. Yet 'three times as many women in fact receive pensions on their own contributions rather than as dependants' (Wilson, 1987: 46), and frequently therefore they receive benefits lower than they would have done as fully dependent wives because of inferior contribution and earnings records. The majority of older women who have had both periods of unpaid home making and periods of paid employment often fail to get any benefit from their social security contributions because of the eligibility rules (Forman, 1983: 38). Divorced, disabled and widowed home makers are also disadvantaged by patriarchal eligibility rules. Pressure from the women's movement succeeded in achieving some modest reforms which assisted divorced and disabled widows and spouses (Forman, 1983: 37–8), but proposals for radical reforms towards establishing equal rights for women in old age benefits have been thwarted (Aschenbaum, 1986:

Chapter 6). The OASDHI benefits system may therefore be mildly redistributive on a class basis, but certainly not on a gender basis.

In 1980, 20.5 per cent of elderly families were poor in the US, not much more than in the UK, but more than double the rate in the FRG (Table A.6). In March 1985 15 per cent of households with the householder aged sixty-five or over were living below the official poverty line; 20 per cent of all elderly households were claiming at least one non-cash benefit such as food stamps or Medicaid, but only 9 per cent were receiving means-tested assistance in cash to supplement or to substitute for the social insurance pension (Duensing, 1988: Table 6-15). Almost all of this means-tested assistance for old people comes from a programme called, since 1974, Supplemental Security Income (SSI), which also originated with the 1935 Social Security Act and covers means-tested assistance to disabled and elderly people. About half of all SSI claimants are receiving social insurance benefits, the rest being uninsured. In 1985 65 per cent of SSI claimants were women and 25 per cent were black, and in that year the average monthly SSI payment to elderly people was $164. SSI is the only nationally uniform means-tested benefit in the US, though most states supplement the federal minimum benefit levels. In 1985 31.5 per cent of black people and 24 per cent of Hispanic people over sixty-five were living below the poverty line, compared to 11 per cent of white people. All these statistics suggest therefore that a substantial proportion of old people in the US are left behind by the social insurance system and live near or below the poverty line, frequently with little support from the welfare state. The inequalities amongst old people are very significantly structured by 'race' and gender. During the 1970s and 1980s the improved coverage of OASDHI has halved the proportion of the elderly living below the poverty line, but the improvement has been much more significant for white people than for black and Hispanic people (US Bureau of the Census, 1987: Table 748).

Social Assistance

By far the most important benefit targeted at poor people is the programme called Aid to Families with Dependent Children (AFDC), popularly known as 'welfare'. Along with SSI this forms the bottom rung of the welfare state in the US. The origins of the scheme go back to the early years of the century, when progressives, including some early feminists, campaigned successfully for states to award benefits to poor lone mothers to prevent children being taken into care. The Social Security Act 1935 made it mandatory for states to provide such a benefit with a matching federal subsidy, the principle of the programme being to direct financial aid to poor lone mother families to prevent them breaking up. It was never conceived as a social assistance safety net akin to Income Support in Britain, but that is what, in a piecemeal and inadequate form, it has become. Two striking features of AFDC are, first, that each state has its own programme, leading to very different local benefit levels and eligibility, and, second, that the eligibility of two parent families for welfare has never been consistently recognized. This may appear anomalous, but as Piven and Cloward (1971) demonstrated, the system has played a central role in forcing people into low-paid work, both 'welfare mothers' and unemployed men, by threatening denial of the means of subsistence. The great variety of local discretion and benefit levels allows the welfare system to be adapted to local political and labour market conditions, not unlike the administration of the poor law in the nineteenth century. But it is not an outdated vestige of the past, it is the kind of system advocated by the New Right in Britain to force down wages in areas of high unemployment. In 1984 the average monthly welfare payment in Mississippi was a mere $91, compared with $489 in California, the national average being $325. Clearly the cost of living in California is not five times that in Mississippi. Plotnick (1989) calculated the extent to which welfare reduced the gap between the pre-benefits income of the poor and the poverty line in the mid 1980s. This allows a measure of the effectiveness of welfare in mitigating poverty, though it is never sufficient to lift a household without any other income to the poverty line. Plotnick (1989) calculated that the median reduction in the pre-welfare gap was 20.2 per cent, varying from 42.0 per cent in generous Wisconsin to 10.9 per cent in stingy Nevada. After 1961, states were allowed to award AFDC to families with an unemployed father, but this is still rare in practice. The proportion of two parent families dependent on AFDC has risen very gradually since the 1970s to around 10 per cent in the late 1980s, virtually all the rest being lone mother families. It is still widely considered that giving welfare to unemployed fathers undermines work incentive. Under the Family Support Act 1988, states are required to extend AFDC entitlement to all two parent families in need for a limited period, but in practice this has not changed the situation fundamentally. The administration of AFDC has always reinforced the status of the applicant as undeserving:

> AFDC welfare centers are typically dingy, forbidding places; long waits for attention and a clinical atmosphere set a dehumanizing tone. Once applicants are called to meet a caseworker, their lives are probed in intimate, exhaustive detail . . . Routinely they are kept under surveillance, exhorted by welfare workers to 'rehabilitate' themselves, and asked to prove that they are not welfare chiselers . . . This process of systematic degradation also works to discourage *potential* welfare clients, who will accept subsistence wages rather than suffer the consequences of being on welfare. (Katznelson and Kesselman, 1979: 193–4)

AFDC was a relatively minor part of the welfare state in the US until the so-called welfare explosion of the 1960s, when in the course of the decade the number of families receiving welfare quadrupled. During the 1980s the number of beneficiaries stabilized at around eleven million, about 5 per cent of the population. The welfare explosion was one of the major achievements of the civil rights movement, which enfranchised most black people in the welfare state for the first time. In part it was 'a response to the civil disorder caused by . . . the modernization of Southern agriculture' (Piven and Cloward, 1971: 249) and the consequent mass unemployment of black southerners and their migration to the northern cities from the 1930s on. In part too, the welfare explosion and the Great Society programmes of which it was a part were a response to the emergence of black voters as a new political constituency. The federal government was forced to intervene in local welfare administration by funding welfare rights services, by challenging local laws and regulations in the courts and by supporting local organizations of the poor. Thus 'man-in-the-house rules, residence laws, employable mother rules and a host of other statutes, policies and regulations which kept people off the rolls were eventually struck down' (Piven and Cloward, 1977: 272). The 1970s and 1980s have witnessed a continual struggle between liberals and conservatives over welfare reform. To outside observers this has been the most visible form of conflict between poor people and the state. Both liberal proposals for a guaranteed minimum income (Moynihan, 1973) and neo-conservative ideas of abolishing welfare (Gilder, 1981) have failed. Since the late 1960s federal and state governments have sought to strengthen the work incentive pressures in the programme. Under Reagan's Omnibus Budget Reconciliation Act 1981, or OBRA, AFDC claimants suffered significant cuts in eligibility and benefits: payments are now made in arrears; assistance to people in low-paid employment has been all but withdrawn; related benefits such as food stamps and housing benefit have been cut back sharply; the means test has been made much tougher; and benefit levels, which are not indexed, have fallen well behind inflation (Bernstein, 1984; Hanson, 1987). As a result of OBRA about 400,000 families lost their entitlement to AFDC and another 260,000 had their benefit cut.

Unemployment and Labour Market Policies

Official unemployment rates in the US on the OECD basis were much higher in the post-war boom years than in Britain, Sweden and the FRG, and the OECD average (Table A.10). Official unemployment peaked in 1976 and 1983 during the two recent recessions, reaching 9.5 per cent in 1982 and 1983. During the 1980s, however, official unemployment in the US has kept close to the OECD average, reflecting the substantial employment growth in the US, while European employment growth has been modest. These official unemployment figures do not, of course, include people who are out of the labour market – the hidden unemployed. There appears to be no reliable estimate of their numbers in the US, but the number of adults of working age outside the labour force is probably much greater than in Western Europe. For example one survey quoted by Marable (1984a: 19) suggested that 20 per cent of all black men of working age were outside the labour force, apparently beyond the reach of official surveys.

Unemployment insurance is the other major plank of the New Deal social welfare reforms alongside OASDHI, SSI and AFDC, originally legislated in the Social Security Act 1935. The scheme is financed by a federal payroll tax, but within certain parameters each state administers its own scheme, reimbursed from the federal fund. Benefits are earnings-related up to a maximum determined by each state and vary between 50 and 70 per cent of previous gross wages for up to twenty-six weeks, extended in certain cases and certain states for up to a year. Taxation of unemployment benefit was introduced in 1978 to save money and to target benefit on the less well off. Around 90 per cent of the official labour force is covered by state unemployment insurance. Reflecting the diversity of schemes and of wages from state to state, the average weekly unemployment benefit payment in 1985 varied from $89 in Tennessee to $153 in Minnesota, with the average for the US being $127. During the early 1980s with the ascendance of neo-conservatism at federal and state levels, eligibility conditions, extensions of benefit beyond twenty-six weeks and funding of the schemes were significantly tightened. Benefit levels only just managed to keep pace with inflation in the years 1973–82 (Reubens, 1989: Table 1). There are few links if any between unemployment insurance programmes and labour market or retraining measures, such as those in the FRG and Sweden. US public expenditure on employment measures is dominated by expenditure on unemployment benefits, while in Sweden at the other extreme it is dominated by positive labour market measures (Reubens, 1989: Table 2). In common with France but unlike most other capitalist welfare states, there is no means-tested assistance for the long-term unemployed who have exhausted entitlement to unemployment benefit or for those not covered at all. This remains perhaps the most explicit example of how the welfare state by default pressurizes people to find paid employment, however poorly paid, or illicit and other informal sources of income. An indication of the level of hidden unemployment and the extent of the failure of unemployment insurance to reach the black community was revealed in a major survey in 1979 quoted by Hill (1988: 312). This showed that only 11 per cent of jobless black household heads were receiving unemployment benefit, 18 per cent had exhausted their unemployment benefit and the rest had no entitlement. The majority of these people had never enjoyed paid employment, but even amongst those who had and had been laid off, only 20 per cent were currently receiving benefit, while 56 per cent never had any entitlement to unemployment benefit. Unemployment insurance is clearly very far from being a universal programme for black people.

Ever since the welfare explosion of the mid 1960s, federal and state governments have developed an array of policies to put pressure on welfare beneficiaries to leave the welfare rolls and find paid employment, notably the Work Incentive Programmes of 1967, 1971, 1975 and 1980. Essentially all these measures have involved sticks and carrots, the sticks being both the threat and the reality of benefit withdrawal, and the carrots being day care, birth control services, job clubs, training, counselling, travel costs and so on. The Omnibus Budget Reconciliation Act 1981 (OBRA), which promulgated most of the cuts in the welfare state under Reagan already referred to, required all 'able-bodied' AFDC recipients to register for employment or training, except mothers with a child under six, amended in 1988 to under three. OBRA also encouraged and assisted the states in introducing 'workfare' schemes, which require AFDC recipients to 'work' for their welfare benefits in unpaid jobs. Although workfare has been greatly admired by the New Right in Britain (Burton, 1988), its direct impact in the US has been fairly modest, though indirectly of course its existence puts more pressure on poor people. As Burghes (1987) has shown, only about 20,000 people are in workfare programmes at any one time and only four states are fully implementing the scheme, with widely differing philosophies. Burghes's review of policy research on the workfare schemes suggests that they did little to help those people who had had previous experience of paid employment in terms of either finding a job or improved wages. Modest gains were achieved from workfare by those who had had little or no experience of paid employment. Almost everyone in workfare programmes ended up in low-paid, unskilled employment or returned to unemployment.

Women, the Labour Market and Income Maintenance

The increase in women's participation in paid employment in the US over the post-war period has sustained a very steady momentum, moving from a level well below the OECD average in the late 1950s to well above the OECD average in the late 1980s (Tables A.12 and A.13). This is largely accounted for by the increase in the numbers of white, married women taking up paid employment; paid employment amongst black women has always been much more common. As in other countries there is a distinctly gendered occupational structure, a segmentation of the labour force which has been consolidated with the growth of the welfare state as a major employer of women. Thus, according to Gordon *et al.* (1982: 206), 'four categories of female workers – those in the peripheral manufacturing industries, in the retail trade, in clerical occupations, and in the health and educational sectors – accounted for 95 per cent of female employment in 1970.' From the 1950s to the 1970s the expansion of employment in the welfare state was 'the single most important impetus behind the greater economic mobility of women and minorities' (Eisenstein, 1984: 118) but the employment of women and minorities in health care, education and social services has been hit hard by public expenditure cutbacks in the 1980s (Eisenstein, 1984: 117–18).

The proportion of part-time paid employment amongst women is significantly lower than in Britain and Sweden, but again close to the OECD average (OECD, 1985a: Table 1.3). As in the FRG, Sweden and most of the OECD states, standardized unemployment amongst women has been consistently higher than amongst men (Table A.14). During the 1980s, despite the budget cuts, the female unemployment rate remained roughly constant as private, service sector employment expanded, while the male unemployment rate continued to rise, the opposite of the case in the FRG. The earnings gap between men and women has not altered very dramatically over the post-war period. Women's actual earnings for every dollar earned by men in fact fell from 63.9 cents in 1955 to 56.6 cents in 1973, though it has risen modestly since (DiNitto and Dye, 1983: Table 11-2). The welfare state makes a very significant contribution to the stratification of women in the US by class, and by family structure (see below on lone mothers) and by 'race' (see below). Power (1988) suggests that women in the US are usefully divided into three groups, which is essentially a class division: first, marginalized women in poverty; second, the mass of women workers in clerical, service, social services and blue collar employment; and third, women in professional and managerial positions, of whom a small elite group have 'made it'. Women in poverty are typically in and out of paid employment, but equally typically dependent on welfare, even when they have low-paid employment. Many poor women

> 'cycle' between periods of total self-support, where they require supplementary welfare, and periods of full dependence on welfare, depending on such factors as the state of the economy, the seasonality of jobs, and their own and their children's health. (Power, 1988: 148-9)

It is widely recognized that welfare has the effect of encouraging the use of this marginalized group of women as a reserve army of labour. The growing mass of women workers in the second group have played a crucial role in sustaining median family incomes in the 1970s and 1980s, decades when for several years individual real wages fell. For these women the most significant aspect of social policy should perhaps have been the equal rights legislation and enforcement machinery established in the 1960s and 1970s. The impact of these measures is extremely difficult to unravel. The overall position of women workers relative to men may possibly have worsened in terms of earnings and in terms of horizontal and vertical gender segregation. There is some evidence that the affirmative action, contract compliance and other anti-discriminatory measures may have been counter-productive in encouraging a male backlash and because 'underlying stereotypes cannot be effectively changed with the legal mechanisms developed to date.' Yet 'the situation of women might be substantially worse without the regulations concerning discrimination, harassment and the overall economic status of women' (Larwood and Gutek, 1984: 255). The women's equal rights movement has suffered two major setbacks in the 1980s. First, in 1982 there was the narrow defeat of the Equal Rights Amendment (ERA) to the constitution, after many years of campaigning by the women's movement. Second, without repealing the existing equal rights legislation, the Reagan administration successfully weakened the administration of the laws by cuts in funding and staffing for the regulatory agencies (Bawden and Palmer, 1984: 201–8). In the mid 1980s the Justice Department launched a series of legal offensives against affirmative action and contract compliance policies in the public sector (Power, 1988: 153). Despite these setbacks campaigning for the ERA and in defence of the equal rights machinery has kept going, and the Reagan administration was by no means fully successful in its onslaught on women's rights. Though hard evidence is rather scanty, it would seem that middle class women in professional and managerial positions have bene-fited more widely from equal rights policies than the women in more working class occupations, both blue collar and white collar. Comparing women workers in the US and Britain, Dex and Shaw (1986) concluded that equal rights policies in employment have had a much more positive impact in the US than in Britain for the majority of women workers. One important reason for this is the predominance of full-time employment of women in the US, which in turn is encouraged by tax relief on child care expenses (see below) and the employer-paid health insurance programmes which accompany most full-time (but not part-time) employment. In general the strength of the women's movement is reflected in tougher legislation than in Britain, leading to a 'more aggressive pursuit of equal opportunities for American women' which has 'raised the overall status [of women workers] in the eyes of employers' (Dex and Shaw, 1986: 128). They suggest that British employers tend to see their women workers as more 'marginal and disposable' than their counterparts in the US.

On the basis of the available evidence it is impossible to delineate very precisely the changing boundaries between these groups or classes of women. It has always been the case that a substantial majority of poor people are women, and, as Table 4.1 indicates, that a very substantial proportion of lone mother families are in poverty. The impact of the US benefits system in lifting lone parent families out of poverty is extremely limited. On the LIS basis for 1980, cash benefits achieved only an 11.6 per cent reduction in the number of lone parent families in poverty, leaving 51.7 per cent of these families in post-transfer poverty (Table A.6). Hence, although AFDC is targeted at single parents, it is insufficient to take a majority of them out of relative poverty, in stark contrast to the situation in the FRG and Sweden. The net income of single parent families in the US as a proportion of that for two parent families is only 57 per cent, by a long way the lowest proportion amongst our four welfare states (Table A.18). This is despite the fact that a much greater proportion of lone mothers in the US are in paid employment than in the UK and the FRG (Table A.17). The structure of families has changed quite dramatically in recent decades with the rising number of lone mother families. By 1984 over a quarter of US families with children were lone parent families: 89 per cent of these were lone mother families. This is by far the highest proportion of lone parent families amongst the OECD states, considerably higher even than Sweden (Table A.16). Lone mother families therefore form an increasing proportion of poor people. At the same time the proportion of poor people who are women has not changed dramatically over the past three decades, which means that more of them are living in lone mother families. Strictly speaking therefore, as Gimenez (1989) has argued, there has not been a feminization of poverty, but there has been some considerable shift in poor women's dependence away from poor men and onto the welfare system.

Racial Inequalities, Racism and the Welfare State

The 'Race' Context

Issues surrounding racial inequalities and racism have probably played as prominent a role in the politics of the modern welfare state in the US as issues of class inequality and oppression have done in Western Europe. Like class of course, 'race' is a socially constructed category with deep historical and cultural roots; groups of people are 'racialized' by various social processes, and the boundaries are frequently vague and subjective. The 1980 US census started from the premise that there were fourteen significant 'racial groups' in the US, relying on self-classification by respondents. A fifteenth category allowed for people who did not identify with the fourteen named groups. The three biggest groups were what the Bureau of the Census described as 'white' (83.2 per cent), 'black' (11.7 per cent) and 'American Indian' (0.6 per cent), with the other twelve categories amounting to 4.5 per cent of an official total population of 226 million. In contrast with much of Western Europe, during the last two decades the US population has continued to increase by about two million a year, around a quarter of which is accounted for by refugees and immigrants for permanent settlement. In addition there are a substantial number of illegal immigrants, particularly from Mexico, possibly equalling the number of legal immigrants at about half a million a year (Carens, 1988). Legal immigration by non-whites has been severely restricted since the early 1920s. In a separate census question, people of 'Spanish/Hispanic origin' were invited to identify themselves, and 6.5 per cent of respondents identified themselves as such. Clearly there are many other cultural and ethnic minorities amongst the 'white' and other groups, who have been and are racialized. Here we shall concentrate on African Americans, almost all of whom trace their ancestry to slavery and thus to Africa, and who continue to use the term 'black people' to describe themselves. They are certainly the largest and arguably the most politically significant racialized social group in the US.

In most positive respects the welfare state was a dead letter for black people in the US until the 1960s. Thus, for example, despite the large numbers living below the poverty line, there were very few successful applicants for AFDC. The explanation for this lies in the explicit institutional racism promulgated from the Supreme Court down to the humblest local authority. Paralleled perhaps only by South Africa and Nazi Germany, the US has been both a stubbornly capitalist and a stubbornly racist state. Up to the Civil War in the 1860s, this was enforced above all through slavery in the southern states. After the Civil War, the federal government engineered policies which fundamentally altered the legal and welfare status of black people, but by the 1880s this phase of Reconstruction gave way to a sustained period of overtly racist policy lasting into the 1950s. In the southern states where almost 80 per cent of black people still lived in 1940, what amounted to an apartheid system was enforced through local legislation, known as the Jim Crow laws, and by terrorist white violence. The system was legitimated by the Supreme Court decision in 1896 that the constitution allowed for 'separate but equal' protection under the law for black and white people, thus allowing segregation in education, public transport, leisure and welfare services. Where these services were available to black people, they were generally much inferior. In response to this and hastened by the mechanization of southern agriculture, black people migrated north and inaugurated the transformation of the black working class from being southern farmers and domestic servants to being industrial and service sector workers in northern (and southern) towns and cities. In 1975 52 per cent of black people lived in the southern states, compared to 89 per cent in 1910; in 1970 19 per cent of black people and 28 per cent of white people lived in rural areas, compared to 73 per cent and 51 per cent respectively in 1910 (US Bureau of the Census, 1979: Tables 5 and 6).

The Second Reconstruction: Black People and the Welfare State

After decades of lobbying and protest by organizations such as the National Association for the Advancement of Colored Peoples (NAACP), in 1954 the Supreme Court reversed the 'separate but equal' doctrine applied to schooling on the grounds that it retarded black educational advance. The decision was implemented by allowing the federal government to deny grants to segregationist school boards. The intensified struggles for desegregation and for black civil rights were essentially black workers' movements, as Marable (1984b: 129) says, demanding 'social guarantees for jobs, housing and health care . . . the premises of democratic socialism – the politics of much of the working class in other advanced capitalist nations'. This was in many respects a struggle for the welfare state. Pushed on by the civil rights movement through the 1960s, the process of dismantling Jim Crow culminated in the Civil Rights Act 1964 and the Voting Rights Act 1965. The Civil Rights Act outlawed explicit forms of racial discrimination and segregation, legalized the notion of affirmative action to ensure equality of opportunity, outlawed institutional discrimination by contractors to the federal government (contract compliance), and allocated federal funds for desegregation and other aspects of the Act's implementation. The emergence of the Black Power movement in the mid 1960s ensured that this Second Reconstruction, as Marable (1984b) and Pinkney (1984) describe these and other Great Society measures, enfranchised black people politically in a reformed welfare state. This was accompanied by the growth of black businesses and a new black professional and managerial elite, alongside much increased black political representation particularly in local government.

The Second Reconstruction appears to have achieved a modest narrowing of the welfare inequalities between black and white people from the early 1960s to the mid 1970s. Yet the flight of white people from the cities into the suburbs has, if anything, intensified residential segregation. *De facto* segregation in schooling is still common because 'though a court may find a school district to be unconstitutionally segregated, it cannot order cross-district busing as a remedy unless the suburbs . . . have engaged in *intentional* segregation' (*Economist*, 1990: 44). Since the economic recession of the mid 1970s, and furthered by the recession of the early 1980s and the Reagan onslaught against the welfare state and affirmative action, racial inequalities have widened, wiping out to an extent the gains of the 1960s. Thus black families' median income as a percentage of white families' rose to a peak of almost 62 per cent in 1975, falling back to below 55 per cent in 1988, the same level as in 1967 and 1953. The gap in infant mortality rates narrowed quite sharply between 1960 and 1975, but began to widen increasingly during the 1980s. Wilson (1987), Farley (1984) and Esping-Andersen (1990) offer more optimistic data, which suggest a sustained upward mobility of black people in the occupational class structure. Marable (1984b) and Pinkney (1984), however, argue that the Second Reconstruction fell apart during the 1970s and that its primary beneficiaries were the new black middle class, comprising up to 10 per cent of the black population. In particular they had gained from better access to college education, creating a growing class division amongst black people. Collins (1983) argues that the upward mobility of middle class black people is not secure, because their positions are frequently dependent on insecure public funding or insecure markets mediating white corporations and black consumers. Ironically the successes of the black elite encouraged the view that the sociological significance of race was declining (Wilson, 1978), that equality of opportunity had been achieved or even that affirmative action had gone too far and was now discriminating against white people. However, in many respects for the mass of the black working class, social and economic conditions remained much the same, while for the poor the situation worsened after the mid 1970s. The statistics above may reflect a stretching of the black class structure at the top and the bottom, with a growing affluent elite and an even faster growing underclass of poor and unemployed people.

By the 1960s most black people were urbanized and living in the inner cities and inner suburbs, where they faced institutional and structural racism more sophisticated than the overt racism of the traditional south. Above all, structural racism took the form of mass unemployment amongst

black men and women, even in the booming 1960s. The official unemployment rate in 1985 for white people was 6.1 per cent for men and 6.4 per
cent for women, compared to 15.3 per cent and 14.9 per cent respectively
for black men and women. According to a survey quoted by Marable
(1984a: 19) about 20 per cent of working age black men were 'out of the
labour force' in 1982, a threefold increase since 1960, so that in total almost
half of all black male adults of working age are jobless, either officially
unemployed, out of the labour force, institutionalized in prisons and
mental hospitals or otherwise unaccounted for. Table 4.1 shows that the
proportion of black families living below the poverty line has remained at
around 28 per cent over the past two decades, between three and four
times the percentage of white families. Black people have adapted to urban
poverty and unemployment in many ways – men joined the armed forces,
many men ended up in prison, families split up in order that mothers could
apply for welfare, women took extremely low-paid casual jobs as domestic
servants and in service industries (Marable, 1983). Black sociologists
charted the emergence of a black, urban underclass, a term used by
Glasgow (1980) to describe 'a permanently entrapped population of poor
people', rejected by the labour market in terms of secure employment and
numbering anything between a quarter and a half of the black adult
population. For the underclass the welfare system 'does not encourage or
provide the means to mobility or to a secure working status; rather it
maintains the status of the poor, often punishing those with incentive and
serving as a system to monitor parts of the underclass' (Glasgow, 1980: 12).
The welfare benefits system, alongside the law enforcement, health care
and social services agencies, functions to maintain and control the
underclass. Ironically the enfranchisement of black people in the welfare
state created a system which entraps and polices many of them, while
preventing absolute destitution. Like most analysts, Wilson (1987: 110)
suggests that 'the race-specific policies emanating from the civil rights
revolution, although beneficial to advantaged black people . . . do little for
those who are truly disadvantaged.' The political conclusions drawn by
analysts vary across the spectrum from radical socialist (Marable, 1983;
1984b) to neo-conservative (Murray, 1984). Wilson (1987), from a social
democratic perspective, argues that the problems of the underclass can
only be solved by universal social welfare programmes along West
European lines, augmented by affirmative action and targeted programmes.

Women and Family Policies

Ideology

The US is the only major capitalist state to have no universal child benefit
and no statutory maternity leave, and there is little likelihood of either
being enacted in the foreseeable future. Clearly there is no federal family

policy in terms of universal programmes aimed at securing the welfare of mothers and children or in encouraging people to have (or not to have) children. Although this is obviously a considerable contrast with Sweden and France, the situation in states like the FRG and Britain is becoming closer to that in the US. Both the FRG and Britain have allowed inflation to eat away at child benefit, with pronatalism almost off the political agenda since the 1950s. In the US the idea of 'family policy' is generally antithetical to the ideologies of voluntarism and liberalism which have shaped social policy. President Nixon vetoed a national programme for day care because it threatened to 'Sovietize' the American family. The corollary of this is that the family is conventionally portrayed in the US, possibly even more than in Europe, as the 'haven in a heartless world' (Lasch, 1977), the bastion of responsible individualism. The traditions of both voluntarism and liberalism in the US emphasize the responsibility of families to support themselves. When Nixon proposed a Family Assistance Plan to replace welfare and give a guaranteed minimum income to all families, Congress threw it out because it would allegedly undermine family responsibility and the work incentive. Another central issue lying behind the apparent absence of family policy in the US is the question of the politics of the birth rate. In Europe, state family policies have frequently been guided by a concern to stem a fall in the birth rate through pronatalist measures. Universal pronatalist measures have never been on the national policy agenda in the US, in part because the population has continually expanded, but above all perhaps because of the institutionalized influence of class- and race-biased eugenics and neo-Malthusianism. Public and private bodies, often working in partnership, have thus sought to limit the birth rate amongst poor white people and amongst black people, native Americans and other minorities, while at the same time attempting to encourage middle class women to have more children. President Theodore Roosevelt in a famous remark in 1905 attacked the use of birth control by respectable women as 'criminal against the race . . . the object of contemptuous abhorrence by healthy people' (quoted by Gordon, 1977: 136). The term 'race suicide' was used to describe this widely held view, undercurrents of which are still apparent. Liberals in the US, since the late nineteenth century, have energetically sought to save children, and to a lesser extent mothers, from destitution or institutionalization. In the 1950s and 1960s the Cold War, and in particular the successful Soviet space programme, generated concern about underinvestment in children as human capital, with Soviet success being attributed to their apparently interventionist family policies (Ehrenreich and English, 1979: 232–4). There have been a series of Presidential Conferences on Children since 1909, almost as a substitute for federal policy intervention. At the local level such liberal pressures helped to create the network of social work, family planning, residential care and community care agencies at the base of the welfare state with relatively little federal coordination or finance. Thus family policy in the US has had two facets – disciplinary benefits and services aimed at the poor and the racialized minorities alongside an ideology of privacy, self-sufficiency and the celebration of motherhood in the 'normal', patriarchal family. However this orthodoxy has certainly never been entirely secure or unchallenged. Black people have accused liberal birth controllers of promoting genocide. The welfare system is widely believed to be undermining the two parent family structure.

Perhaps the most important challenge of all has come from women's movements, which have played a leading role in the development of family policies. From the 1870s women campaigned for voluntary motherhood, birth control and mothers' pensions alongside the demands for political and economic rights. Then as now the feminist movement in the US has united principally around demands for equal rights under the law, but social feminism – demands for social benefits and services for women – has frequently been closely linked with equal rights campaigning. In recent years the women's movement has struggled to extend and defend abortion rights and services, women-centred health care services, services for battered women, child care services, maternity leave and so on.

In the midst of all these manifold political pressures and structural economic changes, family policies have developed piecemeal and erratically. Only 14 per cent of families conform to the traditional male breadwinner pattern, outnumbered by the number of lone mother families. The dual wage-earning family is by far the most common family form, and hence

> the welfare state has arisen in part out of changing patterns of family life and has also created intended and unintended consequences for family life. White married women's entry into the labor force, increased divorce rates, changes in the structure of the economy, and the growth of a feminist movement have all served to reveal the outmoded aspects of the traditional (white) patriarchal family. The state is being forced to reformulate a dynamic of patriarchal privilege that no longer rests solely on the traditional family model. (Eisenstein, 1984: 114)

The 'new patriarchy' which has emerged under Social Democratic family policy in Sweden is also therefore apparent in the US, where women are now also much more dependent financially on the welfare state and/or on paid employment. Because of the greater wages gap between men and women, and the inadequacies of the welfare state in the US, Hewlett (1987) has even argued that the majority of women in the US are in many respects living a 'lesser life' and that so far women's liberation has been something of a myth. In reaction to many of these changes, in the 1970s the New Right, in particular the evangelistic Moral Majority, launched an onslaught on the welfare state as a threat to traditional family values. This was bolstered by the Reagan presidency in the 1980s, and the 1981 OBRA cuts in welfare and related benefits and services were legitimated in terms of traditional family values. Perhaps the New Right's most significant campaign has centred on the question of abortion but they have sought to reform the welfare state on a broad front. In the early 1980s the New Right put their Family Protection Act onto the congressional agenda, which, although it failed to be ratified, laid out their plans. The Act sought to redefine and extend parental responsibilities, for example requiring parental consent for prescribing contraceptives to or performing an abortion on a minor, and the withdrawal of federal funding from agencies which contravened these conditions. The Act sought to deny federal funds to schools which 'did not permit voluntary school prayer, parental participation in decisions relating to the study of religion and . . . parental previews (or as Petchesky has translated it, "censorship") of textbooks' (David, 1983: 36). The Act also proposed that federal funds should not be invested in educational materials which did not reflect conventional patriarchal family values and traditional roles for women or which put homosexuality in a neutral or positive light. Such ideas have had a continuing impact at the local level. The lack of success of the New Right and the Moral Majority at federal government level reflects their lack of support from neo-conservatives, who are relatively libertarian about the family and abortion. The neo-conservatives have concentrated on welfare budget cuts and blunting affirmative action programmes. As Eisenstein (1984: 58) concludes,

> the neo-conservatives are putting in place a state that rejects equality between the sexes and opts for sexual difference, but within the liberal rhetoric of equality of opportunity. As such they do not assert an antifeminist stance but . . . one where the issues of sex and politics and the personal as political are mystified once again.

Even this project has by no means been successfully implemented in the 1980s, as our discussion of the black family, abortion, day care and parental rights below will attempt to show.

The Black Family

A central focus of family policy and poverty policy debate in the US has concerned the growing numbers of lone mother families in particular amongst the black community. The proportion of lone mother families amongst black families rose from 25 per cent in 1964 to 59 per cent in 1984. About 60 per cent of these families live in poverty. For almost three decades there has been widespread concern about this so-called crisis of the black family, for it is widely assumed that the apparent move away from the patriarchal family model has been an altogether destructive and negative feature of the lives of black people. Both liberals and neo-conservatives see it as a fundamental cause of the underclass phenomenon, a social pathology which social policy should tackle. Hence Moynihan's notorious statement in 1965 that 'at the heart of the deterioration of the fabric of Negro society is the deterioration of the Negro family' (Valentine, 1968: 29). As a liberal Democrat, Moynihan advocated a guaranteed minimum income as one means of restoring the two parent family. Neo-conservatives such as Murray (1984) would sweep away welfare and its associated benefits in kind, pushing the poor into paid employment and/or reliance on charity, relatives and friends. He implies that this enforcement of the work incentive would somehow encourage conventional parenthood in an unexplained way. The research evidence indicates that the level and accessibility of welfare benefits has little or no effect on family formation (Neckerman *et al.*, 1988). Marable (1984a) traces 'the destruction of black households' to the structural unemployment of late capitalism, particularly the growth of black male unemployment and the institutionalization of black men in prisons, the armed forces and mental hospitals. This is not necessarily to accept the patriarchal family as a desirable norm. The growing numbers of black lone mother families is a rational adaptation to a number of severe pressures including structural unemployment, the denial of welfare to two parent families, and the hopelessness and search for self-esteem amongst the black teenage underclass. Indeed the departure from the patriarchal family norm can be seen as reflecting the strength of the black community under pressure, not dissimilar to the informal kinship patterns developed under slavery. The increasing proportion of mother-only black families is also a part of the decline of the conventional European-American nuclear family and the rise of alternatives including cohabitation, gay and lesbian parenthood, and absent, supportive father-hood. The latter phenomenon was found to be quite common in an ethnographic study of a poor black community by Stack (1974). Whether it would be desirable or not, thus far neo-conservatives and liberals have signally failed to revive traditional family forms, particularly amongst black people. The structural and social forces which have led to the growth of lone motherhood show little sign of weakening.

Abortion and Sterilization

The abortion question in the US is conventionally discussed in terms of the constitutional rights of women and the rights, if any, of the foetus. In fact the central issue should be the problems of access, particularly for poor women and minority women, to a safe and legal termination in an essentially private health care system. Before the liberal abortion law reform in 1973, women's access to a hospital abortion was controlled largely by private doctors with the result that poor and minority women had little or no access. Thus hundreds of thousands of abortions were performed 'in a class-divided system that relegated poor women to the dangerous and sordid conditions of "back-alley" abortionists while rich and middle-class women usually had access to safe, sanitary abortions in hospitals and private physicians' offices' (Petchesky, 1985: 153). Although the 1973 reform swept some parts of this class differentiated system away, the absence of public funding and cheap, accessible services means that in many parts of the country, especially for poor women, their constitutional right to an abortion up to the twelfth week of pregnancy is academic and cannot be made a reality. The 1973 reform has to be examined in the context of the 'race' and class divisions.

The origins of the 1973 reform lie in two phenomena emerging in the 1960s: the rise of the modern women's movement, which put abortion rights very high on its agenda; and a modification of liberal, neo-Malthusian ideology towards population control, which increasingly supported abortion as a means of controlling the fertility of poor people and ethnic minority people. Significantly, the American Medical Association in 1967 agreed that abortion could be indicated where a woman's health was threatened. Thus 'after a century of medical and eugenicist domination of reproductive politics, abortion became legal . . . because at a particular historical moment social need, feminist activism and populationist ideology came together' (Petchesky, 1984: 132).

The 1973 liberal reform was the result of the Supreme Court's decision in the *Roe* v. *Wade* case, which legalized abortion on demand in the first twelve weeks of pregnancy. Between twelve and twenty-four weeks, a state legislature may regulate abortion procedures in the interests of maternal health. After twenty-four weeks, a state legislature may prohibit abortion, except where the woman's life or health is threatened. In 1976, under the Hyde Amendment, Congress confined federal Medicaid funding (for the health care of poor women) to women whose lives were threatened or whose pregnancy had resulted from rape or incest. In 1981 Medicaid funding for rape and incest victims was withdrawn. Ten states continued to fund Medicaid abortions on demand, and another four where they were considered 'medically necessary'. Since 1973 deaths and illnesses caused by backstreet abortion have declined dramatically, just as the rate of legal abortion per thousand women aged fifteen to forty-four increased from 13.2 in 1972 to 27.4 in 1983. The overall rate has remained at between 25 and 30 since 1977, while the rate for non-white people has fluctuated between 50 and 60. The abortion rate for poor women is around three times the norm, suggesting that, despite the blocks on public funding, the reform has significantly improved the access of poor and working class women to abortion services, even though many of these women have to incur substantial debts to get a termination. According to Morgan (1984) '18 to 23 per cent of women eligible for Medicaid who wanted abortions were unable to obtain them because of lack of funds.' The abortion rate varies dramatically from one area of the country to another, reflecting the unwillingness of many doctors and hospitals to perform abortions. In 1982 the rate of abortions per thousand women aged fifteen to forty-four varied from 169.9 in the District of Columbia (covering the capital city) to 7.7 in West Virginia. Private charitable and for-profit clinics have developed to meet the demand, but their accessibility is uneven. In 1983 90.5 per cent of abortions were performed by the twelfth week, compared to 85.4 per cent in England and Wales. The rate of abortion in the US is more than double that for Britain, Sweden and the FRG. This may reflect the more liberal legislation, but also higher proportions of unwanted children, inferior sex education and less use of birth control measures. Francome (1986: 155) suggests that 'the abortion rate in the US could be greatly reduced by a more rational and open approach towards sexuality', but in the light of the New Right's 'family protection' drive this seems unlikely to emerge. Petchesky (1985: 159) concludes that the reality of abortion in the US is complicated: 'poor women, it would seem, often cannot get abortions when they want to; are sometimes pressured to get abortions when they do not want to; but most frequently seek and get abortions because they need to – necessity, not freedom, dictates "choice".'

Since 1973 the anti-abortion 'right to life' movement allied with the Moral Majority and many supporters of the New Right have waged a militant campaign against the reform. Abortion clinics have been fire-bombed and picketed. Demonstrations and counter-demonstrations have proliferated, as the women's movement has strongly defended the reform. The legal struggle came to a head over the Supreme Court decision in July 1989 to allow state legislatures to restrict access to legal abortion, including banning abortions in publicly funded facilities and effectively making abortions beyond twenty weeks' gestation illegal. So for example the state legislature in Idaho decided in March 1990 to take up these powers, passing legislation which would render illegal 95 per cent of all abortions in the state and impose criminal sanctions on doctors who do not comply. However, the measure was vetoed by the state governor. Similar anti-abortion bills have been failing all over the country, as conservative politicians discover that an anti-abortion stance can be politically damaging. The political reality is that the 1973 reform commands majority support, not only amongst the general population, but also amongst the political and judicial establishment, whether it be in support of women's rights or population control. So far the advance of the anti-abortion movement has been stalled.

The pervasive influence of eugenicism and racism in 'family policy' in the US is highlighted by the struggle over the issue of sterilization abuse. Thirty-two of the state legislatures passed eugenic laws between 1907 and 1940, and they remain on the statute book in many states. These laws allow involuntary sterilization of women alleged to have hereditary disorders, sometimes including those labelled as 'socially inadequate' or simply people with physical handicaps. Under these laws 63,000 people were sterilized between 1907 and 1964 in the US and its colony, Puerto Rico. Most of them were mentally ill and most were poor black or Hispanic women. More recently at least ten states have considered compulsory sterilization of welfare applicants, though this has never become law. According to Rodriguez-Trias (1982: 149), 'hysterectomy, now the most frequent major operation, with rates in the US four times greater than Sweden, is an indication of still another way of sterilizing women without their consent. Black women on welfare suffer the most abuse.' Medicaid will cover 90 per cent of the cost of voluntary sterilization. Under population control programmes of 'voluntary' sterilization, it has been estimated that in 1982 41 per cent of native American women had been sterilized (Morgan, 1984: 704). During the 1970s and 1980s black and other minority women stepped up the resistance to sterilization abuse, attempting to force the federal government and local authorities to regulate the operation and to develop informed consent (Rodriguez-Trias, 1982).

Day Care and Parental Leave

Given the family policy context already described, it is hardly surprising that federal and local government in the US have rejected comprehensive, publicly funded day care for pre-school children. Exceptionally and temporarily, during the Second World War the federal government funded nurseries to enable women to take up factory work. In 1971 Congress passed the Comprehensive Child Development Act, which would have provided federal funding for a network of day care centres across the country, but the Act was vetoed by President Nixon, who conveyed the policy orthodoxy very precisely thus:

> Good public policy requires that we enhance rather than diminish both parental authority and parental involvement with children – particularly in those decisive early years when social attitudes and a conscience are formed and religious and moral principles are first inculcated . . . For the federal government to plunge headlong financially into supporting child development would commit the vast moral authority of the national government to the side of communal approaches to child rearing and against the family approach. (quoted in Ellis and Petchesky, 1972: 12)

The private sanctity of the family and of motherhood has to be protected from the interference of the state. Yet three factors have punctured this orthodoxy over the past three decades, all of which have been reflected in continued Congressional support for day care. First, day care and early educational intervention are seen as a fundamental means of tackling poverty and child abuse, not least by encouraging mothers living in poverty to find paid employment. Second, the benefits to the development of all children of good quality care outside of the family have been increasingly recognized, particularly in the US where educational achievement is seen as so vital to 'making it' competitively. Finally the expansion of women's paid employment has created a huge demand for day care from almost all social classes, which the women's movement has supported as a key element in furthering equal opportunities. All these pressures have fuelled a considerable expansion of day care since the early 1960s, in which federal and local government have played a significant role.

The proportion of children under six with mothers in the paid labour force increased from 29 per cent in 1970 to 49 per cent in 1985 and is projected to rise to 65 per cent by 1995. Table 4.2 shows that in the period 1965–85 for the under threes there was a sharp decline in the proportion of day care by relatives and nannies, and a corresponding increase in the proportion by childminders and particularly by day care centres or

Table 4.2   *Day care arrangements for children under three of employed mothers in the US*

Type of care	Maternal employment	1965	1985
Relatives	Part-time	56	35
	Full-time	49	
Sitter, in-home	Part-time	19	9
	Full-time	22	
Family day care home (childminder)	Part-time	23	34
	Full-time	24	
Day care centre (nursery)	Part-time	2	22
	Full-time	6	

Source: Phillips, 1991: Table 9.2

nurseries. Similar trends have emerged in the care of three to five year old children with mothers in paid employment, accompanied by a sharp increase in kindergarten (nursery school) places in both public and private sectors since the mid 1970s. According to Kahn and Kamerman (1987: 4), 'half the states require all their school districts to offer kindergarten [to three–five year olds], and five states actually mandate kindergarten for all five year olds . . . no state provides prekindergarten programs for all four year olds, but clearly development is beginning in this direction.' The growth of family day care (childminding) has been largely unregulated, since in most states only minders with three children or more are supposed to be regulated. Little is known about the quality, working conditions and finance of family day care in the US. It would appear that family day care is used by parents who are neither poor nor affluent – not poor enough to qualify for anti-poverty day care programmes, and not affluent enough to afford private day care centres. Hewlett (1987: 89) found many parents desperately juggling 'packages of multiple informal arrangements, where [they] piece together a mixture of their own time, relatives' time, neighbours' time, and paid help to provide enough child care to get through the working day'. Day care centres (nurseries) fall into two categories, the for-profit sector used largely by middle-income families and the non-profit sector which is more of a mixed bag, frequently supported from public funds. There are only about 500 employer-provided workplace nurseries, which is a fairly insignificant contribution. Government funding contributed 17 per cent of day care centres' income in 1988 compared to 29 per cent in 1977, with as much as a quarter of for-profit centres receiving federal funds. The number of places in for-profit centres has more than doubled since the mid 1970s, particularly in the franchised day care chains, led by Kinder-Care Learning Centers Inc. which has 1200 centres in forty states. In 1988 for-profit centres had 51 per cent of the children in day care centres, compared to 37 per cent in 1977. Most of the non-profit centres are privately administered by churches, charities and so on, frequently operating in partnership with the public authorities. In recent years a significant privatization of day care has taken place. The proportion of children in day care centres who were black fell from 28 per cent to 21 per cent between 1977 and 1988, indicating the relatively increased influx of middle class children. A recent survey of day care centres found that wages, conditions and quality of care were significantly higher in the non-profit sector, and that 'children from middle-income families were enrolled in centers of lower quality than were children from low- and high-income families' (Whitebook *et al.*, 1989: 16). Ironically high-income parents appear to get access to the best quality day care in the non-profit sector, confirmed by Walker (1990) who discovered affluent fathers camping all night outside centres in Washington DC. They were queuing for 'the handful of free kindergarten places at the handful of free schools to which middle class parents are prepared to risk sending their children' (Walker, 1990: 23). In the big cities the annual costs of a for-profit kindergarten place start at $5000 a year and can go above $10,000, when average middle class incomes are around $50,000.

Aside from federal funding of nursery education, direct federal funding for day care centres and family day care comes largely from three programmes targeted at poor people – Project Head Start, the Social Services Block Grant and the Child Care Food Program. Project Head Start, one of the centrepieces of the era of War on Poverty and the Great Society, was initiated in 1965 to provide part-time education, health and social services to poor pre-school children and their families, though it reaches only about 16 per cent of those eligible. Head Start continues to enjoy considerable political support, but under the post-1981 OBRA cuts, all the other forms of federal funding for day care have suffered real cuts. Indirect federal support for day care takes the form of federal income tax relief (sometimes with additional state income tax relief) on up to 30 per cent of the costs of day care. In 1986 the cost to the Treasury of this Dependent Care Tax Credit has been estimated at over $3.4 billion, more than double its cost in real terms in 1980 and 1.7 times more than the direct expenditures on day care. There is also tax relief on day care expenses as an employees' fringe benefit. These forms of fiscal welfare benefit middle- and upper-income families, and have little impact on poor and low-income families. From all this data it is apparent that the day care system is riven with class divisions, which have become more striking in the past decade. Federal policy has been adjusted to cater for the affluent working class and middle class demand for day care at the expense of funding for services to the less affluent working class and the underclass. The positive aspect of recent developments is that the Nixon orthodoxy is increasingly being rejected by parents, and day care is losing some of the stigma of being associated with 'welfare'. In 1990 Congress approved another Child Care Bill which sought to shift the balance of federal funding away from tax credits and towards services for low-income groups, with an injection of $5 billion a year and more in the future to improve and expand day care provision. President Bush, however, has vetoed the Bill in favour of keeping the budget deficit down.

There is no statutory parental leave or parental benefit in the US. A decade of political pressure and legal wrangling led to the passage of the Pregnancy Discrimination Act 1978. Under the Act employers merely have to give pregnant women the same rights as other temporarily 'disabled' workers. The legislation said that

> discrimination based on pregnancy, childbirth or related medical conditions was illegal . . . [and] outlawed a host of discriminatory practices: stipulating larger deductibles [expenses not covered] for pregnancy than for other disabilities; subtracting maternity leave from an employee's accumulated seniority . . . ; paying pregnancy benefits to employees' wives, but not to female employees. (Adams and Winston, 1980: 34)

This was a hard-fought gain for the women's movement, though very far from being a universal maternity leave provision. Only a few states have compulsory disability insurance. Hence in the mid 1980s 60 per cent of mothers had no maternity rights at all and 40 per cent of mothers in paid employment had no maternity insurance coverage. Although some women get disability leave for pregnancy and childbirth, maternity leave for the child's first few months is not guaranteed and 'employers still routinely fire women if they take even a short leave of absence to have a baby' (Hewlett, 1987: 72). Additionally,

> since one third of single women and one quarter of married women have no health insurance, childbirth can be an expensive proposition . . . even if women have some coverage . . . it is rarely comprehensive. None of the 100-odd working mothers I interviewed was completely covered for the expenses of childbirth. (Hewlett, 1987: 72)

Inevitably women's access to insurance for maternity leave and the costs of childbirth is structured occupationally. The large corporations generally make provisions comparable to the minimum statutory provisions in Western Europe, but this covers less than a quarter of the women in paid employment. There is therefore a marked class structure in eligibility with professional and managerial women working for large employers relatively well catered for in comparison to many working class women who have little or no coverage.

The Health Care System

Private Health Insurance and Public Expenditure

The US is unique amongst the OECD states in that the bulk of health expenditure is privately incurred. In 1984 only 41.4 per cent of health care expenditure in the US came from public funds, compared to an OECD mean of 78.7 per cent (Table A.19). Public spending on health care in the US moved from 24.7 per cent of total health care spending in 1960 to a peak of 42.5 per cent in the late 1970s, indicating the impact of the Great Society period of welfare state expansion, with a slow decline since reflecting the contemporary stagnation of the welfare state. The funding of health care services is no longer dominated by direct patient payments (Table 4.3), as the costs of scientific medicine have escalated. About three-quarters of finance now comes from either private insurance or public funds.

Table 4.3   *US expenditure on health services and*
supplies as percentage by source (does not include all
medical research and construction)

Source	1970	1985
Private		
Direct patient payments	38	26
Insurance premiums	24	33
Other private	2	1
Total	64	60
Public		
Medicare	11	18
Medicaid	10	11
Other public	15	11
Total	36	40

Source: US Bureau of the Census, 1987: Table 126

However, in relation to national economic resources as measured by GDP, total health care spending (public and private) in the US has led the world since the early 1960s, commanding 10.7 per cent of GDP in 1984, compared with an OECD mean of 7.5 per cent (Table A.20). The growth of total health spending in relation to GDP growth over the period 1960–84 was close to the OECD mean (Table A.22). Compared to other states, however, a greater proportion of this growth is accounted for by demographic change, particularly the growing number of old people, rather than real increased use of services in general (OECD, 1987: Table 22). Surprisingly perhaps, comparing public health care spending per head of population, the US overtook the UK between 1970 and 1984 and closed the gap on Sweden (Table A.21), reflecting the higher level of GDP and of economic growth in the US. The US welfare state in the form of public health care spending therefore makes a major contribution to the health care system, with private and public spending and services intertwined in a complex way.

Up to the middle of this century, the health care system in the US was in many respects not that different from those in Western Europe, with a mix of public and voluntary hospitals and with most doctors practising as solo professionals, funded by fees, charity, public funds and non-profit health insurance. With the rapid expansion of hospital-based scientific medicine, the system has gradually changed, but in contrast to Western Europe, that change has been led by private forces, both for profit and not for profit. Not only is the supply of health care technology and plant commodified as it is elsewhere, but increasingly both health insurance and health care services themselves are being commodified, that is provided by profit making corporations (Salmon, 1985). The original mass health insurance organizations emerged in the 1930s in the shape of the local non-profit making Blue Cross and Blue Shield funds, organized by hospitals to protect themselves and their patients against the rising cost of hospital hotel and medical charges respectively. After the war, commercial insurance companies expanded their market share substantially by offering employer group health plans at competitive premiums related to occupational and class status. The for-profit and not-for-profit health insurers have shared the market over recent decades. In the last two decades, a new form of health care provider called Health Maintenance Organizations (HMOs) has come to prominence. Instead of being a passive third party like conventional insurance organizations, an HMO offers a complete local health care package to members who pay an annual fee. Many members have some or all of the fee paid for them by their employers. The HMO either contracts with providers or directly provides the health care service to the patient. HMOs, which can be profit making or non-profit making, covered about 12 per cent of the population by the late 1980s.

The commodification of the hospital system has been the other major new development in the past two decades. For-profit hospitals are described by their supporters as 'investor-owned' or by neutrals as 'proprietary'. Until the 1960s there were only a handful in the US, but in 1960 the first private hospital corporation was formed. By the late 1980s around 30 per cent of beds were in for-profit hospitals, and much of this expansion has been publicly funded in a largely unplanned way. Himmelstein and Woolhandler (1984: 20) found that in Oakland and Boston the major private hospitals received 'more than 60 per cent of their revenues from government sources'. In addition an increasing number of voluntary and public hospitals have management contracts with the for-profit corporations. In the 1980s leading corporations such as Humana and AMI opened their own community health centres to provide ambulatory care and have also begun to take over HMOs. It seems likely that by the end of the century a few, giant transnational corporations will dominate the production of health care in what has been described as 'the new medical-industrial complex' (Navarro, 1989: 205; Bergstrand, 1982: 50). The old two tier voluntary (non-profit, private) and public (state or municipal) hospital system now has another, increasingly powerful upper tier, creaming off the profitable patients and sending unprofitable ones to the non-profit hospitals. In order to compete for funding, the voluntary hospitals are having to emulate or buy in the harder, corporate approach, while the public hospitals have suffered severely from budget cuts and underinvestment. Himmelstein and Woolhandler (1984: 19) reported that 'six of New York's nineteen public hospitals have been closed, as have the only public hospitals serving Detroit, Philadelphia, and twenty-nine of California's sixty-six counties.' By the end of the century, a new hospital system will have been created, with two levels both supported by public funds, an upper class of essentially commercial hospitals and a lower class of impoverished public and voluntary institutions for the poor and uninsured – the twenty-first century version of the workhouse hospital.

Public money from a wide variety of local and federal programmes is injected into this essentially private health care system. Table 4.4 indicates the basic structure and coverage of health insurance in the US. The most

Table 4.4   *Percentages of population covered by sources of health insurance in the US, 1983*

Medicare	12
Medicaid	8
Military/institutional	5
Group insurance plans through employment	58
No health coverage	15
Personal insurance, not provided through employment	2

Source: Staples, 1989: Table 1

striking feature is that substantial proportions of the population either have no health insurance or are inadequately insured to cover the potentially massive costs of a personal/family health problem, but this cannot be reliably quantified. On the basis of official statistics Renner and Navarro (1989: Table 6) suggest that in 1984 17.4 per cent of non-elderly people had no health insurance. In 1980 62 per cent of employees had an employer plan (occupationally based health insurance, usually requiring employee contributions) covering the costs of hospital and out-patient care and prescriptions, but only up to certain ceilings. Of those covered by employer plans, 37.5 per cent were not covered for 'extended care', that is protection against the enormous costs of chronic illness, and 49.5 per cent were not covered for routine dental care (Renner and Navarro, 1989: Table 5). Therefore anything between 20 and 60 per cent of the population are either inadequately insured or not insured at all. The proportion of employees covered by an employer health plan fell from 62 per cent in 1980 to 59.8 per cent in 1984, suggesting that underinsurance was increasing in the 1980s. According to Bodenheimer (1989: 536) the number of people lacking health insurance for all or part of the year has increased by 50 per cent over the 1980s. Renner and Navarro (1989: 438) found 'a substantial and increasing gap between the average employee's income and that of employees with direct employer health coverage' which they link directly to the growth of non-union, low-wage and part-time jobs. Naturally the distribution of health insurance reflects the occupational class structure, with managerial and professional employees having the best coverage, low-paid non-unionized workers in the service and retail sectors having poor or no coverage, and the organized working class in an intermediate position. Thus

> a worker's access to health insurance varies with other indicators of labor market success, primarily wages; and health care coverage is one of the fringe benefits that characterizes a good job in the US economy. However, even when workers with 'good jobs' are laid off or quit, they also lose their health benefits. (Staples, 1989: 418)

Given that the labour market is firmly stratified by 'race', class and gender, private health insurance closely reflects these inequalities. In the early 1980s 14 per cent of white people, 22 per cent of black people and 29 per cent of Hispanic people were uninsured for health care (Bodenheimer, 1989: 536).

Two of the outstanding reforms from the Great Society era introduced in 1965 are Medicare and Medicaid, health insurance programmes for old people and poor people respectively. The two programmes are quite different in funding and status, Medicare being associated with the popular universalism of social security, and Medicaid equally identified with the stigma of welfare. Medicare is the contributory health insurance element of the OASDHI social security programme, offering uniform national standards of eligibility and benefits with reasonable reimbursement of doctors and hospitals. Nevertheless there are prescribed ceilings to entitlements, such as ninety days' stay in hospital, so that it only covers about 40 per cent of the actual health care costs of the average person over sixty-five. The post-1981 OBRA cuts took about 6 per cent off the Medicare budget by increasing deductibles, that is expenses not covered. Since 1985 'old people have been paying a higher proportion of their income for health care than they did before Medicare came into being' (Bodenheimer, 1989: 535).

Medicaid is far from uniform nationally, each state having a different programme with the costs shared equally between the states and the federal government. The schemes are obliged to cover welfare recipients and their families, but eligibility beyond this varies from state to state, sometimes including other people on low incomes and people receiving SSI and unemployment benefit. Although 'all states must cover hospital and physician expenses and may cover optional benefits such as prescription drugs and dental care . . . most states limit the use of benefits by restricting days of hospital care [and] number of physician visits or by imposing copayments' (Raffel, 1987: 219). For many poor families Medicaid is the most vital element of the welfare state, which frequently confines them in a poverty trap, where any rise in money income might lead to the loss of this vital benefit in kind. About 60 per cent of the poor are either not eligible for or not receiving Medicaid to which they are entitled because of its administrative complexity. Generally the rates of reimbursement for doctors and hospitals under each state's Medicaid programme are very low. This 'discourages hospitals and doctors from providing good care or any care at all' for Medicaid patients (DiNitto and Dye, 1983: 189); hospitals and doctors will tend to rush these patients and perform unnecessary treatments and tests to maximize the relatively meagre income. The post-1981 OBRA cuts retrenched the funding of Medicaid by around 5 per cent. Medicaid is a last resort for many elderly and chronically sick people whose entitlements under Medicare and private insurance have been exhausted. Seventy per cent of Medicaid expenditure is devoted to elderly and chronically sick people who have fallen through the insurance system and whose families are unable to bear the costs of care. This is the modern version of the workhouse for people who are not able-bodied.

Power Struggles in the Health Care System

There are essentially three parties to the struggle over health care in the US: the medical profession, the corporate/bureaucratic health care management, and the popular movements for health care reform. Alford (1975) suggests that these are the powerful 'structural interests' in health care, describing them as the 'professional monopolists', the 'corporate rationalizers' and the 'equal-health advocates'. Although unquestionably much weaker than the predominant interests, the underlying and continuing influence of popular movements for egalitarian health care reform are frequently underestimated. As Navarro (1989: 888) points out, 'the majority of the US population is in favor of the government . . . establishing a universal and comprehensive health program even at the cost of paying higher taxes', but the unyielding opposition of the medical profession and the corporate rationalizers prevents its realization. Navarro emphasizes the relative economic and political weakness of the working class in the US as the fundamental explanatory factor. Since at least the beginning of this century, there have been major campaigns for national health insurance (NHI) and national health programmes going beyond NHI. Increasing health care costs and falling patient incomes during the depression years of the 1930s prompted a revival of NHI campaigning which it was hoped would be part of the New Deal. However, hospital managers supported by doctors energetically developed mass voluntary health insurance schemes as a substitute, and the 1935 Social Security Act studiously avoided NHI. After the war, Truman initially supported strong popular demands for NHI, but in the Cold War atmosphere it failed again. In the late 1940s the industrial trade unions began to conclude employer agreements for greatly expanded employer health plans. These collective bargaining processes alongside social security were organized labour's greatest gain from the New Deal. At the very same moment in the late 1940s the American Medical Association (AMA), representing the medical profession, began to campaign explicitly for the first time in favour of voluntary health insurance as 'the American way' (Starr, 1982: 313), contrasted with the introduction of alien national health services in Britain and Sweden. Employer health plans tied workers more firmly to their jobs by controlling their access to health care, as well as undermining support for NHI. In the 1960s under the added pressure of the civil rights movement and the commitment to the Great Society, the federal government introduced Medicare and Medicaid. Since then, many liberal Democrats have continued to campaign for NHI. Recently the National Rainbow Coalition, working within and outside the Democratic Party with Jesse Jackson as its president, has campaigned for a comprehensive national health programme. The programme would guarantee universal access to a health care system funded by taxation and federally administered. Local planning and public accountability would provide a check on the federal bureaucracy, while the providers of health care would continue to be largely voluntary, non-profit making institutions (National Rainbow Coalition, 1988).

As well as the campaigns for NHI and national health programmes, innumerable struggles by women, ethnic minorities, health care workers, disabled people, gay and lesbian people and many other groups for health care reform have made a positive impact on the system at the local level. Foremost amongst these perhaps is the women's health movement, which has established well-woman clinics, abortion clinics and health centres under women's control, and challenged patriarchal medical practice in many fields, particularly the management of childbirth and the treatment of mental illness (Ruzek, 1978). In the 1980s the gay movement has led the campaign for health care services for AIDS victims. An important, contradictory aspect of the private health care system in the US is that, in some respects, it offers more room for manoeuvre to popular interest groups, particularly those with middle class consumer muscle. The more bureaucratized systems of Western Europe are more immune to such forms of popular pressure.

It is no exaggeration to suggest that the medical profession in the US has probably been the strongest and most successful interest group the world has ever seen. The basis for their power derives not only from the immense authority of scientific medicine, but specifically from the reconstruction of the profession in the early 1900s. On the basis of the Flexner Report of 1910, the AMA succeeded in restricting entry to the medical profession essentially to middle class, white men. Over half the medical schools were closed, including virtually all of those who enrolled black and women students, and those from less affluent backgrounds (Brown, 1979). Medical school admissions did not reach their 1905 level until 1955. Despite affirmative action policy in medical school admissions, by the late 1970s only 20 per cent of medical students were women and only 6 per cent were black, still a considerable improvement on the 1960s. By the 1930s the AMA not only had firm control of medical education, but 'also controlled the practice and economics of medicine through local medical societies'

(Brown, 1979: 7). By the 1970s office-based physicians had reached the top of the class structure, with earnings in 1976 five and a half times greater than average full-time earnings. In 1984 their average gross earnings were $181,300.

To some extent in conflict with the medical profession, but on a class basis in partnership with it, the corporate rationalisers are a disparate group, including hospital managers and corporations, insurers, medical school foundations and federal/local government. Their politics ranges from those who would expose health care entirely to free-market forces to those who would institute federal planning of health care resources and tight regulation of doctors' expenditure. What unites the corporate rationalizers is the struggle for cost containment in the context of the explosion of health care spending and costs, the issue which dominated health care policy making in the 1970s and 1980s. The real pressure for cost containment has come from employers, particularly the major corporations, who since the recession of the mid 1970s have sought to cut back the health care plans achieved by union collective bargaining. In 1979 health insurance accounted for 7.8 per cent of gross wages in the steel industry and 8.1 per cent in the car industry. In 1984 health insurance took up 38 per cent of businesses' pre-tax profits. Since the mid 1970s corporations have negotiated to get employees to bear a greater proportion of the direct costs of health care, so that employer health plans cover less and less of the full cost. In 1974 200 leading corporations formed a powerful pressure group for health care cost containment, and by 1986 'over 200 business-dominated local health care coalitions existed compared with only twenty-five . . . in 1982' (Bodenheimer, 1989: 535). Such pressures from business in the 1970s encouraged the federal government to promote the allegedly more efficient HMOs. Since the mid 1970s a whole raft of federally inspired, bureaucratic cost containment measures have been developed, essentially struggling to enforce financial self-regulation on the medical profession. In reviewing these measures Björkman (1989: 72) concludes that 'in matters of cost, peer review, health planning and resource allocation the American profession remains well placed' and continues to dominate the health care sector. Starr (1982), however, suggests that the increasing cost containment pressures from government and employers have eroded the authority and strategic position of the medical profession. It is also theoretically possible that the rapid expansion of the for-profit health care corporations will 'proletarianize' doctors. Yet

> because of their dependence on physicians, the corporations will be generous in granting rewards, including more autonomy than they give to most workers . . . Nonetheless, compared with individual practice, corporate work will necessarily entail a profound loss of autonomy. (Starr, 1982: 446)

There seems little doubt that the emergence of the medical-industrial complex is shifting power towards private corporate management, whose lack of political accountability may make the struggles of the popular health movements much tougher.

Health Status and Health Inequalities

In terms of the health status of the population as measured by seventeen age- and sex-specific mortality rates in 1975, the US ranked ninth out of ten leading industrial states (Table A.23). The infant mortality rate in the US has consistently been the highest amongst the four capitalist states examined in this book. In a recent review of the impact of medical measures on mortality and morbidity in the US, McKinlay *et al.* (1989: 204) confirmed the generally accepted view that 'medical care has contributed little to the modern decline in mortality and therefore to any improvement in health.' Like the National Rainbow Coalition they advocate 'an effective public health program [which] could, by a conservative estimate, save annually 600,000 lives, six million person years of life and $5 billion in medical costs' (McKinlay *et al.*, 1989: 205). Data on health inequalities seems largely confined to racial inequalities, though we have already discussed the question of class differences in women's access to abortion services. In some respects 'race' can be taken as a metaphor for 'class' given the racialization of the class structure. In a local study of racial differences in preventable deaths, Woolhandler *et al.* (1985: 9) found that 'the black/white differential was significantly greater for preventable causes than for the non-preventable group.' In this case therefore differential access to health care services was critical to the outcome and explained much of the observed differences in preventable death rates. Clearly the accessibility and the structure of a health care system are significant factors in explaining geographical and sociological differences in health status.

Table 4.5 *US infant mortality by 'race' (deaths under one year per 100,000 live births)*

	1960	1983
White	22.9	9.7
Non-white	43.2	16.8
Black	44.3	19.2

Source: US Bureau of the Census, 1987: Table 112

Table 4.6 *US life expectancy at birth (age in years)*

	1920	1970	1984
White	54.9	71.7	75.3
Non-white	45.3	65.3	71.3
Black	N/A	64.1	69.7

Source: US Bureau of the Census, 1987: Table 105

Tables 4.5, 4.6 and 4.7 suggest that the health status gap between black and white people has barely changed despite the expansion of the welfare state, with infant mortality for black people remaining since 1960 at twice

Table 4.7   *US maternal deaths per 100,000 live births*

	1960	1983
White	26.0	5.9
Non-white	97.9	16.3
Black	103.6	18.3

Source: US Bureau of the Census, 1987: Table 112

the rate for white people. Racial differences in life expectancy have narrowed since the 1920s, but the narrowing has slowed up in recent decades, and the gap between black and white people is still more than five years. The decline in maternal deaths was dramatic for all groups during the 1960s and 1970s, indicating perhaps the impact of welfare state expansion and the women's health movement, but the rate for black women was three times that for white women in 1983, compared to a difference of almost five times in 1960. Geographical differences in infant mortality rates provide another indication of race and class inequalities in health status. The infant mortality rate (per 100,000 live births) for white people in 1983 (US Bureau of the Census, 1987) was lowest in Delaware (7.3) and highest in the District of Columbia (11.6), while for black people it was lowest in Oklahoma (14.9) and highest in Illinois and Milwaukee (both 23.1). In 1983 the overall maternal death rate increased for the first time in decades. Infant mortality rates rose in eleven states between 1981 and 1982 at the height of the recession. There is some evidence that, with the fading of the Second Reconstruction and increased unemployment since the recession of the mid 1970s, the health status of the population and the class/racial differences in health status are worsening.

Conclusion

The so-called backlash against the welfare state in the US began almost as soon as the expansion of the welfare state took off in the 1960s, reflecting the prevailing influence of voluntarism. The struggle over the welfare state has remained intense ever since, culminating thus far perhaps in the conflict over the Reagan tax cuts and social spending cuts in the early 1980s. The outcome of the conflict has not been a clear-cut victory for the conservatives, nor has it left the welfare state undamaged. Almost all of the New Deal programmes and many of the Great Society programmes have survived with significantly retrenched budgets. The financial burden of the welfare state has been shifted somewhat from the federal government to local government, employers and employees. Decentralization has been accompanied by privatization, particularly in areas such as day care, residential social services and health care. This privatization has largely taken for-profit, proprietary forms, rather than non-profit, voluntary forms. Entrepreneurial and corporate capital, substantially supported by public funds in the shape of social security for example, has established profitable markets in welfare services, which hitherto were simply not profitable.

The impact of this restructuring of the welfare state and the continuing high levels of unemployment (much of it hidden) has been to widen class, 'race' and gender inequalities. It has also had the effect of increasing class divisions *amongst* women and *amongst* black people. New professional and managerial elites amongst women and black people have benefited most clearly from civil rights reforms. For the mass of women and black people in paid employment, their continuing, inferior structural position in the labour market engenders a continuing inferiority in social welfare, which is predominantly derived from occupational status. The federal enforcement of equal rights legislation for black people and women has atrophied and in certain aspects it has turned against its intended beneficiaries. Thus in some respects, the welfare state in recent years has contributed to deepening social inequalities. Perhaps the most vivid index of the increasingly authoritarian response to social problems and social inequalities in the US is the explosion of the prison population and of drug-related crime. This has a very distinct class, 'race' and gender dimension. According to Walker (1991: 11) one in four black men aged twenty to twenty-nine is either in prison, on probation or on parole, while less than one in five of the same group are in college. Yet the annual cost of college education is about half the annual cost of imprisonment. Thus

> the criminal justice system has increasingly been used as the main vehicle through which America handles its social problems, a catch-all device which scoops up drug users, the mentally ill, the homeless and other social 'failures', and puts them out of sight and out of mind into its prison system. (Walker, 1991: 11)

The proportion of the US population in prison is the highest in the world, way ahead of the Soviet Union, and a black man is four times more likely to be in prison in the US than in South Africa.

However, any appraisal of the recent history of the welfare state in the US should not be entirely pessimistic. There was and there still is a feasible project on the right of US politics to dismantle the welfare state. So far this project has lamentably failed, and conservative forces are in some disarray over their future strategy. Welfare liberalism is very much alive and well in the US; social security is popular and widely supported. The middle classes, just as in Western Europe, are realizing some of the benefits of the welfare state, such as the need for subsidized day care and community care. Even the reform of 'welfare' is stalemated between conservatives and liberals, just as it was in the 1960s. Popular pressure in support of civil and welfare rights remains formidable. Nowhere has this been better illustrated than in the struggle over abortion rights. The long-awaited 'reversal' of the liberal abortion reform in 1989 has been staunchly opposed by the women's movement, liberals, libertarian conservatives and popular opinion. The anti-abortion movement seemed to be in retreat once again as the 1990s opened. The experience of the 1980s in the US shows that the welfare state is neither irreversible nor doomed. In a period in which working class and popular movements have been on the retreat in the face of capital's forward march, the welfare state has been restructured to reflect new balances of power.

5

Britain: the Liberal Collectivist Welfare State

Unlike Sweden, Germany and the US, the slump of the 1930s did not produce a radical shift in British social policy. Cuts in unemployment benefit and deflationary economic policies were deployed to discipline the working class and poor people. At the same time however governments became more embroiled in infrastructural investment, industrial relations and macroeconomic management. The decisive ideological shift towards the modern welfare state occurred near the end of the Second World War with the adoption of Keynesian economic policy and Beveridgean social policy. The British welfare state has since occupied a middle ranking position amongst capitalist states. It has not been dominated by Social Democratic ideology like Sweden, nor has it been dominated by voluntarism and reluctant collectivism as in the US. The 'mixed economy of welfare' in Britain shares something in common with the notion of the Social Market Economy in the FRG, but with lower levels of welfare expenditure, a more egalitarian ethos and more emphasis on direct, public provision of services. Also as in the FRG the Conservative Party has been the dominant force in post-war politics particularly in the 1950s and 1980s. In the face of union and employer resistance, Labour governments have been unable to sustain social democratic corporatist structures in the long term. The commitment of the Conservative Party to the welfare state has always been ambivalent and opportunistic. Hence, with the collapse of Labourism amidst the fiscal crisis of the state in the 1970s, Thatcherism succeeded to some extent in moving the British welfare state away from European models and more towards the model of the US.

The political economy of the British welfare state in the post-war period is usefully divided into two periods, that from the 1940s to the mid 1970s, and that since the mid 1970s. From the 1940s to the mid 1970s the informal post-war settlement between capital and labour was based on the apparent commitment to full employment, fairly steady if unspectacular economic growth and the incremental expansion of a universalist welfare state in line with economic growth. This period of the post-war settlement itself divides into two eras. The 1940s to the early 1960s was an era of austerity in material welfare terms, of great optimism about the benefits of the welfare state and of relatively little conflict and pressure over welfare issues. The period from the early 1960s to the mid 1970s by contrast saw a rediscovery of mass poverty, unprecedented expansion of welfare expenditure and the emergence of pressure groups and new social movements advocating a wide range of unmet welfare needs amongst poor people, elderly people, the black communities, women and so on. During this period welfare politics broke out of the embrace of class politics to a greater extent than in the FRG and Sweden. The pluralism of welfare politics in Britain since the 1960s is thus closer to the situation in the US, with the important difference that the British trade unions representing welfare state workers have played a prominent role in the 'welfare lobby'.

The second period, since the mid 1970s, saw the withering of the post-war settlement in the context of stagflation with mass unemployment, retrenchment of the welfare state, anti-union measures and other devices being used by governments in the attempt to restore capital to health. The years from 1974 to 1979 saw the Labour governments wrestling with the pressures from the 'welfare lobby' in the context of recession and inflation. Between 1976 and 1979, legitimated by a corporatist social contract with the unions, the Labour government inaugurated the transformation of the welfare state consensus, a task taken up with greater enthusiasm after 1979 by the Thatcher governments. During the 1980s cuts in social welfare, permanently high levels of unemployment, and regressive reform of personal taxation succeeded in significantly increasing the level of poverty and widening the inequalities between the affluent and those on below average incomes. Finally in the wake of the 1987 election, 'third term' Thatcherism tackled the restructuring of the welfare state more directly and thoroughly than ever before. This project, so far unfinished, essentially sought to change the role of the welfare state in Britain from being a direct provider of welfare to being a regulator of privately provided welfare. The project has been seriously thwarted by many obstacles and forms of resistance from consumers, welfare professionals, the Treasury, local government and so on.

Throughout this chapter reference will usually be made to the British welfare state, that is the welfare state in England, Wales and Scotland, though most of the statistical material covers the United Kingdom (UK). In the areas of social security and health care, policy making and administration in the post-war period have been highly centralized, compared to other welfare states. Thus the British social security system and National Health Service operate in Northern Ireland in much the same way as on the mainland. In the fields of education, housing and personal social services, there are significant policy and legislative differences between England and Wales, Scotland and Northern Ireland. In Northern Ireland the involvement of the local state in the provision and funding of education and public housing prior to 1973 maintained institutional discrimination against Catholics and contributed to the rise of the Catholic civil rights movement in the 1960s. The extent to which direct rule from

London since 1973 has been able to curb these processes is debatable, to say the least.

Ideology and Welfare Expenditure

Liberal Collectivism and Thatcherism

The term Liberal Collectivism comes closest to encapsulating the post-war welfare consensus, against which Thatcherism pitted itself. The 'Liberal' element is appropriate because the architects of the consensus were Keynes and Beveridge, both of whom were Liberals. Beveridge himself was very much identified with and involved with the new liberalism of the Edwardian era prior to the First World War, when free-market liberalism was modified by the introduction of social insurance and elements of Bismarckian social policy. Of course the 'one nation', Disraelian strand of the Conservative Party and the moderate social democrats of the Labour Party have always had much in common with Beveridgean and Keynesian liberalism. Indeed the phrase 'Butskellism' has been widely used since the early 1950s to describe the post-war political consensus embracing one nation Tories like Butler and moderate Labour leaders like Gaitskell. The term 'Collectivism' signals the emphasis in the post-war settlement on direct public provision of welfare benefits and services, the commitment to universal access to those benefits and services, and the national uniformity of the system. Thus at the centre of the post-war Liberal Collectivist consensus is an ideology which accepted an extended role for the state in economic and social policy and implicitly guaranteed social rights of citizenship for the whole population. Defining the precise extent of the state's welfare obligations and the welfare rights of citizens was left to political pragmatism and social struggle. In reality the welfare citizenship of women, black people, and poor people was not secured by the post-war welfare state. Indeed the whole notion of welfare citizenship at the heart of the post-war consensus is ideological in the sense that it carries nationalistic overtones and implies the exclusion of certain people from the benefits of citizenship (Taylor, 1989: 25–6).

Dunleavy (1989) has aptly described the Liberal Collectivist consensus as based upon an 'ungrounded statism' inherited from war-time mobilization and relying heavily on direct state provision of benefits and services with relatively little emphasis on voluntary, trade union, charitable, communal and, indeed, for-profit forms. Nor was local government given much room for positive manoeuvre except to some extent in the fields of schooling and caring services. In Britain statism was ungrounded in that it did not have secure roots in a strong Social Democratic movement as in Sweden or within a more conservative corporate statist tradition as in Germany. Thus in Britain

a statist pattern of intervention was established in a political system characterized by the predominance of the right and the incomplete establishment of social
democratic ideas in a non-hegemonic position. It flourished in a society with a
notably weak development of corporatism; an absence of policy stability in
macroeconomic management [stop–go etc.]; and a low level of substantive
welfare benefits provision. (Dunleavy, 1989: 256)

The extent of 'statism' in the Liberal Collectivist consensus must not be
exaggerated however. Central to Beveridge's conception of the welfare
state was the idea of the 'social minimum' of welfare based on contributory
insurance principles, the welfare state as a safety net which would
nevertheless encourage people to make their own private welfare provisions over and above the minimum. Indeed 'compulsory contributions to
provide more than a minimum would, in Beveridge's view, be an attack on
the individual's freedom to spend his money as he thinks best' (George and
Wilding, 1985: 64). Anti-collectivists within the Conservative Party, who
believed that the post-war welfare state constructed in the 1940s already
went far beyond the necessary social minimum, played a major part in
limiting the resources and the further development of the welfare state
from the early 1950s onwards, as highlighted in the fifties by Titmuss (1958:
35, 148).

In the mid 1970s amidst the disarray of Keynesianism, the 'overload' of
pressures reflecting unmet needs and the fiscal crisis of the state, the anti-
collectivist wing of conservatism exploited the ungrounded nature of post-
war statism. The New Right, led by Mrs Thatcher, attacked the Liberal
Collectivist consensus as an old order which had failed, filling the
ideological vacuum with monetarist, supply-side macroeconomics and
privatization and market-led competition for the public sectors of industry
and social welfare. Comparable responses to the recessions of the mid
1970s and the early 1980s emerged in Sweden, the FRG and, above all, the
US in the form of Reaganomics. However the shift in Britain was more
radical for two reasons. First, the fundamental weakness of the British
economy, particularly manufacturing industry, diminished the supply of
resources for the welfare state to a comparatively much greater extent.
Second, on the demand side, popular pressures and political support for
publicly provided welfare benefits and services were comparatively well
organized and, if anything, increasing in strength in the 1970s with the rise
in unemployment and the emergence of new social movements. Hence the
1980s in Britain saw a terrific ideological struggle between defenders of
Liberal Collectivism and supporters of Thatcherism. The latter claim to
have achieved nothing less than a revolution and to have established a new
consensus based on competitive individualism and market forces, nour-
ished enthusiastically by the state. The Thatcher governments purposefully
sought to stifle and discourage the pressures and the social movements
pushing for extension and improvement of the welfare state. This has not
been entirely successful by any means, provoking, for example, a further

rediscovery of poverty, championed by the Church of England. However, the more radical social policies of post-1987 Thatcherism successfully attacked the Beveridge social minimum and transformed the statism of British social policy.

Welfare Expenditure

Britain has occupied a middle ranking position amongst the capitalist welfare states in terms of public expenditure on social welfare as a proportion of national economic resources over the post-war period. Table A.1 shows that real social expenditure as a proportion of GDP was a little above the OECD average in 1960, and a little below it in 1981. In 1981 Britain lagged far behind Sweden and the FRG on this measure, and the US had narrowed the gap. The so-called welfare expenditure boom in Britain between the early 1960s and the mid 1970s was quite modest by international standards. The figures on real income elasticity in Table A.1 suggest that, unlike the US and the FRG, the welfare state in Britain was cushioned from the recession in the mid 1970s. In other words the growth of real social expenditure as a proportion of GDP was sustained in the 1975–81 period, though the welfare state did not survive as well as in Sweden. This certainly reflects the struggle by the Labour governments of 1974–9 to protect key elements of the welfare state. Analysis of welfare expenditure since the advent of Thatcherism is hampered by an important change in the basis for the government's published statistics on public expenditure. Since 1979 the government has used cash figures for public expenditure adjusted for general inflation in the economy. Prior to 1979, as in the OECD, price deflators specific to each welfare sector were used, giving a more precise picture of the real input into each sector, because price inflation tends to be higher in these sectors (the relative price effect). Public expenditure figures for the 1980s therefore tend to disguise the extent of real expenditure restraint, particularly in labour intensive services like education, health care and social services. The government finds itself in a quandary in the presentation of public spending statistics. It wants to claim both great success in cutting public expenditure and full support for popular elements of the welfare state such as the health service, state pensions and free state schooling. Thus on the one hand central and local government spending (excluding public corporations and proceeds of privatizations) declined from almost 47 per cent of GDP in 1982–3 to just below 40 per cent of GDP in 1988–9 (HM Treasury, 1989: Section 4), reflecting the government's achievement in restraining the welfare state in a period of buoyant economic growth. On the other hand over the period 1979–80 to 1989–90 the government could claim a 37 per cent real rise in spending by the Department of Health and a 36 per cent real rise in spending by the Department of Social Security, though it is probable that these increases were more than cancelled out by the impact of the relative price effect and the increased numbers of social security claimants and elderly people. The British welfare state since the mid 1970s has undoubt-edly suffered real retrenchment both in relation to GDP and in relation to needs.

Income Maintenance Policies and Outcomes

The ranking position of Britain in terms of combined de-commodification of social security benefits (Table 1.1) is considerably below the mean for capitalist welfare states. In other words social insurance benefits in Britain blunt the impact of labour market inequalities modestly compared with most capitalist welfare states, particularly in comparison to most of those in Western Europe. Britain with Australia, New Zealand, Canada, the US and Ireland is described by Esping-Andersen (1990: 48) as having a benefits system based on an Anglo-Saxon 'social-assistance tradition . . . characterized by the application of a means- or income-test . . . these systems do not properly extend citizen rights.' In Britain the Liberal Collectivist notion of 'the social minimum' grafted onto the far from moribund poor law tradition resulted in an uneasy combination of means-tested assistance and social insurance. The resulting income maintenance system is unique amongst capitalist states in two key respects. First, means-tested social assistance throughout the post-war period has operated on a nationally uniform tariff of benefits and entitlements, administered by central government with millions of people totally dependent on it. Second, the social insurance system has consistently offered low replace-ment of earnings, poor coverage of risks and relatively tough eligibility conditions in exchange for modest contributions from employers, employees and the state. The social insurance system is comparatively underdeveloped; hence the mass role of social assistance. It is widely recognized that this is not what Beveridge envisaged, and that the dominance of social insurance in Scandinavia, the FRG and even the US is more in keeping with his ideas. In Britain the Labour government of the 1940s failed to establish an adequately funded social insurance system on the dubious grounds that employees, employers and the state could not afford the contribution burden. Egalitarian views on the left dictated opposition to earnings-related social insurance benefits, which inevitably reinforce the social inequalities generated by the labour market.

The 'universality' of the post-war social insurance schemes in Britain is also something of a myth. A considerable number of people, mostly women, are either not covered at all or have an inadequate contribution record, thereby denying them access in their own right to unemployment, sickness, maternity and other benefits as well as the National Insurance pension. Many married women continue to derive entitlement to the pension from their husbands' contributions. This includes the large number of women in paid employment, who took Beveridge's married women's option of paying greatly reduced National Insurance contributions, exclud-ing them from rights to unemployment, sickness and pension benefits in their own right. This option was withdrawn from new entrants to the labour market in 1978, but it continues to affect many women who were in paid employment before April 1978. In addition to these women, Hakim (1989) estimates that in the mid 1980s there were about two million people, about 7 per cent of the labour force, in regular paid employment but not covered by National Insurance, of whom about 80 per cent were women, mostly in part-time, low-paid work at home or from home. If one also takes into account other features of the casual economy such as the use of unregistered migrant workers, then it is likely that over 10 per cent of the labour force is not in fact covered by National Insurance, a proportion that is rising with the growth of part-time employment and the casual economy.

Income Inequality

Data on the distribution of net income adjusted for household size in 1972/3 and 1980 puts the UK in a middle ranking position in terms of the gap between rich and poor people, not as unequal as the FRG and the US, but less equal than Sweden (Tables A.3 and A.4). The redistributional impact of the taxation and social security systems was also in the middle range comparatively, not as significant as in the US and Sweden, but more significant than the FRG (Tables A.2 and A.5). For the UK it is possible to compare the impact of the welfare state in the mid 1970s with the mid 1980s (Table 5.1) using data on the distribution of 'final income' from the Family Expenditure Survey (FES). Here 'final income' is calculated by taking into

Table 5.1   *UK percentage distribution of final household income by quintile groups of households*

	Bottom fifth	Next fifth	Next fifth	Next fifth	Top fifth
1976	7.4	12.7	18.0	24.0	37.9
1986	5.9	11.4	17.0	23.9	41.7

Source: CSO, 1989: Table 5.18

account cash benefits, direct and indirect taxation (including mortgage tax relief) and welfare 'benefits in kind' such as state education, the NHS, housing and public transport subsidies. According to the government statisticians 'at least part of the change is because the mix of households [by size] within each quintile group has changed' with 'less elderly and more young families in the lowest quintile' (CSO, 1989: 97). O'Higgins has compared the distribution of unadjusted household income (as above) with 'equivalent household income', that is adjusting for household size and composition in terms of adults and children. He found that 'the use of equivalent rather than unadjusted income reduces the apparent inequality of the distribution of quintile income shares, but makes relatively little difference to the picture of the trends over the 1976–82 period in the distribution and redistribution of income' (O'Higgins, 1985: 300). This is confirmed by Stark (1988: Table E) and CSO (1990b: 93–6). We may therefore safely conclude from Table 5.1 that over the 1976–86 period in the UK there was a widening distribution of final income within the 'working class', with poor people in particular falling much farther behind. The top fifth of the income distribution achieved a substantial increase in their proportion of final household income over the period. As O'Higgins (1985) pointed out, the main reason for this was the worsening distribution of original (market) incomes, caused by recession and unemployment. Tax changes in the period were less significant, while changes in the rest of the welfare state have had only a small effect, on this particular statistical basis.

These changes are also illustrated by the history of the Gini coefficient in the UK at different stages of the tax/benefit system (Table 5.2). The really

Table 5.2   *UK Gini coefficients for the distribution of household income at different stages of the tax–benefit system*

	1975	1979	1983	1986
Original income	43	45	49	52
Gross income[1]	35	35	36	40
Disposable income[2]	32	33	33	36
Final income	31	32	33	36

[1] Gross income is original income plus cash transfers and mortgage tax relief.
[2] Disposable income is gross income less income tax, employees' National Insurance contributions and rates.

Source: CSO, 1988: Table 11

dramatic change between 1975 and 1986 in the Gini coefficients was the growing inequality in original or market income from employment, investments and occupational pensions. The growing inequalities in gross, disposable and final incomes have been more modest. However welfare 'benefits in kind' are calculated on the basis of age and sex only, regardless of income, so that their apparent lack of impact on the distribution of income is something of a statistical artefact. The growth in original income inequality was occurring throughout the 1980s, while the growth in the other forms of income inequality was concentrated in the mid 1980s. On the basis of the same FES data, it has been estimated that between 1979 and 1988 the disposable income of the bottom 20 per cent of the income distribution fell by 6 per cent, while that of the top 20 per cent rose by 38 per cent (Labour Party, 1989a).

The FES data also indicates just how vital the welfare state is for the least affluent in Britain. The poorest 20 per cent of households had an average original income from earnings and wealth of just £130 in 1986 without the welfare state, which brought their final income up to an average of £4130. The CSO has calculated the cash value of the welfare state to the quintile groups of households ranked by original income, as in Table 5.3. This table underestimates the extent to which the welfare state is

Table 5.3 *UK distribution of welfare state benefits in cash and kind, 1986: quintile groups of households ranked by original income (£ per year)*

Bottom fifth	Next fifth	Next fifth	Next fifth	Top fifth
4880	4220	2760	2530	2390

Source: CSO, 1989: Table 5.17

benefiting the more affluent by not including tax relief on pensions and by the built-in assumption that each quintile division gains equally from 'benefits in kind'. In fact the middle class pro rata consume more of these 'benefits in kind', i.e. public services such as the NHS and higher education, as documented by Le Grand (1987). The top 20 and 40 per cent of the income distribution have been gaining an increasing share of the welfare state, a process which seems to have accelerated since the advent of the welfare crisis in the mid 1970s. Indeed it has been demonstrated quantitatively that from 1979 to 1984 the Conservative policy of cutting welfare expenditure and privatizing the welfare state was hampered to some extent by a willingness to favour those state-provided services that were 'predominantly used by members of the middle classes' (Le Grand and Winter, 1987: 165). Third term Thatcherism reached its zenith with the March 1988 budget which, in the most radical reform of income tax since the war, slashed the five higher rates of tax to leave just two bands, 40 per cent for higher earners and 25 per cent for the rest. It is likely that this reform has led to a further substantial increase in the gap between the top 20 per cent of the income distribution and the rest. One political commentator wrote on the day after the 1988 budget speech that it represented 'the Thatcherite catharsis . . . it takes us in one giant stride towards American levels of taxation, in support of an American view of the proper relationship between social justice and individual wealth, between equality and opportunity as values society should uphold' (Young, 1988: 1). Net income inequality is certainly moving gradually towards becoming comparable with that in the FRG as well as the US, so that Britain is probably losing its middle ranking status in this respect.

Poverty

The politics of poverty in Britain has been quite vibrant compared with the rest of Western Europe since the rediscovery of poverty in the early 1960s. At the heart of this phenomenon lies a determination by the working class, supported by the liberal middle class, to turn welfare state rhetoric into reality, particularly in the context of the failure to implement an adequate and reasonably just social insurance system after the war. For cultural and historical reasons, poor people were possibly less marginalized in Britain in the post-war decades than in other capitalist states. Certainly the needs of poor people have been capably represented at the national level by pressure and interest groups (MacGregor, 1981: Chapter 7), and by the liberal wings of the mass media and the Church of England. As in the US, poor people in Britain have also kept their needs on the political agenda by the threat and the reality of demonstrations and uprisings. The riots of 1887, the Hunger Marches of the inter-war years and the uprisings of 1981 and 1985 are but the most dramatic examples. The so-called inner city riots of 1981 and 1985, and the threat they represented, had an incalculable and underestimated impact on Thatcherism, unquestionably slowing down and reforming the onslaught on poor people. Nevertheless, with the return of permanent mass unemployment since the mid 1970s and the pruning of the welfare state, there is a widespread perception that the gap between affluent and poor people has widened, with the latter becoming a new underclass of unemployed people and lone mothers, more cut off from the mainstream of the working class. A similar phenomenon has, of course, been observed in the other capitalist welfare states, but its development in Britain was comparatively accelerated during the 1980s.

There has never been an official poverty line in Britain, but until recently either the social assistance level or 40 per cent above the social assistance level has been unofficially accepted as the poverty line. It is widely recognized that these are inadequate measures of poverty, because they only indicate the performance of social assistance in bringing people up to an arbitrarily defined social minimum. Nevertheless since these measures have been widely used, Table 5.4 shows the chronological changes over the past three decades. The apparent increase in poverty between 1960 and

Table 5.4   *Percentage of the population (i) in receipt of social assistance (SA), (ii) not in receipt of SA but living at or below the SA threshold, (iii) not in receipt of SA and living at between 100 and 140 per cent of the SA threshold, Great Britain*

	1960	1975	1979	1981	1983	1985	1987
(i)	n/a	6.8	7.3	9.1	11.4	12.9	14.6
(ii)	n/a	3.4	3.9	4.9	5.1	4.5	6.8
(i) + (ii)	3.8	10.2	11.2	14.0	16.5	17.4	21.4
(iii)	10.7	12.9	10.1	13.4	19.1	15.6	n/a
(i) + (ii) + (iii)	14.5	23.1	21.3	27.4	35.6	28.5	n/a

Sources: Townsend, 1979: Table 4.21; Parker and Mirrlees, 1988: Table 12.33; Nolan, 1989: Table 1; House of Commons, 1990

1975 mostly reflects improvements in social assistance benefit levels and take-up thereof. The increases since 1975 probably reflect the growth of unemployment and the underclass phenomenon, since there have been few real improvements in social assistance since then.

A more adequate measure of poverty is the percentage of people living in households or families whose disposable income is below 50 per cent of the average (mean) equivalent income. This measures the 'economic distance' between poor people and the average, but it is therefore only a measure of *relative* income poverty. On this basis the European Commission found that the percentage of the UK population in poverty grew from 6.7 per cent in 1975 to 12.0 per cent in 1985, while for the Community as a whole it grew from 12.8 per cent to 13.9 per cent in roughly the same period (Labour Party, 1989a). Since the early 1970s the UK shifted from having the second lowest poverty level of the twelve EC states to being ranked sixth in 1985. In comparison with the other states examined in this book, the 'economic distance' poverty level in 1980 in the UK was in the middle range, somewhat higher than that in Sweden and the FRG, but much lower than that in the US (Table A.6). In 1988 the British government officially adopted the economic distance method of presenting 'low-income statistics' (the term 'poverty' is not officially recognized by the government). These figures also show an escalation in poverty between 1981 and 1985 (Nolan, 1989: Table 2), but it is a more modest increase than that suggested by the EC figures. Understandably the government prefers to highlight a modification to the statistics which actually shows a fall in economic distance poverty between 1981 and 1985 (Nolan, 1989: Table 3)! In this and other ways the government like its opponents has shaped the poverty statistics to its own ends (Johnson and Webb, 1989). Like the evidence on the distribution of income, most of the evidence on poverty suggests that a significant increase has occurred since the mid 1970s.

Old Age Pensions

Britain like most other states has a mixture of four forms of income maintenance for old people – social assistance, social insurance, occupational pensions or superannuation (in both the public and private sectors), and private individual annuities and pensions plans. Until very recently there were very few of the latter. Table A.7 indicates that as a proportion of national economic resources, Britain spends significantly less on pensions (public and private) than Sweden and the FRG, but rather more than the US. In terms of the total amount spent on pensions contributions the balance between social security and occupational pensions is similar to that in the FRG and the US, with about two-thirds of expenditure devoted to public social security programmes for old people (Table A.8). This however ignores the impact of fiscal welfare in the form of various tax reliefs on occupational pensions. The Treasury finds it impossible to calculate the total 'cost' of these reliefs because of multiple counting. However to give some idea of their scale, in 1987/8 the raw total was over £10 billion, compared with the £23 billion spent on public pensions and benefits to elderly people (Hogwood, 1989: 118; HM Treasury, 1989: 40–2). Thus if tax reliefs are included in pensions 'expenditure', as much or more than 40 per cent of total pensions spending may be devoted to occupational schemes.

Occupational pension schemes expanded steadily between the 1930s and the 1960s, but since the mid 1960s their membership has stuck at around 50 per cent of the labour force. The expansion occurred in part because of the inadequacy of the National Insurance pension, which was reformed in 1961 and 1978. The Labour government's reform of 1948 introduced only a flat-rate National Insurance scheme, which offered a pension at less than the social assistance poverty line and was not indexed to inflation. This did not therefore fulfil even Beveridge's idea of the social minimum, let alone more social democratic notions of welfare citizenship. Thus a large proportion of old people remained dependent on social assistance, though some refused to claim it because they associated it with the stigma of the poor law. In response to the rediscovery of poverty among elderly people and the glaring class and gender inequalities wrought by the development of occupational pensions, the Conservatives introduced a modest earnings-related (graduated) National Insurance pension in 1961. State pensions were not indexed to inflation until 1978, far later than most other capitalist welfare states, reflecting perhaps the weakness of pensioner power in Britain and also the relative disinterest of the trade unions in social security issues. Instead state pensions were cynically uprated in the run-ups to general elections by Labour and Conservative governments. Finally in 1978, in the wake of the Social Security (Pensions) Act 1975, a fully fledged and indexed State Earnings Related Pension Scheme (SERPS) was introduced to supplement the basic flat-rate pension, though it will not be fully operational until 1998 because the pension is based on the best twenty years' earnings. Employees could 'opt out' of SERPS into an occupational pension scheme of comparable or better quality. The Thatcher government turned its attention to SERPS in 1985 essentially with the intention of privatizing it in order to relieve the escalating burden on the exchequer and to offer entrepreneurial opportunities to the private pensions industry. During a heated public debate it became clear that the pensions industry was rather wary of taking on such a colossal and potentially risky responsibility, and that popular opinion supported the retention of SERPS. Hence the government made a partial retreat in the eventual Social Security Act 1986, implemented in 1988. SERPS was retained in a considerably diminished form, with the pension in future to be based on whole lifetime earnings, not the best twenty years, and further induce-ments to opt out of SERPS into occupational or private individual schemes. The government hopes that these measures will reduce the eventual cost of SERPS by more than half, largely at the expense of manual and women workers, who generally have lower lifetime earnings. Alongside the diminution of SERPS in 1988, the government introduced new financial inducements to encourage expansion of occupational pen-sions and private personal pensions. In theory the development of private personal pensions (including portable schemes) could benefit workers in semi-casualized occupations such as farming, construction and retailing. In practice they are only likely to benefit the highest earners amongst these workers, such as small business people and skilled tradespeople. The 1988 reform seems likely to increase the occupational social class inequalities in pensions eligibility, as well as to add to the confusion and complexity facing individuals and employers left to the mercy of pensions salespeople (Kaye, 1987: 25).

By 1985 51 per cent of pensioners were receiving an occupational pension, though occupational pensions accounted for only one-fifth of the gross incomes of pensioners as a whole. The quality of occupational pension schemes naturally reflects the occupational class structure quite closely, with the young, part-time women workers, short-service workers, older new employees and unskilled manual workers unlikely to be covered (Brown and Small, 1985: 169). Although many blue collar and lower-status workers are now members of occupational pension schemes, the benefits are often little better, if at all, than the state scheme. Indeed according to Walker *et al.* (1989: 575), 'many of today's pensioners receive little or no financial benefit from their occupational pension.' Retired people, formerly in low-paid or intermittent paid employment, particularly women, are often caught in a 'pension trap' in which their occupational pension merely lifts them a little above the poverty line and out of eligibility for social assistance. The present and future beneficiaries of decent occupational pensions are, of course, white collar managerial and professional employees, predominantly male and white. These are the elite 10 per cent or so of pensioner households who enjoy an income above the average for all households. Although the degree of poverty amongst pensioner households has declined in recent years with the extension of state and occupational pensions, in 1985 65 per cent of pensioner households in Britain had incomes below 140 per cent of the social assistance (supplementary pension) poverty line and 36 per cent of pensioner households were actually eligible for social assistance (Walker *et al.*, 1989: 576). Comparative data for 1980 shows that the income of pensioner households as a proportion of the average for all households in the UK is by far the lowest amongst our four welfare states (Hedström and Ringen, 1990: Table 4.3), while the poverty rate amongst pensioner households in the UK is almost as high as that in the US, and substantially greater than in the FRG and Sweden (Table A.6). Income inequality amongst pensioner households is significantly less in Britain than in the FRG and the US, but more than in Sweden, reflecting quite closely the general distribution of net equivalent income in these welfare states (Achdut and Tamir, 1990: Table 5.8).

The gender dimension of inequality and poverty amongst present and future pensioners is difficult to quantify, but it is produced by the structure of the labour market, women's unpaid caring roles and other patriarchal assumptions built into both state and occupational pensions schemes (Groves, 1987). With the greater longevity of women, these factors mean that poverty and unmet need continue to be experienced more profoundly amongst elderly women than elderly men (Walker, 1987). In the past two decades women have been engaged in a protracted struggle to remedy this situation, centred in the 1980s around the 1979 EC Directive on Equal

Treatment. Direct gender discrimination has been reduced, and the government is being forced by the courts to equalize the retirement age. Nevertheless issues such as the position of widows, provision for carers, and independent pension rights for women are far from even being recognized as legitimate claims, as shown for example in House of Lords (1989: 106). Despite SERPS contribution credits for years of unpaid caring for dependants, 'unpaid work still incurs a pensions penalty, particularly in the private sector' (Owen and Joshi, 1990: 71). The concept of equal treatment is deployed on a narrow, actuarial basis in the legislation and by the courts (Owen and Joshi, 1990: 70), and therefore does little to redress gender inequalities of outcome which are caused by deeper structural and institutional factors than simply direct discrimination (Millar, 1989b: 316).

Social Assistance

Means-tested social assistance has played a central role in the post-war British welfare state, as already noted, because of inadequate funding of social insurance. One of the great ironies of British welfare history is that, after prolonged and bitter struggles against 'the household means test' in the inter-war years, the post-war settlement was popularly assumed to mean that 'never again' would workers and their families be subjected on a mass scale to the degradation of means-tested poor relief, with much of its Victorian associations still thriving. As Table 5.4 shows, in fact this is precisely what has happened, and this is often portrayed, understandably, as a severe indictment of the British welfare state. From a radical and comparative perspective, however, the central role of social assistance in Britain appears a more complex and contradictory phenomenon. Despite all its manifold failings, the social assistance system in Britain provides more universal, less discretionary and arguably less stigmatized cash benefits to poor people than any other capitalist welfare state. Britain is one of very few welfare states to provide such benefits on a nationally uniform basis, and certainly the only example amongst the four states examined here. This is a feature which important figures on the New Right such as Minford (1983) have long argued against. Minford would like to see benefit levels linked to local wage levels for unskilled work to stop the benefits system 'pricing people out of jobs' in areas of high unemployment. This would be similar to the situation in the US in many respects. The fact that through the twelve years of Thatcherism such a proposal did not reach the policy agenda, is an index of the strength of the 'poor people's movement' and its supporters in Britain.

The comparatively positive aspects of social assistance provision in Britain are a direct result not only of the struggles of the 1930s, but of the continuing popular struggles of poor people in Britain to defend and improve this most essential element of the welfare state. As Piven and Cloward (1971) have argued, poor relief and social assistance have been a key site of confrontation and popular resistance against the class disciplinary, patriarchal and racist functioning of public welfare institutions. In terms of reinforcing the class structure, social assistance has played a central role in enforcing labour discipline or 'work incentive'. Throughout the post-war period benefit levels for unemployed claimants have fluctuated narrowly at between 17 per cent and 21 per cent of gross average earnings of male manual workers (Parker and Mirrlees, 1988: Table 12.32), ensuring that there is little incentive to refuse low-paid employment. The stigma of claiming assistance, which continues to be cultivated by its administration following the poor law tradition, has the effect of deterring claims (take-up is estimated at around 75 per cent) and of promoting the values of individual and family self-help in the working class as a whole. The great majority of social assistance claimants are women, which is in part a reflection of the failure of the social insurance system to protect women and give them an independent income. Nevertheless the state has sought to force patriarchal dependence upon women who claim social assistance through the cohabitation rule and measures against deserting male partners (Ginsburg, 1979: 83–8). Racism is institutionalized in the administration of social assistance in several ways. Access to social assistance is lawfully denied to 'persons from abroad', so that actual or alleged immigrant status leads to people being denied benefits. The implementation of this policy

> leads, inevitably, to passport checking and liaison between immigration authorities and the DHSS, with the result that for many people the DHSS is seen as an arm of the immigration authorities. The practice is racist in that it flows from a system of immigration control which is itself racist and because it is applied primarily to black people. (Gordon and Newnham, 1985: 29)

Incoming settlers in Britain have to be 'sponsored' by a British citizen (usually a close relative), who is then legally responsible for ensuring that the settler has no 'recourse to public funds' particularly social assistance. In practice this has led to passport checking and surveillance of black British citizens, as well as creating a group of permanent British residents who are denied access to the benefits system in perpetuity (Gordon, 1986). There is also evidence of racist attitudes and racial stereotyping amongst DSS (formerly DHSS) officers, which is facilitated by the continuing tradition of administrative discretion in the determination of claimants' needs (NACAB, 1991; Gordon and Newnham, 1985: Chapter 3).

At a largely hidden, day-to-day level, claimants' resistance to all these processes has been hard fought in Britain over the post-war period, and essentially it lies behind the three major reconstructions of the scheme as well as numerous other changes made since 1948, as governments have struggled to seize more of the initiative, as well as responding to 'pressure from below' (Alcock, 1987: Chapter 7; Novak, 1988: Chapters 5, 6). The rediscovery of poverty and the growth of the 'poverty lobby' in the early 1960s prompted the recasting of National Assistance as Supplementary Benefit (SB) in 1966. This reform strengthened claimants' legal rights, particularly their rights to positive discretionary grants and additions to benefits. The stigma of claiming assistance lessened and take-up increased substantially. Over the next decade claimants and their advocates became more confident and organized, so much so that, with the fiscal crisis in the mid 1970s and the return of mass unemployment, the Labour government sought means of restraining the alleged 'overload' on the system. This resulted in the 1980 Social Security Acts implemented by the Conservative government which sought to cut down positive discretion, without much success as the welfare rights movement managed to neutralize most of it, so that 'by 1984 entitlement to SB was more unwieldy and confusing than ever' (Alcock, 1987: 91).

This situation satisfied neither the 'poverty lobby' nor the government, and the latter responded with the Social Security Act 1986, implemented in 1988, which recast Supplementary Benefit as Income Support (IS). Eligibility for benefit was changed in order, it was said, to 'target' people the government believed were more deserving such as families with children and disabled people. Young people, unemployed people and generally able-bodied people without dependants were targeted as less deserving. Claimants' rights to grants and additions were abolished and replaced with a much more discretionary, arbitrary and disciplinary regime in the shape of the local, cash limited Social Fund. The impact of the 1988 reforms has been furiously contested by the government and the welfare rights movement. However the government has not seriously challenged statistics which show a 9.8 per cent fall in the number of SB/IS claimants between 1987 and 1988 (House of Commons, 1990) and, for example, benefit cuts (in real terms) between 1987 and 1990 of 4 per cent and 15 per cent respectively for a couple with two young children and for a single disabled person. The Conservative government found itself in a familiar contradictory position. On the one hand it wanted to claim success in cutting the cost of social assistance and disciplining poor people more severely, which is what has actually taken place. On the other hand it has been anxious to present a humane face to the electorate by alleging (without much conviction) that it is giving more help to the deserving poor.

Unemployment and Labour Market Policies

On a comparative basis the unemployment level in Britain in the 1960s and 1970s was close to the OECD average, that is at a level much higher than in the FRG and Sweden and much lower than in the US. In the years 1980–7 UK unemployment rose far higher than the OECD average, reaching 12.4 per cent in 1983, the highest level ever recorded by OECD amongst the top seven industrial states (Table A.10). With the economic recovery after 1984, the unemployment rate fell steeply, almost back to the OECD average, but with the recession of the early 1990s it has, once more, risen well above the OECD average. Recent figures have to be treated with particular caution, however, since the government has made numerous changes to the way unemployment and availability for employment are measured, as well as expanding the Youth Training Scheme. Although some of these changes are discounted in the OECD basis, it has been estimated that administrative and policy changes between 1981 and 1986 accounted for a reduction in the number of registered unemployed people of 1.38 million, about 30 per cent of the 'real' 1986 total of 4 million (Meacher, 1989: 137–8). In 1986 the government introduced Restart, a programme of compulsory interviews every six months for long-term unemployed people; non-attendance can lead to loss of benefits. The government claims that these interviews offer counselling and a menu of options to help long-term unemployed people back into the labour market. Independent evidence (Meacher, 1989: 139–44; Harper, 1990: 17) suggests that Restart simply recycles long-term unemployed people through various schemes or, ironically, has encouraged many of them to register as long-term sick or disabled. It has been estimated that almost half the fall in the numbers of registered unemployed people between 1986 and 1989 (a total fall of 1.7 million) is accounted for by Restart, though very few of these people have found 'proper jobs' (Harper, 1990: 17).

A comparatively low proportion of unemployed people received unemployment insurance benefit (UIB) in Britain in the period 1973–83, covering two recessions, and the real level of UIB was almost halved in this period, whereas it increased in the other three welfare states examined in this book (Reubens, 1989: Tables 1 and 2). This data reflects the running down of UIB in Britain with the return of mass unemployment, so that means-tested social assistance (SA) has taken the leading role in supporting unemployed people. In May 1986 around two-thirds of registered unemployed people either had no entitlement to UIB or had exhausted their entitlement. Particularly since the advent of the Conservative administrations in 1979, there have been a considerable number of changes in income maintenance for unemployed people, whose cumulative effect has transformed the system into a much less generous and more disciplinarian regime. The single most dramatic change was the withdrawal in 1981/2 of the earnings-related supplement (ERS) to UIB, first introduced in 1966, ironically, to facilitate redundancy (Ginsburg, 1979: 67–72). In terms of 'linking living standards while unemployed to those when previously in work for a wider section of the workforce, the [ERS] scheme was poorly designed' (Micklewright, 1989: 535) in comparison with the schemes in other West European states. The flat-rate UIB benefit level fluctuated between 17 per cent and 22 per cent of average earnings of male manual workers over the post-war period up to the mid 1980s, maintaining a close proximity to social assistance benefit levels (Parker and Mirrlees, 1988: Table 12.32). Statutory indexing of UIB to inflation has now been abandoned. Atkinson and Micklewright (1989: 145) have estimated that the cumulative effect of all the changes between 1979 and 1988 was to reduce total benefits expenditure (UIB plus SA, in real terms) devoted to unemployed people by around £500 million, or 7 per cent of the total which would have been spent if the 1979 system had remained unchanged. The purpose of all these changes is obviously not only to cut public expenditure, but also to reinforce the incentive to take and hold down paid employment. The labour disciplinary functions of the benefits system have been stepped up significantly, but the extent to which this has pushed people into paid employment is debatable and impossible to quantify.

The objective of British labour market policy throughout most of this century has been 'that of keeping government intervention in the labour market to a minimum' (Lonsdale, 1985: 167), relying on the indirect influence of macroeconomic industrial relations, immigration control and social security measures to regulate employment and unemployment. Experiments with regional employment policies and incomes policies to hold down unemployment are believed to have failed, undermined by corporate and/or union strategic resistance. British governments, like those in the US and unlike those of Sweden and the FRG, have essentially adopted the view that the recruitment, the shedding and the training of labour should be 'employer-led'. Thus the total spending on the Swedish labour market programmes (benefits, training, grants, support of disabled workers etc.) is 'sixteen times the sum spent in the UK per unemployed person' (Meacher, 1989: 152). Partly as a result of this, since the mid 1970s the British labour market has exhibited two chronic problems in addition to the high level of unemployment – a 'skills gap', that is shortages of skilled labour and oversupply of unskilled labour, and sharp regional and local disparities in the supply of and demand for labour. Labour and Conservative governments' response to these problems has been confused. Labour hankers for traditional apprenticeships in manufacturing industry, while Thatcherites want to see unemployed people turned into a pool of casualized, low-paid workers in an expanding services sector of the economy. In reality, the most significant development has been the Youth Training Scheme (YTS) established in 1983 on the basis of Labour's temporary Youth Opportunities Programme, which originally sought just to keep unemployed young people off the streets. Besides continuing this function, YTS has aimed, fairly successfully, to remove sixteen and seventeen year old school leavers from the labour market. The government in effect took over the funding of firms' training schemes for school leavers, as well as funding other schemes with little or no training content, which exploited the free labour of the YTS 'trainees'. By the mid 1980s YTS was costing around £1 billion a year, a rare example of the expansion of the welfare state under Thatcherism, for which much of the credit must go to the 'inner city riots' of 1981 (Finn, 1987: 141–2). Despite a strong rhetoric of equal opportunities associated with YTS, the scheme has manifestly failed to challenge firmly established racial and gender divisions in the labour market, not least because being 'employer-led' the MSC had little means to confront racist and sexist processes in careers guidance, schooling and the workplace (Wrench, 1987; Cockburn, 1987). The YTS concept of sponsoring and funding training privately provided by employers and agencies was extended to adult unemployed people with the launch of the Employment Training (ET) programme in 1988, linked to Restart. The considerable cost of YTS and ET has prompted the government to begin the process of privatizing them, offloading the costs and the administration onto employers by establishing in 1989 local Training and Enterprise Councils (TECs). The government has encountered considerable resistance from employers and unemployed people to both ET and the TECs. Nevertheless at the end of the 1980s

> the welfare principle and provision of indefinite benefit to unemployed people until they find a job has ended . . . In its place a form of workfare has been introduced under which all unemployed people are required to work or train in order to qualify for benefit . . . The major criticisms will continue to concern the quality of provision and income [for unemployed people] and the non-availability of real jobs. (Meacher, 1989: 153)

The government has succeeded in greatly strengthening the labour disciplinary functions of the welfare state without changing the 'employer-led' or 'market-led' tradition of British labour market policy.

Women, the Labour Market and Income Maintenance

The steady growth of women's paid employment in Britain is documented in Tables A.12 and A.13, showing that the female share of the total labour force increased from 30.7 per cent in 1950 to 41.4 per cent in 1987, and the female labour force as a proportion of the female population of working age increased from 42.9 per cent in 1950 to 62.6 per cent in 1987. These figures are close to the OECD averages and are similar to the pattern in the US, but contrast dramatically with the very modest increase in the FRG and the very large increase in Sweden. Like Sweden, and less like the US and the FRG, much of the increase is accounted for by the growth of women's part-time employment. Women's employment in Britain is marked by persistently high levels of occupational segregation by gender, both vertical (women relatively concentrated at lower levels of pay and status) and horizontal (women concentrated in particular occupations). A large proportion of the post-war growth in women's paid employment is accounted for by the expansion of employment in the welfare state, particularly education, social services and health care, but far from challenging gender divisions in employment, this has often reinforced them (Beechey and Perkins, 1987: Chapter 3). Thus

> far from stagnation in the sexual division of labour there has been the recreation of equivalent levels of segregation around higher rates of female participation and new job structures . . . the overall effect has been to retain the same level of over-representation and under-representation of women within occupations because of the rapid increases in women's share in already feminised occupations. (Rubery, 1988: 256)

Implementation of the 1970 Equal Pay Act initially achieved a modest increase in women's wages relative to men's, but since the late 1970s there has been little or no further improvement. Women's earnings as a percentage of men's are considerably lower in Britain than in much of Western Europe and slightly better than in the US (Rubery, 1988: Table 9.1). According to the European Commission, women working full-time in manufacturing industry in Britain earned 68 per cent of the wages of men in 1988, compared to 80 per cent or more in France, Italy, Denmark and Greece (*The Guardian*, July 6th 1990). As Table A.14 shows, the UK female unemployment rate in the 1980s was more than six times the rate in the post-war boom years, double the increase for men. However Britain is unusual in having consistently lower levels of unemployment on the OECD basis amongst women than amongst men, the reverse of the norm in our other three countries and in the OECD in general. There is no simple explanation of this phenomenon. Since the early 1960s male-dominated manufacturing workforces have been most drastically affected by mass redundancies, while the services sector expanded to offer more employment for women in particular. The lingering strengths of the 'family-wage' and 'women's wages as pin money' ideas have discouraged many women from seeing themselves as seeking paid employment. Finally the linked administration of benefits and the employment service has always discouraged women from registering as unemployed, and the partners of unemployed men tend to withdraw from the labour market to avoid their earnings leading to the loss of benefits.

Post-war Liberal Collectivism, Butskellism, one nation Toryism and Labourism all enthusiastically embraced the traditional view of women's role as unpaid home maker supported by a male breadwinner. Despite protests from women's groups, the post-war Labour government followed Beveridge's explicit recommendations in this respect, so that the social insurance and social assistance benefits system enforced women's financial dependence on men (Land, 1971; Pascall, 1986: Chapter 7). Since the recession of the mid 1970s, government ministers have attempted on occasion to rejuvenate the ideology of domesticity, implying that mothers should not be in the labour market. Patriarchal assumptions based on the model of the full-time male employee with dependants continue to govern the benefits system, which is therefore increasingly out of step with reality, given the central importance of women's earnings in most households, growing numbers of lone mother families and inadequate maintenance from fathers. Over the past twenty years the women's movement has been an important influence within the poverty lobby and poor people's movements, successfully defending the payment of child benefit to mothers and seeing off some of the more explicit aspects of unequal treatment by the benefits system. More substantial demands for women's financial independence from men, fair recognition of women's unpaid caring work and affirmative action to undermine structural divisions in the labour market have made little headway. In general women's welfare has suffered much more than men's since the recession of the mid 1970s, particularly under Thatcherism. The cuts in welfare benefits and services, the deteriorating pay and conditions in public services, privatization of welfare services, the growth of part-time and casual employment without employment protection and social insurance, the increase in poverty and unemployment – all these processes have had a differentially adverse impact on women in Britain, particularly for black women and working class women. This is the consequence of the decline of the welfare state and the rise of the 'enterprise economy'. Yet the ideology of domesticity has not been successfully re-established and women's paid employment has increased substantially since the recession of the early 1980s, with much anticipation of further increases in the 1990s. The bolstering of women's disadvantages in the labour market resulting from government policies has caused them to become 'an attractive source of labour supply to employers for particular types of jobs . . . [which] provides a relative advantage in finding employment, although not necessarily secure or adequately remunerated employment' (Rubery and Tarling, 1988: 126). An increasing proportion of the growth of women's paid employment is accounted for by part-time and casual employment and homeworking, particularly amongst working class women. Women in professional and managerial jobs are much more likely to be employed full-time with statutory employment protection rights, and with pensions and social insurance cover. Asian and black women (except Muslims) are also much more likely than white women to be employed full-time, but their pay and employment status is much inferior to that of white women (Breughel, 1989; Cook and Watt, 1987). Class and 'race' divisions cut across gender divisions in the labour market. Hence the impact of government policies on women's employment and incomes has been uncoordinated, indirect and contradictory throughout the post-war period, because the ideology of domesticity is constantly confronted by the reality of employer demands for women workers, the willingness of women to supply their labour power and gathering party political support for equal opportunities for women.

Racial Inequalities, Racism and the Welfare State

This section discusses social policy and 'race' in post-war Britain, focusing on the experience of black people, who for the most part trace their origins to the post-war migration of workers from the former colonies in the Caribbean, East Africa and the Indian sub-continent. There are many other ethnic minority groups in Britain including Irish people, whose experience of the welfare state has much in common with black people's, but over the post-war period the racialization of domestic politics and immigration policy has put people of colour into a distinct category of lesser welfare citizenship.

Migration and Immigration Policy

The great majority of Afro-Caribbean migrants came to Britain in the late 1950s and early 1960s, but Asian migration has been much more evenly spread throughout the post-war period, reaching a peak however in the late 1960s. Some migrant workers were recruited directly in the former colonies by both private and public sector employers. Black settlers were exploited as a cheap labour reserve. The National Health Service, for example, has been critically dependent on migrant workers and black settlers throughout its existence (Doyal *et al.*, 1981). The post-war Liberal Collectivist settlement not only involved the domestic reconstruction of class relations and citizenship on the basis of the welfare state, but also brought the reconstruction of colonial relations on the basis of the Commonwealth. Following the granting of independence to India, the 1948 British Nationality Act confirmed the rights of Commonwealth and colonial citizens to enter and settle in Britain. Ever since then governments have developed gradually more effective measures to undermine these rights in respect of black people without destroying entirely the concept of Commonwealth citizenship. By the early 1950s the 'Labour and Conservative governments had . . . instituted a number of covert, and sometimes illegal, administrative measures to discourage black immigration' (Solomos, 1989: 46). The 1950s saw intense policy and public discussion about the impact of black settlement on the welfare state. In reality black people were denied access to some welfare services such as council housing or received inferior, racialized treatment from others. The prevailing ideology was that black people had come ' "individually and on their own initiative" and thus there was no need to make welfare provision for them. There was thus *no intention* to provide for them, and when Black immigrants *did* use welfare services they were seen as scroungers' (Williams, 1989: 180). Prompted by overt racist pressures from white people, notably the riots of the late 1950s, Powellism in the late 1960s and the rise of the National Front in the late 1970s, Labour and Conservative governments, starting in 1962, established increasingly restrictive immigration and nationality laws and rules differentially affecting black people from the former colonies, which give enormous discretionary power to immigration officers. The intent and the effect of the legislation and its implementation is racist in almost innumerable respects. Most notably perhaps the 1971 Immigration Act finally removed the right of black Commonwealth citizens with a work permit to settle in Britain. The 1988 Immigration Act requires that all British and Commonwealth citizens settled in Britain who want to be joined by spouses and/or children from abroad, must 'sponsor' them and prove that they are able to support them without resort to 'public funds'. Between 1973 and 1988 this stipulation only applied to people who settled in Britain after 1973. Such measures differentially affect black settlers, and Asian people in particular, leading to the separation of family members sometimes for years. Thus immigration officers assess aspiring 'sponsors' and visit their homes, and they investigate kinship relations with the possibility of fraud very much in mind. The legitimation for racist immigration control is that the people most likely to want to come to Britain will be from poor countries and, according to a government policy statement in 1986, in terms of housing, education, social services and, of course, jobs, the country could not support all those who would like to come here. Firm immigration control is therefore essential in order to provide the conditions necessary for developing and maintaining good community relations. (quoted by Solomos, 1989: 60)

It is therefore the pressure on a welfare state in the process of retrenchment, as well as accommodation to white concern about black welfare scroungers, which expressly concerns government. The result is a growing number of removals and deportations of allegedly illegal immigrants from the black and other ethnic minority communities. Individuals and communities, supported by lawyers and campaigning groups, devote enormous resources to resisting and challenging the administrative discretion wielded by immigration officers.

Not only the police and immigration officials, but employers and welfare agencies now assist in enforcing the immigration laws through passport and identity checks on black people (Gordon, 1985). This 'has led to a fear of harassment among many black people, who do not claim benefits or services to which they are entitled for fear that their status and eligibility too, may be called into question' (Gordon, 1985: 94). The immigration laws have created growing numbers of black people excluded from welfare citizenship by the rules concerning 'resort to public funds' as mentioned already. This contributes to a political atmosphere surrounding the welfare state in which the legitimate claims of welfare need amongst black people may be seen as suspect. Thus it becomes more possible for local education authorities, housing departments, benefits offices, hospitals and so on to consider the legitimate claims and needs of black people as a lower priority, particularly when expenditure is being cut back. So, for example, in the late 1980s many Bangladeshis in the East End of London found that the local authority, backed by the courts, was unable to help them if they were homeless and was unable to provide schooling for their children, essentially legitimated by assumptions and rules about immigration status. The ramifications of racist immigration policy extend deeply into the day-to-day operation of welfare eligibility in Britain, as in the other three welfare states examined here.

The Status of Black People in the British Welfare State

By the late 1980s over 40 per cent of black people in Britain were born in Britain and over two-thirds had British citizenship. The formal status of most black people within the British welfare state is therefore much more secure than the status of former guestworkers in the FRG. In the late 1980s, people of Afro-Caribbean and African origin numbered around 625,000 and people of Asian origin around 1.25 million, making black people about 3.5 per cent of the population of Britain. It is difficult to assess the extent to which the welfare state has mitigated racial inequalities in basic welfare to counter the negative forces already discussed. Certainly in the 1970s and 1980s black people became more vociferous and better politically organized to assert their rights within the welfare state, particularly in the areas of housing and education. If the welfare state, including anti-discrimination legislation, did not exist or was severely retrenched, it would have a differentially adverse impact on black people, just as it would also have on women and poor people. Indeed the retrenchment of the welfare state, sharply increased unemployment and poverty, and widening income inequalities since the mid 1970s have had a differential impact on the black communities. At around the very time that black politicians were making inroads into local government and black professionals were beginning to influence the welfare state from within, and when equal opportunities and ethnic monitoring policies were beginning to be adopted by some employers and welfare agencies, this was the moment in the mid 1970s when Liberal Collectivism was transformed and the new orthodoxy suggested that the welfare state had overextended itself. In other words, as the welfare needs of black people became more effectively represented, so the retrenchment of the welfare state gathered momentum, paralleling similar developments in the US. To give one example, just as black people had begun to establish their right to publicly financed, low-cost rented housing, governments severely cut back the council house building programme and subsidized the sale of council houses to sitting tenants. This reinforced the inequalities created by thirty years of institutionally racist allocation policies (Ginsburg, 1989). Yet the black communities have played a central role in defending the welfare state, ranging from the effects of the urban uprisings of 1981–5 to conventional lobbying, self-organization and political representation. So, for example, black groups have had some success in getting public funds for housing associations to provide low-cost rented housing.

The most fundamental aspect of racial inequality is perhaps to be found in the labour market. Black workers are more likely than white workers to be in low-status, low-paid occupations and to experience unemployment. Over the period from the mid 1960s to the early 1980s the evidence suggests that there was 'no convergence of the labour-market situations of black and white workers with respect to industrial or occupational concentration, job levels, pay or working patterns . . . [and] the marked gap between them with respect to unemployment . . . widened' (Jenkins, 1988: 315). The recessions of the mid 1970s and early 1980s differentially increased black unemployment because black workers are

> disproportionately more likely to be in industries (manufacturing and the health service, for example), occupations (unskilled and semi-skilled manual jobs) and locations (inner-city areas and the declining industrial areas of the West Midlands and the North) which are particularly affected by unemployment. (Jenkins, 1988: 315)

These factors can be described as having structural racist effects on employment. In addition there is ample evidence of both institutional racism and direct discrimination in the British labour market (Ohri and

Faruki, 1988; Jenkins, 1988). During the 1980s the unemployment rate (using the OECD basis) for ethnic minority workers has remained at about double that for white workers and, as Table 5.5 also shows, unemployment is experienced particularly by Afro-Caribbean, Pakistani and Bangladeshi men, and also by all black young people.

Table 5.5 *Percentage of unemployed, economically active men and women aged sixteen and over, by ethnic group, Great Britain 1985–7*[1]

	White	All ethnic minorities	Afro-Caribbean	Indian	Pakistani or Bangladeshi
Men	11	20	24	15	29
Women	10	18	18	18	–[2]

[1] The figures are averages from three years' surveys 'to reduce sampling errors and minimise apparent fluctuation between years' (OPCS, 1989: 30).
[2] The number of economically active Pakistani and Bangladeshi women was statistically insignificant.

Source: OPCS, 1989

Policy analysis of racism and racial inequalities in employment and welfare naturally focuses on official anti-discrimination measures. However the most significant challenges to racism and racial inequality take the form of resistance and activity by individuals, voluntary groups and organizations and informal groups of trade unionists, professionals and others taking action at the local level in the neighbourhood and the workplace. Formal policies trail in the wake of these activities, though they often provide an important context or platform for the struggle. Thus, for example, every year hundreds of workers win cases of alleged racial discrimination by employers at statutory Industrial and Employment Appeal Tribunals. Ben-Tovim *et al.* (1986: 173) have documented in the areas of housing, education and social services how 'local voluntary organisations are . . . the principal collective means by which the local struggle for racial equality has been pursued.' At the formal level, the primary instrument of policy is the Race Relations Act 1976, which was the product of the more radical, early phase of the 1974–9 Labour government just prior to the welfare state crisis. Its passage reflected fears about the alienation of black young people, concern to deflect criticism of racist immigration policy and the need to respond to the demands of Labour's black voters for action. Though without it the situation would probably have been worse, there is widespread agreement that the Race Relations Act 1976 has had a minimal effect in reducing racial inequalities of outcome. Some Conservatives use this as a pretext for advocating its abolition, but most anti-racists and advocates of equal opportunities argue that strengthening the legislation on US lines would provide a symbolic and practical platform for challenging the status quo. The 1976 Act made not only direct but 'indirect' racial discrimination illegal, that is where formally equal practices have discriminatory effects. However, in its present form it is a somewhat narrow and awkwardly phrased expression of the idea of institutional discrimination. As such it requires the courts to find 'social facts' about broader societal relationships . . . this is an activity alien to the English courts and one which, to judge from the reported cases, they feel profoundly uncomfortable with. (Lustgarten, 1987: 17–18)

Challenging all but the most overt forms of direct and institutional discrimination is impossible under the present law. Nevertheless the 1976 Act also gave to individuals, for the first time, the right to take cases of alleged direct discrimination to the county courts and the employment tribunals. This right has been taken up predominantly in employment cases, but the effectiveness of the law is severely limited by the paucity of the sanctions available to and used by the tribunals. The statutory levels of fines and compensation are low. In 1989 115 successful individual complaints were supported by the Commission for Racial Equality (CRE) and the average amount of compensation was £1527 (CRE, 1990: 110), which is not much of a deterrent to most employers. Aside from helping complainants, the CRE was established under the Act as a statutory watchdog with limited powers, notably to develop voluntary Codes of Practice for organizations in fields such as employment, housing and education and to make 'formal investigations' into organizations suspected of direct or indirect discriminatory practices. The CRE's activity on these fronts has had some positive impact on agencies of the welfare state, particularly local authority housing and education departments, but its impact on private welfare agencies and private employers has been very limited. Finally the 1976 Act enjoined local authorities 'to promote equality of opportunity', with the result that they declared themselves equal opportunities employers, and this has been mimicked by other big employers in the 1980s. Yet 'there appears to be little or no relation between possession of even a developed and implemented equal opportunities policy (although there are few enough instances of the latter) and stimulating change in employment outcomes, at least in the short term' (Gibbon, 1990: 19). The use of affirmative action and contract compliance measures by local authorities has been rare, and generally frowned on by central government and the courts. Despite the manifest inadequacies of current anti-discrimination policies in Britain, these measures are comparatively much more progressive and explicit than those in other European countries, including Sweden and the FRG.

Under the Thatcher governments there was little significant change in 'race relations policy' aside from the ever tightening immigration rules. The present anti-discriminatory policies of the CRE and other public bodies 'have operated in a vacuum and an environment which has been generally negative, if not hostile' (Solomos, 1987: 48). However abolishing the Race Relations Act would be too overt and too controversial for government to contemplate. Positive legal reform, as advocated by the CRE, the opposition parties and many others, was quite antithetical to the free-market, individualist strand of Thatcherism. The present situation is something of a stalemate, with the structural effects of government policies and the labour market tending to exacerbate racial inequalities, while individual resistance and achievement, local struggles and initiatives and the race relations industry ameliorate the situation.

Women and Family Policies

Family Ideology and Policy

The notions of 'family' and 'nation' have been fundamental, linked organizing principles behind the development of capitalist welfare states, quite explicitly in the cases of Sweden and Germany where the idea of social welfare intervention to promote them has long and contrasting histories in each. In the cases of the US and Britain, their role in policy reform has been less explicit, but they have played a central role in orchestrating the ideological environment for social policy, particularly in Britain as Williams (1989) has shown. Britain, like the US, does not profess an interventionist 'family policy', though British politicians and the wider establishment have always been at pains to express their support for 'family values'. Liberal Collectivism, post-war social democracy and Thatcherism all shrink from the idea of family policy as antithetical to liberal individualism and extending the boundaries of the welfare state too far. Inevitably, however, almost every aspect of social policy carries with it and reinforces orthodox assumptions about family structure and responsibilities, and about gender roles within the family. Thus the ideology of British family policy embraces several principles, sometimes labelled rather awkwardly 'familism' or 'familialism', which share a great deal in common with prevailing ideology in the US, and to some extent in the FRG. First, the sanctity and privacy of 'the family' is always invoked to counter proposals for material welfare support for families. Individual privacy and freedom is commonly equated with family privacy and freedom, where the 'individual' is conceived as the father. Looked at from the point of view of women, children and other dependants, their individual freedom and privacy is by no means guaranteed by family privacy, quite the opposite in many instances (Barrett and McIntosh, 1982: Chapter II).

The second principle of British family policy is to support the two parent, married, heterosexual model of the family household. Other 'family' structures – cohabitation, lone parenthood, 'absent' parenthood, gay and lesbian parenthood – are less eligible forms. Alternative forms of care in residential homes, day centres, nurseries or even independent living for handicapped people are constructed as 'second best' substitutes because 'inadequate people are not fully entitled to "family privacy" [which] is a right they forgo when they ask for help or are seen to have need of it' (New and David, 1985: 77). Third, family and community care policies reinforce a gender division of labour within families, in which the primary role of women is to be informal, unpaid carers of children, elderly relatives and other family members unable to 'support themselves' (Lewis, 1989).

Finally, like many other welfare states, Britain has a long-established eugenicist, neo-Malthusian tradition. This has continued to surface in the post-war period, and suggests that social policy should encourage white, middle class, married couples to have many children, and working class couples, particularly poor people and people of ethnic minority origin, to limit their family size. It remains true that 'official policy assumes that "good parenting skills" are found in intact, white, middle-class, two-parent family households' (New and David, 1985: 79). All these assumptions have come under increasing challenge from feminists, gay men, lesbians, anti-racists and many others over the 1970s and 1980s. At the same time Thatcherites in particular have sought to bolster conventional principles, though as in the US the New Right is sorely divided over some of the issues. The conventional principles of family policy have also been directly undermined by the growth of women's paid employment, the increasing burden of informal care for elderly people, changes in household/family structure such as higher divorce rates and more lone mother families, and the growing visibility of violence and abuse of women and children in families. There has therefore been a series of struggles, moral panics and policy debates around discrete aspects of family policy, some examples of which we shall now examine.

Child benefit, paid universally to all mothers, has been symbolic of the condition of British family policy. It was first advocated by women, as in many other Western nations, in the early years of this century as an endowment of motherhood, and a pronatalist measure which would strengthen the imperial nation. The campaign was sustained for almost half a century until 1946 when the 'family allowance' was introduced (Macnicol, 1980). The explicit support of Keynes as well as Beveridge played an important part in its implementation, since Keynes saw the family allowance as important in generating aggregate consumer demand in the economy and furthering the multiplier effect to secure post-war economic growth (Land, 1975). In its first decade the family allowance kept pace with average earnings, but thereafter its real value fell consistently as it was allowed to stagnate. The poverty lobby and the women's movement have been strong supporters of child benefit because it is universally taken up and it is paid direct to mothers. The growing strength of both movements built up pressure for reform in the 1970s, but there was also a lobby for the abolition of the family allowance in favour of enhanced income tax allowances for children, following the US model. After a furious struggle by women's organizations and anti-poverty groups (Field, 1982), the Labour government agreed to phase out child tax allowances and consolidate them into the new child benefit. Under the Thatcher governments there was a continuous campaign to maintain the level of child benefit, which had not kept pace with inflation and was frozen for four years from

1987 to 1991. In April 1991 child benefit was increased in line with price inflation over the previous twelve months, which signalled a modest reversion to one feature of Liberal Collectivism by the post-Thatcher Conservative administration. In 1989 the level of child benefit in Britain was in the middle range of the EC countries, neither especially generous nor parsimonious (Brown, 1990: 27). Conservatives appear to be in considerable disarray on the issue, with many continuing to support index-linked child benefit, alongside the opposition parties. The withering away of child benefit and the stalemate over its abolition or reform is symbolic of the hesitancy of British governments over family policy, just as earlier Labour governments fumbled the introduction of the family allowance and the abolition of child tax allowance. This reflects the struggle between the women's and poor people's movements on the one hand and supporters of conventional, patriarchal principles on the other hand.

Lone Mothers

Lone parent families as a percentage of all families with dependent children in Britain increased from 8 per cent in 1971 to 14 per cent in 1987, not as high as in Sweden or the US, but significantly higher than the FRG and most other European countries (Table A.16). This reflects increases in the numbers of divorced and never-married mothers. As elsewhere, the great majority of lone parents are women, nowadays mostly divorced women. Historically the treatment of lone mothers has varied enormously according to status, widows having always enjoyed a relatively deserving status while unmarried mothers were seen as less deserving and not infrequently treated punitively. These status distinctions have blurred significantly over the post-war period with the rise in divorce, and slowly changing attitudes towards unmarried motherhood. The women's movement and the poverty lobby have played a central role in undermining some of the stigma of lone motherhood, with the National Council for One Parent Families being an important element of the poverty lobby. The generic terms 'one parent family' and 'lone motherhood' have only become widely used in the past twenty years. In policy terms, this was most significantly reflected in the government commissioned report on one parent families (Finer, 1974) which advocated a means-tested, guaranteed maintenance allowance for lone parents. The means-tested basis was criticized by many in the poverty lobby and the women's movement, and the proposal has never been implemented. As a modest substitute, the Labour government in 1975 instituted for lone parents a higher level of child benefit and of earnings disregard for social assistance. According to the Secretary of State for Social Security at the time, this was 'the most' that could be done for lone parents (quoted by Millar, 1989a: 28).

During the post-war period the incidence of poverty amongst lone parent families (based on net incomes in relation to the social assistance level) has fluctuated around levels between three and six times that amongst two parent families (Millar, 1989a: Table 2.1). In 1981 55 per cent of lone parent families had net incomes below 140 per cent of the social assistance level. The net income of lone parent families as a proportion of that of two parent families is much lower than in Sweden, much higher than in the US and around the same level as in the FRG (Table A.18). Lone mothers in Britain have always depended very significantly on social assistance and child benefit for their income, but this dependence has increased over the past two decades. In 1978/9 Millar (1989a: 114) found that only 17 per cent of lone parents did not claim social assistance at some point in the course of a year. Pressure from social security officials on lone mothers to find paid employment and/or to get maintenance from fathers relaxed somewhat in the 1970s and 1980s, possibly in the light of Finer's rather utopian view that 'mothers, particularly when they have very young children, should not feel under any pressure to take paid employment' (Finer, 1974: 279). Between 1981 and 1988 the number of social security staff pursuing absent fathers fell by a third and the proportion of lone parents on social assistance who were also receiving maintenance fell from 50 to 23 per cent (DSS, 1990). While in the 1960s, lone mothers were more likely than married mothers to be in paid employment, the opposite has been the case since the early 1970s. In this respect, Britain is quite different from the other countries in this study, where lone mothers are more likely to be in paid employment than married mothers (Table A.17). This may be explained by the comparatively less pressurizing benefits system, the poverty trap (loss of welfare benefits when taking up low-paid employment) and the low quality of employment opportunities and training available to women in Britain (NCOPF, 1990).

In 1982/3 a secret Cabinet committee considered the question of whether 'present policies for supporting lone parents strike the right balance between ensuring adequate child support to prevent poverty and encouraging responsible and self-reliant behaviour by parents' (*The Guardian*, February 17th 1983). The government was considering whether to shift that balance in the latter direction, for example by abolishing the post-Finer benefit changes and putting more pressure on lone mothers to find employment as in the workfare regimes in the US. These specific proposals came to naught, after secret minutes of the ministers' meetings were leaked to the press, provoking a sharp response from women's and poor people's organizations. In 1990 the government returned to the question of lone motherhood with modest proposals to get the courts to deduct maintenance directly from absent fathers' earnings. This will do nothing to raise the incomes of lone mothers, but, if successful, will shift some of the cost of maintenance from the state onto fathers. The response of the Thatcher governments to the question of lone motherhood was confused, but lone mothers have certainly suffered differentially from the increase in poverty and income inequality, the rise in unemployment and the withering of the welfare state. It may be argued that this in itself discourages lone motherhood, though not with much apparent success. The confusion rests on the contradiction between on the one hand wanting to support families in which mothers stay home to care for children, and on the other hand wanting to lessen the dependence of lone mothers on the social security system by encouraging them to be self-sufficient by finding paid employment or by getting maintenance from fathers.

Abortion

In Britain as in the US 'abortion is the central feminist issue of our time' (Simms, 1985: 78) and the conflict over abortion policy therefore illustrates very sharply the nature of Liberal Collectivist family policy. The centrepiece is the 1967 Abortion Act which legalized abortion up to twenty-eight weeks' gestation, where two doctors believe that continuing with the pregnancy 'would involve risk to the life of the pregnant woman, or of injury to the physical or mental health of the pregnant woman or any existing children of her family, greater than if the pregnancy were terminated'. In effect, because continuing with a pregnancy is statistically always a greater health risk, this gives doctors the unhindered right to decide. The 1967 Act is not in force in Northern Ireland, because of opposition from both religious traditions. Britain was amongst the first Western states to liberalize abortion policy in the post-war period, but unlike Sweden and the US for example, women do not have the right to abortion on demand, even early in pregnancy. In some respects policy and practice in Britain is similar to the situation in the FRG since 1974, where counsellors have the right to decide. A host of immediate factors explain the particular origins of the 1967 Act such as the Thalidomide tragedy, the more libertarian moral climate, the rediscovery of poverty and the effective pressure group politics of the Abortion Law Reform Association (ALRA). Underlying this was the growing influence of women within the trade union movement and upon the political parties. To some extent a fusion of class and feminist politics was taking place around the abortion question. During the 1960s the class inequalities amongst women in gaining access to a safe termination were exposed as unacceptably unjust. Many affluent women could get a safe termination privately and out of reach of the law, whether legal or illegal. Working class women faced the risk of a backstreet termination or an unwanted pregnancy.

The original Medical Termination of Pregnancy Bill introduced in parliament in 1966 sought to specify acceptable social grounds for termination, for example where 'the pregnant woman's capacity as a mother will be severely overstrained by the care of a child' or when 'the pregnant woman is a defective or became pregnant while under the age of sixteen or became pregnant as a result of rape' (quoted in Greenwood and Young, 1976: 25). These clauses were abandoned because the medical profession saw them interfering with their clinical discretion, but the debate over them illustrated parliament's anxiety not to be supporting abortion on demand. ALRA and parliament were anxious for legal abortion to be accessible to 'marginal women' (such as those above) and maybe to 'normal women' whose contraception had failed. Abortion on demand, however, might encourage normal women to ignore contraception and to reject motherhood and 'family life'. Thus parliaments and governments have firmly resisted the feminist call for abortion on demand as a matter of family policy. The 'liberal consensus' offloads the implementation of this aspect of family policy onto physicians, because although they have no training in social work or abortion counselling, 'doctor knows best'. The state prefers to trust doctors rather than women. This aspect of the consensual opposition to abortion on demand was most explicitly articulated in the government commissioned Lane Report in 1974:

> To expect doctors to operate under orders without reference to their judgement would be contrary to good medical practice . . . some women would find the burden of making their own decision, unsupported, a heavy one . . . they would be vulnerable to pressure from parents, husbands or boyfriends. Another disadvantage of permitting abortion on demand might in some cases be to encourage neglect of contraceptive precautions. Furthermore, the already high number of abortions would almost certainly be inflated and we consider it probable that many obstetricians and gynaecologists would be unwilling to operate under such a system. (Lane, 1974: 65)

The German system of leaving the decision to counsellors was also rejected by Lane as interfering with clinical decision making. The Lane Report therefore suggested, without evidence, that the medical profession would refuse to implement abortion on demand and that women (whether with or without counselling support) were unable to make the decision themselves. It went on to criticize doctors and others who interpreted the law as meaning that 'an undesirable environmental situation of the mother of itself suffices to justify abortion . . . There is no justification for performing abortions merely because inconvenience would otherwise result' (Lane, 1974: 69–70). Here the report betrays a more authoritarian tone, hinting at the view that to allow 'normal' women easy access to abortion would threaten family values. Despite the hostility of the state to abortion on demand, by the late 1980s the idea was supported by 79 per cent of the general public and 73 per cent of consultant gynaecologists according to Savage and Francome (1989: 1323).

The 1967 Abortion Act has swept away backstreet abortion. The annual number of abortions to women resident in Britain has risen steadily from 101,000 in 1971 to 180,000 in 1988, due in part to an increase in the number of women of childbearing age, but also reflecting changing attitudes amongst women and their concern about the health risks of the pill. The demand for abortion services after the passage of the Act produced little or no earmarked resources and investment by the NHS. In general neither the Department of Health, the health authorities nor senior consultants have given priority to the needs of women seeking abortion services, which are integrated somewhat uncomfortably into obstetrics and gynaecology services. The Health Department and health authorities feel little pro-abortion pressure and fear the anti-abortion lobby, while many consultants see terminations as routine, low-status and unrewarding work (Paintin,

1984: 18). As a result, the majority of terminations are performed in the private sector, in licensed charitable or for-profit clinics with little delay and therefore more safely than the NHS. Women seeking an NHS abortion are confronted by many obstacles, particularly unsympathetic doctors and administrative delay. In 1984 the Royal College of Obstetricians and Gynaecologists found that there was avoidable delay at many stages in the NHS abortion service (Francome, 1986: 54). The inadequacy of the NHS abortion service is most vividly illustrated by the massive local differences in public and private provision, the latter probably being most prominent where the NHS is least adequate. In 1983 the NHS performed 87 per cent of terminations in the Northern region, but only 21 per cent in the West Midlands region. At the level of health districts the extremes were Gateshead with 93 per cent NHS and Dewsbury with a mere 4 per cent. The ironical outcome of the Abortion Act is that it is more educated and more middle class women who continue to have easier access to abortion by being able to surmount the administrative and financial obstacles more easily. The less affluent and more 'marginal' women whom the legislators wanted to target are likely to be seen as more 'deserving' in the NHS, but may still suffer delay and therefore higher risk. Francome (1986: 56) concludes that 'abortions are much simpler to obtain in the US and are performed on average much earlier.' The same may also be said of Sweden, but the situation in the FRG seems closer to that in Britain.

Amongst British resident women with two previous children, the rate of concurrent sterilization with an NHS abortion is 22 per cent compared to 6 per cent with non-NHS abortions (WRRC, no date: 5). This is very high by international standards even compared to the US. There is a strong suspicion that such concurrent sterilization is differentially experienced by black women and by poor women. Certainly the long-term contraceptive Depo-Provera with dangerous side-effects has been prescribed differentially for Asian women in Britain, which has been the subject of a long campaign. For black women, and for some white working class women too, the racist and eugenicist dimension of birth control and gynaecological services requires a continuing struggle for the right to choose to have children (Bryan *et al.*, 1985: 100–7).

The abortion question has never been far from the headlines in Britain in the 1970s and 1980s, as the 'pro-life' anti-abortion activists have sought to amend or abolish the 1967 Act. Parliament has considered numerous bills to this end, all of which have been defeated by the women's movement, which has defended the Act, supported by the majority of the trade union movement and the medical profession. In the late 1980s the anti-abortion movement concentrated on trying to reduce the legal time limit for abortion from twenty-eight weeks to twenty-two, eighteen or even fewer weeks. In response to this pressure the most significant amendment to the 1967 Act so far was enacted in 1990, when the legal time limit for abortion was reduced to twenty-four weeks. However, at the same time, the House of Commons voted that there should be no time limit on abortions needed 'to prevent grave permanent injury to the physical or mental health' of a pregnant woman or where there was 'substantial risk that if the child were born it would suffer such physical or mental abnormalities as to be seriously handicapped'. Previously the limit had been twenty-eight weeks in both cases. In 1988 of only twenty-two abortions carried out after twenty-four weeks, eighteen were done for foetal abnormalities and four because of risk to the mother's life, so that the liberalization of the law simply amounts to a legal clarification of the existing situation (*The Guardian*, April 24th 1990: 6). The struggles to defend and extend abortion rights and the right to have children will continue for many years.

Day Care and Parental Leave

The intimate association of post-war Liberal Collectivism with a patriarchal, conventional view of the family and gender roles within it, is very clearly illustrated by policy on the care of children under five. During the Second World War, over 1600 local authority day nurseries were established in industrial areas to encourage women into factory employment in aid of the war effort. During the late 1940s educationists and women trade unionists struggled to have nurseries integrated into the welfare state, exploiting the pronatalist 'baby boom' atmosphere and the unanticipated continuing demand for women's paid labour (Riley, 1981). By the early 1950s, as pronatalism waned and the ideology of women's domesticity triumphed, only a few hundred local authority nurseries had survived. The policy of the Ministry of Health, expressed in a widely quoted circular issued in the very month the war ended, eventually prevailed and has remained the basis of government policy ever since, and in practice has been extended to include most children under four. The Ministry accepted

> the view of medical and other authority that, in the interest of the health and development of the child no less than for the benefit of the mother, the proper place for a child under two is at home with his mother . . . the right policy to pursue would be positively to discourage mothers of children under two from going out to work; to make provisions for children between two and five by way of nursery schools and classes; and to regard day nurseries as supplements to meet the special needs of children whose mothers are constrained by individual circumstances to go out to work or whose home circumstances are in themselves unsatisfactory from the health point of view or whose mothers are incapable for some good reason of undertaking the full care of their children. (Ministry of Health, Circular 221/45)

This policy was endorsed in a further circular in 1968, by the Finer (1974) Report on one parent families, the Plowden (1967) Report on primary schooling and Mrs Thatcher's education policy White Paper (DES, 1972). During the 1970s and 1980s the policy has come under considerable pressures – the increasing numbers of mothers in paid employment needing day care, child development experts advocating the long-term benefits of quality day care for children, and the clear implication of equal opportunity employment policy in favour of day care provision. For a moment in the late 1970s these pressures built up so strongly that a celebrated writer of popular child care manuals was moved to conclude that official policy had changed in favour of day nurseries for all, much to her regret (Leach, 1979). In fact the Labour government was unmoved by the pressures upon it, in the context of its firm restraint on welfare state growth after 1976 and a reiteration in that same year of ideological (but not financial) support for childminding as a low-cost, familial form of day care (DHSS, 1976). Under the Thatcher governments these same pressures continued to build up, added to which, more recently, with increased skilled labour shortages anticipated in the 1990s, employers have begun to realize the necessity of day care provision to secure and retain the services of skilled women workers. In May 1990, responding specifically to all these pressures for day care, Mrs Thatcher herself 'dismissed the need for a national child care policy, saying it could lead to "a whole generation of crèche children . . . [who] never understood the security of home" ' (*The Guardian*, May 18th 1990: 2). Ministerial statements have been more non-committal, merely emphasizing that 'day care will continue to be primarily a matter for private arrangement between parents and private and voluntary resources, except where there are special needs' (quoted in Moss, 1991: 133). In 1982 the government inaugurated the taxation of workplace nurseries as a 'company perk', but this was rescinded in the 1990 budget as a minor concession to the 'day care lobby'. John Major, the Chancellor of the Exchequer at the time, argued that 'it is not for the government to encourage or discourage women with children from going out to work.' Recent Conservative governments, while tacitly recognizing the suppressed demand for day care, maintain very firmly that local and central government have no part to play in meeting that demand.

The outcome of this 'hands off' day care policy is a curious patchwork (Table 5.6) of public, private and voluntary provisions and informal arrangements of very varied quality and cost to meet the continually rising demand. State maintained schools cater for about half the three and four year olds, with around half of these places being full-time. Part-time nursery schooling expanded significantly in the 1970s in the wake of the White Paper (DES, 1972), but the great majority of the under fives in state schools are four year olds in primary schools, which are sometimes unsuited to the needs of young children. The 1980 Education Act removed the obligation of local education authorities to consider nursery education needs, and since then specialist nursery schooling has begun to wither away slowly. In line with the White Paper's stipulation that schooling should not encourage mothers into paid employment, schooling is an unsatisfactory form of day care for parents in paid employment because of school holidays and the short school day, which means more juggling with childminders, nurseries and informal care.

Local authority day nurseries offer full-time places, catering almost exclusively for children deemed to be 'at risk' by social services departments, who administer them. The pay, working conditions and status of

Table 5.6   *UK non-parental day care provision for the under fives, 1985*

Type of provision	% of population aged 0–4 for whom this type of provision is available
State maintained school	17.6
Private school	1.0
Local authority day nursery	0.9
Private or voluntary day nursery	0.8
Registered childminder	4.0
Unregistered childminder	0.7
Nanny, au pair etc.	0.8
Total	25.8

Source: Cohen, 1988: Table 5.1

nursery workers are generally inferior to those of nursery schoolteachers. The number of local authority day nursery places expanded significantly in the early 1970s in response to increased public concern over child abuse, but has since remained static. There are very few integrated or combined day nurseries and nursery schools. Given the lack of central government direction, there is enormous local variation in the provision of local authority nursery schooling and day nursery care, which is certainly more a reflection of varying local politics than actual local needs. Many rural and suburban local authorities have few school places and/or day nursery places for the under fives, while inner city local authorities tend to make more provisions (TCRU, 1990: 4, 6). Private and voluntary nurseries are predominantly at workplaces, particularly in the public sector. A number of community nurseries have been established by groups of women and of black people to provide more participative, anti-racist and anti-sexist child care. In the late 1980s private sector corporations began to show some interest in nursery provision as a means of securing and retaining skilled female employees, most notably the Midland Bank who opened thirty-six nurseries in 1989. However the Confederation of British Industry believes it is unlikely that most employers will respond in this way, despite ministerial exhortation (Brindle, 1990: 4). Childminding is by far the most common form of out-of-home care arranged for the under threes, and the number of places has doubled over the past two decades in response to the demand. Childminding has become a very important source of low-paid employment in the casual economy for working class women. As in Sweden there are great differences of opinion over the quality and desirability of childminding compared to nurseries (Moss, 1987). Child-minders generally receive little or no practical support from social services departments. Governments have rhetorically supported childminding as a low-cost, flexible form of provision, and as the next best thing to the ideal of full-time mothering, a view firmly advocated by Leach (1979). Although local authority supported playgroups are conventionally included as a form of day care service, they are not included here since at most they run for a few half days a week, and are generally run by mothers and childminders themselves. Nevertheless as Table 5.7 indicates some mothers do leave children in playgroups while they are in paid employment. Information about the use of nannies, au pairs and 'mothers' helps' is scanty, but it would seem that an increasing number of middle class parents have been able to afford nannies in recent years. The arrangements made by women in paid employment for the care of their pre-school children are largely informal, as Table 5.7 indicates. Parents, as in many other Western

Table 5.7   *UK arrangements made by women in paid employment for the care of pre-school children, 1980 (percentages)*

Type of arrangement	Full-time workers	Part-time workers	All working women
Husband	13	50	47
Grandmother	44	24	34
Other relative	8	13	13
Childminder or friend	26	14	19
Day nursery	9	4	4
Nursery school	5	4	4
Playgroup	3	3	3
Nanny	6	2	4

Source: Martin and Roberts, 1984: Table 4.10

countries, have to juggle their careers and their child care as best they can, often at great expense and under great stress. Women rely most on husbands, grandmothers and other relatives, and those without such support suffer the most.

On the basis of the available information, it is extremely difficult to draw firm conclusions on class and 'race' stratification in access to and use of day care services. Clearly nannies and private schools are only accessible to the very affluent. It would seem however that working class mothers of pre-school children are more likely either to withdraw from paid employment entirely or only to work part-time and rely on cheap informal care arrangements. The proportion of women with children under five actually in paid employment is lower in the UK than in the other states examined here (Table A.15), including the FRG where the overall labour market activity rate of women is lower. The scarcity and the high costs of day care provision are clearly a major deterrent to working class mothers returning to paid employment in Britain. Middle class, managerial and professional mothers are more likely to return to full-time employment, relying on whatever combination of costly childminding, nannying and nurseries they can come up with. This class difference bears much in common with the situation in the US and the FRG, and to a lesser extent in Sweden. The choices for working class women are more severely constrained by the relatively high and unsubsidized cost of child care, unless their children are deemed 'at risk'.

Admittedly on the basis of limited evidence, it seems that 'local authority nurseries provide more places for ethnic minority children than any other pre-school institution . . . [one study] found that 18 per cent of all children in these nurseries were Afro-Caribbean and nearly 5 per cent Indian/Pakistani' (Cohen, 1988: 28). In many respects this shows the welfare state working well in meeting the needs of hard-pressed Afro-Caribbean and non-Muslim Asian mothers, who are more likely to be in full-time, low-paid employment than white mothers. However, this provision is predominantly identified as being for children 'at risk' and the dominant ideology (Leach, 1979) implies that only 'bad' mothers leave their children in full-time nurseries. Thus to some extent a double standard and a pathology model of black mothers may be being reinforced. Somehow, according to the prevailing ideology, white mothers should be encouraged to stay at home, but black children should be in nurseries to compensate for deprivation at home. In practice, according to a study by Asrat-Girma (1986: 48), 'the message . . . confirmed by the nursery regimes is *black women and black culture are inadequate*.' Such evidence as there is suggests that black mothers have to rely more on poorer quality childminders or relatives, and that black children are strongly underrepresented in playgroups and nursery schools.

Belatedly compared to many other West European states, statutory maternity leave was introduced in Britain in 1975 as part of Labour's corporatist social contract and its obligations to conform with EC directives. The statutory leave period is lengthy by European standards, eleven weeks before the birth and twenty-nine weeks after, but for most of it there is no statutory maternity pay so that it is rarely taken up in full. The qualification rules for maternity leave are comparatively very restrictive. For example, women working more than sixteen hours a week must have worked for the same employer for at least two years. A survey in 1979 found that only 54 per cent of women satisfied the conditions, mostly those in managerial or professional jobs (Daniel, 1980), since when the rules have been tightened further. Small firms with fewer than six employees are in effect exempted from offering statutory maternity leave. There is no statutory paternity leave. Statutory maternity pay (SMP) in Britain is the least adequate amongst the EC states. In 1988 most women in EC states received between 80 and 100 per cent of their full pay for at least sixteen weeks of maternity leave. In Britain qualifying women receive 90 per cent of full pay for only six weeks, with a further twelve weeks at a flat rate. The structure of SMP was radically reformed alongside statutory sick pay in 1987. Prior to that date they were both social insurance benefits; now they are occupational benefits 'in so far as they are administered and delivered by employers and are governed by additional rules of entitlement based upon the employment contract . . . [though] they are paid for out of taxation by the state reimbursing employers for their cost' (Lonsdale and

Byrne, 1988: 149). The eventual goal of the Conservative government is to privatize maternity and sick pay entirely. It has been estimated that 80,000 women have lost entitlement to SMP with the new structure (Lonsdale and Byrne, 1988: 146).

Beyond the inadequate statutory rights, a number of large employers have increasingly developed their own maternity rights agreements since the mid 1970s. Women trade unionists have usually taken the lead in pressing for these agreements, and although it is not known how wide-spread they are, the diversity of arrangements and of women's experiences in taking them up is substantial (O'Grady and Wakefield, 1989). With growing concern about labour shortages in the 1990s, a number of private corporations in retailing, banking and industry have started offering extended career breaks such as five years' unpaid leave to mothers (*The Economist*, July 21st 1990: 29). It appears that women in professional and managerial occupations with big employers are much more likely to be covered by occupational maternity rights agreements, reflecting a similar situation in respect of statutory rights. Women in manual occupations, part-time employment, with small employers and in the private services sector are much less likely to be covered, reflecting very considerable class differences in access to and use of maternity rights.

In part because of the comparatively inadequate day care and parental leave provisions in Britain, the proportion of mothers of pre-school children in paid employment is much lower than in some other states, including Sweden and the US. Nevertheless the proportion of British women with children under five in full-time paid employment increased from 7 per cent in 1981 to 12 per cent in 1989 and in part-time employment from 17 to 28 per cent in the same period. This phenomenon alongside the rapidly increasing proportion of births outside marriage (27 per cent in 1989) has caused a flurry of political debate about family policy, with the Conservative Party split into three camps. The traditional 'family fogies', including Mrs Thatcher, believe that the welfare state does too little to encourage mothers to stay at home with young children. Some of the family fogies would like to restore child tax allowances to fathers or to confine an increased child benefit to mothers of the under fives. At the other extreme are Tory libertarian feminists who believe that the welfare state should enable women to compete in the labour market on fairer terms. This might be furthered by tax relief on child care costs for example. Finally 'the most powerful Tory group is the economic realists . . . In their view the most pressing aim of family policy is to offset the decline in school leavers by increasing the number of women workers' (*The Economist*, August 11th 1990: 27). This might be facilitated, for example, by giving employers tax relief on child care vouchers given to mothers they employ. All these proposals involve public expenditure in effect, and given the party's general hesitancy over interventionist family policy, any significant policy changes in practice seem unlikely. In government, the Labour Party has also exhibited similar divisions and hesitancy about family policies.

Currently the party is committed to improving child benefit and to placing 'a statutory duty on all local authorities to provide comprehensive, integrated childcare services for the under fives' (Labour Party, 1989b: 62) with both equal opportunities and labour market concerns to the fore.

The Health Care System

Finance and Administration

The National Health Service (NHS) is more or less unique among capitalist states in claiming to provide a comprehensive, nationalized service to the whole population, largely free at the point of consumption and largely funded by national direct taxation, with comparatively little finance from social insurance contributions or local taxation. Public expenditure on health care as a proportion of total health care spending has fluctuated at around 90 per cent, far in excess of the OECD mean (Table A.19) and comparable to the proportion in Sweden. Supporters of the NHS have argued that it has always been chronically underfunded, which is partly the result of its severe dependence on the national exchequer and the national politics of public expenditure. Hence total health care spending as a proportion of GDP has remained significantly lower than the OECD mean, and the gap between Britain and the OECD mean has widened considerably since 1960 (Table A.20). In terms of *public* expenditure on health care per head of population, even the US overtook Britain during the 1970s (Table A.21). This underfunding is compensated for by lower administrative and labour costs in the NHS and possibly greater effectiveness and less waste in its use of resources, compared to other systems, though it is difficult to quantify this satisfactorily. Physicians in the US for example earn 5.1 times the national average wage, compared to 2.4 times in Britain. Administration accounts for about 5 per cent of NHS resources, while in the FRG it takes up about 10 per cent and in the US as much as 20 per cent of health care resources. In the post-war boom years 1960–75, total health care expenditure (on a volume basis) in the UK grew twice as fast as real GDP, higher than the mean growth rate for health care spending in the OECD states (Table A.22). In the crisis years 1975–84 this trend was reversed, with health care expenditure growth halted, and then decreasing significantly in the years 1980–4. Between 1979 and 1988 under the Thatcher administration, the average annual real rise in NHS expenditure was 1.7 per cent, by far the lowest amongst the post-war administrations and insufficient even to keep pace with the growing numbers of infirm elderly people (Huhne, 1989).

The NHS, set up in 1948, remains the most popular and most firmly established element of the British welfare state inspired by the Liberal Collectivism of the post-war settlement. The ideology of the NHS is anticapitalist in that it suggests that health care should not be a commodity provided and consumed in a market, and that only public provision can ensure an acceptable level of equity in access to and use of resources, as well as making more efficient use of the resources available for health care. These principles contrast radically with those on which health care finance and administration are based in most other states, even such radically contrasting systems as those in the FRG and the US, and they are also entirely alien to Thatcherism. Yet in several other fundamental respects the NHS is similar to other health care systems. First, hospital-based scientific medicine has increasingly dominated NHS provision, so that it has an intimate relationship with the transnational pharmaceutical and medical technology corporations, whose financial muscle influences the deployment of resources. The internationally spiralling costs of medical technology have particularly affected NHS resources, because governments have tended to link its resourcing to the general level of inflation rather than the higher levels commonly associated with health care industries. Second, the great bulk of NHS resources is devoted to the wages and salaries of its employees. Since at least the late 1960s, the various struggles of NHS employees to defend and improve their salaries, wages and conditions have often taken centre stage in industrial relations and in government determination of the NHS budget. Third, the deployment of NHS resources and to a great extent the demand for health care are shaped by the medical profession. As elsewhere, the doctors' control of medical knowledge creates enormous barriers to achieving accountability for their activities. In the NHS medical professional power is built into the basic administrative and financial structure, which in its essentials remained unchanged between 1948 and 1991.

During the mid 1940s the Labour Minister of Health, Aneurin Bevan, struck a famous deal with the senior representatives of the medical profession. This deal lies at the heart of the NHS. Unlike the medical profession in the US, the British medical profession in the 1940s had little confidence that private insurance lubricated by the state would generate the financial resources required for the development of scientific medicine. Such a system had failed in the inter-war years. The entrepreneurial spirit was largely absent amongst medical professionals and hospital administrators, reinforced by the natural collectivism engendered by the war. In the atmosphere of the 1940s the hospital doctors in particular preferred to embrace popular enthusiasm for a national health service and to look to central government for the big investment demanded by scientific medicine. Hence in return for securing government control over the aggregate resources devoted to the NHS, Bevan largely conceded day-to-day control over the use of those resources and over administration to the medical profession. Senior hospital doctors are even allowed considerable control over their own remuneration through self-conferred merit awards. Bureaucratic structures were therefore created to administer the NHS, which were deliberately remote from consumers, NHS workers (except doctors) and local politics. The regional and district health authorities which manage the NHS have no formal accountability to the communities they serve. General practitioners insisted on having an independent contractual relationship with the NHS and their own local administrative structures, resisting Bevan's notion of health centres integrated into the NHS as the basis for primary care. In retrospect, the stout independence of the GPs may have increased their popularity and saved them from the atrophy of general practice seen in countries like Sweden and the US, where hospital-based health care is even more predominant. Bevan also conceded the right of NHS doctors to practise privately both outside the NHS in private clinics and inside it using NHS pay beds. Hence the notions that some patients would pay for NHS services and that the NHS would 'compete' with private provisions were built in from the start. Although Bevan originally conceived of the NHS as offering free treatment to everyone whatever their residential status, in 1949 he capitulated to pressure to charge 'overseas visitors' for NHS treatment. He even claimed that he had 'arranged for immigration officers to turn back aliens who were coming to this country to secure benefits off the health service' (Cohen, 1982: 6). Subsequent legislation in 1949 gave the Ministry of Health powers to charge people 'not ordinarily resident in the UK' for NHS services. These powers appear not to have been used much until 1982 when the government produced complex rules for charging overseas visitors, which are, in practice, institutionally racist and closely linked to immigration control (Cohen, 1982). Another early break with the principle of free treatment came in 1951 when the Labour government decided to introduce patient charges for spectacles and dentures, a policy change which prompted the resignation of Bevan and Harold Wilson from the government. Later in 1951 the incoming Conservative government introduced prescription charges. Prior to the Thatcher administration, charges to NHS patients accounted for less than 2 per cent of NHS income, but over the 1980s this has risen to almost 4 per cent as prescription and dental charges have been raised sharply and new charges for eye testing and dental examination have been introduced.

Private health care and private health insurance expanded steadily but unspectacularly from 1948 to 1979. However, between 1979 and 1986 under the Thatcher administration the number of private beds and the number of people covered by private insurance doubled. By 1986 15 per cent of hospital beds in England and Wales were in private nursing homes and hospitals, and 9.5 per cent of the UK population had some private health insurance cover (CSO, 1990a: 122). However, because of its popularity with the medical profession and the general public, the Thatcher administration had to tread very carefully in dealing with the NHS. While almost all Conservatives continue to proclaim their full support for the principle of a comprehensive NHS, free at the point of consumption, the free-market Thatcherite wing of the party has searched for means to privatize health care gradually. Hence the expansion of private health care in the 1980s was not an *explicit* government policy strategy, but it was rather quietly and deliberately facilitated by a number of discrete policy changes. In 1980 private health care was deregulated in several respects and NHS consultants were given new contracts enabling them to take on more private work; the 1981 and 1988 budgets introduced personal tax relief on health insurance premiums for people on low incomes and for old people respectively. The 1981 budget also introduced tax concessions which 'encouraged the growth of consultant-owned hospitals . . . [and] also allowed companies to set against corporation tax the health insurance premiums which they paid for their employees' (Higgins, 1988: 88). The 1980s saw a boom in private health insurance as a company perk, largely for professional and managerial employees. In 1987 45 per cent of health insurance policy holders had their premiums paid in part or in full by their employer. The 'enterprise culture' fostered by the Thatcher administration encouraged investment in Britain by for-profit health care corporations largely from the US, whereas previously almost all private care was provided by non-profit organizations or in private NHS pay beds. A campaign led by the NHS trade unions forced the Labour government of the 1970s to reduce the number of private or pay beds in the NHS by half, and their number had fallen further to only a thousand by 1986. Finally the apparently worsening performance of the NHS as a consequence of underfunding and increased consumer expectations, particularly with severe public expenditure restraint since 1976, has generated more demand for private health care in areas such as abortion, out-patient consultation and elective or cold surgery, to enable some people to jump the NHS queue. Predictably the coverage of private health care has a clear class and gender dimension. A substantial proportion of male professional and managerial workers have health insurance cover, while virtually no manual workers do, and very few women workers in any occupation have cover in their own right (Higgins, 1988: 164).

Aside from encouraging the growth of private health care, the other element of post-1979 Conservative strategy for the NHS has been to promote the 'contracting-out' of specific NHS services to non-NHS contractors. This strategy has been given a higher public profile, because it preserves the name of the NHS, though it implies an entirely different conception in which the NHS becomes a regulator and overseer of privately provided services, rather than a direct provider itself. The first major initiative of this kind came in 1983 when health authorities were instructed to put hospital cleaning, catering and laundry services out for competitive tender. Full implementation of compulsory competitive tendering (CCT) has been delayed and undermined by considerable resistance from both the health authorities and the ancillary workers' trade unions. By the end of 1989 77 per cent of contracts had been awarded 'in house', but CCT has significantly depressed the pay and conditions of ancillary workers (JNPRU, 1990), as well as generating enormous job losses. Between 1981 and 1988 the number of NHS ancillary staff fell by 33.5 per cent, while personpower in all the medical grades of staff increased. The performance of private contractors has been found wanting by many health authorities, and by the late 1980s they were winning far fewer new and renewed contracts (JNPRU, 1990). In the absence of any government evidence for increased efficiency in NHS ancillary services it is hard to disagree with the unions' view that CCT is simply 'a means of forcing NHS staff to do the same work or work harder for less money [and] to achieve this the government are prepared to let standards fall to an absolute minimum (and lower)' (JNPRU, 1990: 46). Aside from abortion services and some services for the mentally ill, contracting out of other health care services has so far been rare.

In view of growing public concern about underfunding and other inadequacies of the NHS, Mrs Thatcher herself instigated and chaired a secret 'NHS Review' which was deliberated upon during 1988 and culminated in the publication of a White Paper in January 1989. The White Paper (DOH, 1989) embraces a radical, new conception of the NHS, based on the creation of an 'internal market'. In this model three 'budget holders' (district health authorities (DHAs), contracted-out GPs and private insurance plans) buy hospital care on behalf of consumers from three types of hospital (DHA managed hospitals, self-governing NHS hospitals and private hospitals) who compete with each other. Reacting to the White Paper the editor of the *British Medical Journal* wrote that

> it is not fanciful to talk about the end of the traditional health service, with its low administrative costs and its decent principle of uniform access to a high standard of medical care . . . the proposed new structures, such as budget holding practices and independent hospitals, make it almost axiomatic that they behave like commercial enterprises. (Lock, 1990: 1)

At the time of writing it is impossible to assess at all precisely the likely effects of such a major reform, which could take the NHS various distances and along a number of routes towards privatization. The proposals in the White Paper, legislated for by the 1990 Health Services Act, certainly amount to the 'marketization' of the NHS (Petchey, 1989: 96). Whether the present reform package will worsen patient care and exacerbate health inequalities is fiercely debated and depends on a large number of imponderables. Some GPs and hospital doctors believe that the reforms could make the NHS more effective and more user-friendly (Feinmann, 1989). Other doctors believe that the reforms will exacerbate existing class, 'race' and gender inequalities in the quality of health care (Savage and Widgery, 1989; Rea, 1989) particularly for old and chronically sick people. The medical profession as represented by the British Medical Association (BMA) has mounted vigorous opposition to the White Paper proposals on the basis that they should have been piloted first. There will be a prolonged struggle between the government, NHS administrators, doctors and other NHS workers over the implementation of the reforms in the 1990s, with the consumer as ever largely sitting on the sidelines.

Central Government and NHS Management

As already discussed, the structure of the NHS made it deliberately remote from local party politics and from pressure and interest group politics representing consumers. Pressures from these quarters certainly shape NHS policies, but they are mediated through the medical profession and through central government who both claim to represent the consumer. Hence the major power struggle over health care policy in Britain, probably even more so than in other health care systems, is that between medical professionals and the government. Closely connected with this has been the conflict between the NHS and its workers (including doctors) over their pay and conditions, which since the late 1960s has frequently erupted into industrial action. Here, however, we will concentrate on central government's attempts to shape the management of clinical resources.

Having initially given doctors more or less complete discretion over the management of clinical resources within the overall NHS budget, since the 1960s governments have sought more and more energetically to influence the deployment of these resources. Until the early 1960s central government played little part in shaping the use of NHS resources, but this changed with the 1962 Hospital Plan. The centrepiece of the Hospital Plan was the concept of the district general hospital (DGH), purpose built to provide an integrated hospital service to a large population. These institutions were to be the citadels of the NHS, which, through economies of scale and nationally uniform standards, would improve efficiency and equity. But

> the basic vision of what a hospital service should be like [was] almost entirely determined by the medical consensus . . . there is no indication in the Hospital Plan of other possible criteria being considered, such as accessibility for patients or the effects of hospital size on staff morale and recruitment. (Klein, 1989: 74)

The implementation of the plan has continued sporadically over the ensuing three decades and remains far from completion, though it has prompted the closure of hundreds of local and specialist hospitals. It is the most important and classic case study in the problems of the NHS created by underinvestment, the hegemony of hospital-based scientific medicine, lack of public accountability and bureaucratic inertia. From the late 1960s governments concentrated their energy on attempting to strengthen the hand of NHS administrators as the bearers of managerial efficiency, not only to counter medical professional influence but also in response to the rising power of the NHS trade unions. Resource planning machinery, streamlined administrative structures and professional management were promoted, culminating in a major reorganization in 1974. In the end this reorganization strengthened the power of the medical profession, giving them representation on health authorities and veto powers in the basic unit of management, the district management team, a policy described somewhat fatalistically by Klein (1989: 95) as 'an acknowledgement of the reality of medical syndicalism'.

In the mid 1970s the Labour government faced increasing consumer pressures to redress the enormous geographical maldistribution of health care resources, which if anything had worsened since the formation of the NHS. In 1976 the government instituted a programme (RAWP – Resource

Allocation Working Party) for ongoing geographical, needs-related redis-tribution of resources within the NHS. Over the decade to the mid 1980s RAWP had substantially reduced the resource disparities between the NHS regions, shifting resources from the South East of England to the Midlands and the North. However 'what is not known is how extra resources have been translated into services, and the consequences of this for patient care' (Allsop, 1989: 61). The Labour government also attempted to stem the atrophy of lower-status health care services which had been overshadowed in the drive for acute, high-tech hospital care. Hence the government proclaimed its Priorities policy in 1976, which sought national planning and prioritization of resources for health and community care services for old people, people with learning difficulties and people suffering mental illness. However 'overall target figures for resource allocations were quickly abandoned' (Allsop, 1989: 62) and the Priorities policy turned out to be more a statement of hope than an effective resource management intervention, particularly as it coincided with a much tougher regime of public expenditure restraint.

Not surprisingly the Thatcher administration, while not explicitly aban-doning RAWP and the Priorities policy, concentrated its attention on the question of 'efficiency' rather than equity in the management of NHS resources. Of course in the absence of a clear conception of what real efficiency in health care means, the government has tended to use efficiency criteria from private industry whose application to health care is problematic. Nevertheless a whole battery of measures to cut costs and increase efficiency have been promulgated by the government including compulsory competitive tendering for ancillary services, much increased throughput of patients, much more day care treatment, drives for generic substitution of pharmaceuticals including a 'limited list' of drugs for GPs, and performance-related pay for managers in implementing these meas-ures. In the early 1980s 'gradually the circulars [from the DHSS to the DHAs] began to impose a new set of priorities on the NHS [which] . . . emphasised the enormous importance of management' (Davidson, 1987: 43). The single most important change was the restructuring of NHS management in the mid 1980s in the wake of the Griffiths (1983) Report. Griffiths firmly rejected the 'consensus management' style enshrined in the 1974 reorganization, because 'there is no driving force seeking and accepting direct and personal responsibility for developing management plans, securing their implementation and monitoring actual achievement.' Hence individual managers were introduced at all levels of the NHS, armed with packages of performance indicators to pursue cost efficiency. In the wider Thatcherite context of the 'enterprise economy', the diminu-tion of union power and the attack on professional monopolies, the post-Griffiths NHS management has had greater confidence and willingness to carry out the government's intentions, thereby challenging the traditional relative autonomy of the NHS providers, from ancillary workers to consultants. On the ground 'the threat of managerial scrutiny may have been more important than its reality, to the extent that it persuaded the medical profession itself to examine, if only defensively, its own practices' (Klein, 1989: 212). It remains extremely dubious, however, whether the so-called management revolution can contribute to higher-quality health care in the context of continued underfunding. An NHS district general manager recruited from private industry, who resigned in 1988, complained that he had not envisaged his role as being an asset stripper. The Thatcher government's impatience in struggling with the contradictions of imposing managerial efficiency on the NHS in the context of underfunding and medical syndicalism produced the NHS Review. The 'marketization' of the NHS is a more radical and more risky strategy for squeezing more cost efficiency out of the NHS. Apparently the government has done no cost–benefit analysis of its reform proposals, so that its costs and benefits are entirely uncertain (Robinson, 1990).

Health Status and Health Inequalities

The comparative health status of the British population as measured by mortality status occupies a middle range position amongst the leading industrial countries, significantly better than the US and significantly worse than Sweden (Table A.23). Although the NHS's formal commitment to equity in access to health care provision has not been successfully implemented, the ideology of NHS universalism has generated considerable public pressure to mitigate inequalities in both health care provision and health outcomes, however remote the connections between the two. These pressures reached a climax in the 1970s, to which the Labour government responded with the RAWP programme, the Priorities policy and in 1977 the commissioning of an expert report on inequalities in health. The Black Report (named after the chair of the working group) concentrated mostly on inequalities in health outcome by occupational social class, the parameter of stratification which dominates British social statistics. The report concluded that

> the poorer health experience of the lower occupational groups applied at all stages of life . . . The class gradient seemed to be greater than in some comparable countries . . . and was becoming more marked. During the twenty years up to the early 1970s . . . the mortality rates for both men and women aged 35 and over in occupational classes I and II [professional and managerial] had steadily diminished while those in IV and V [semi-skilled and unskilled manual] changed very little or had even deteriorated. (Townsend *et al.*, 1988: 2)

The report recommended a large injection of money into the NHS to remedy underfunding combined with a comprehensive anti-poverty programme including effective action to implement and improve the Priorities policy, and affirmative action to direct better health care and preventive services towards working class communities. The Black Report was published in 1980 and completely dismissed by the Conservative government. A follow-up to the Black Report called *The Health Divide* published in 1988 confirmed the original findings and concluded that in the decade from 1971 to 1981 there was a fall in 'all cause' death rates in Britain, but these improvements were not experienced equally across the population. Non-manual groups experienced a much greater decline than manual groups; as a result the gap between the groups widened. Furthermore death rates among women from coronary heart disease and lung cancer actually rose in manual groups over the ten year period, while showing a substantial decline for non-manual women. There was also a widening gap between manual and non-manual groups in their rates of chronic sickness from 1974 to 1984. (Townsend *et al.*, 1988: 353)

The Health Divide was as firmly dismissed by the government as the Black Report. The issues surrounding class inequalities in health status and strategies for preventing illness continue to be hotly debated, particularly in relation to heart disease, AIDS, diet and the safety of food. A great variety of discrete public health campaigns and struggles has developed in the 1980s, almost invariably initiated and sustained by lay people in alliance with radical professionals, the most important example being the struggle against AIDS led by the gay movement. At the local level an integrated New Public Health Movement is trying to establish itself (PHA, 1988).

The health status of black people in Britain is not covered by official statistics, which is indicative of a lack of official concern. The class structure of health status and the differential concentration of black people in the less privileged occupational social classes, and their greater likelihood of experiencing unemployment and poverty, would obviously suggest that the health status of black people will be significantly inferior to that of white people in general. The very limited evidence available suggests that this 'structural' effect does indeed operate (Townsend *et al.*, 1988: 248–54; Baxter and Baxter, 1988). Evidence of direct racial discrimination or subjective racism in NHS service provision comes from accounts of individual experiences at all levels of the service including nursing care, clinical consultation and patient consent, patient reception and handling, and general practice (McNaught, 1987: 13–15; Donovan, 1986). However, because of the closed, unaccountable nature of the NHS and the barriers to making effective complaints, challenging subjective racism in the NHS is extremely difficult and rarely taken up successfully. The Commission for Racial Equality makes virtually no reference to discrimination in health care provision in its annual reports.

There have been several campaigns and critical commentaries aimed at undermining institutional racism in the NHS and at the improvement of NHS services to the black communities. Local campaigns have had some success in making health authorities sensitive to cultural differences *vis-à-vis* hospital diet and burial for example and to overcoming language differences. Most attention, however, has been focused on specific illnesses and health problems differentially affecting the black communities, notably sickle cell anaemia amongst Afro-Caribbean people, rickets and osteomalacia amongst Asian people and higher levels of infant and perinatal mortality amongst all the black communities, particularly those of Pakistani and Bangladeshi origin. The sickle cell issue has been pushed onto the NHS agenda by persistent lobbying and local activism which has increased professional and public awareness. Nevertheless for sickle cell sufferers 'levels of services are poor [and] individual patients are still encountering considerable problems in their interaction with the NHS' (McNaught, 1987: 55). The incidence of rickets and its adult equivalent, osteomalacia, amongst Asians became the subject of a government funded campaign in the early 1980s. The disease is linked to low levels of vitamin D, so the campaign focused on advising Asians to use margarine (fortified with vitamin D since the war to prevent rickets) rather than ghee in their cooking, and to expose themselves to more sunlight, which naturally increases vitamin D levels. The DHSS unaccountably rejected the idea of fortifying chappati flour with vitamin D. The Stop Rickets campaign was based on a perception that Asian people had 'an inherently unhealthy diet, because of their "ignorance" about nutrition. The solution to rickets was simple: "the long term answer lies in health education and change towards a Western diet and lifestyle" ' (Pearson, 1986: 49–50). The ethnocentrism of the campaign was widely criticized in the Asian communities, as well as its failure to confront the general effects of poverty and inaccessible health care services on the health status of Asian people. Whether as a result of the campaign, the controversy it raised or other factors, the incidence of the diseases appears to have diminished.

The Stop Rickets campaign evolved into the Asian Mother and Baby Campaign (AMBC) launched by the DHSS in 1984 to improve perinatal and infant mortality rates in the Asian communities. Once again the onus was put on changing the behaviour of Asian mothers, rather than challenging institutional and subjective racism in NHS obstetric and maternity services, let alone the direct links between perinatal mortality and poverty. In practice the AMBC involved recruitment of Asian women as 'linkworkers' to mediate between NHS staff and Asian mothers, which, within the severe institutional limitations imposed by the NHS, has provided a platform for improvements in the service on the ground (Rocheron, 1988). These are but three of many examples of campaigning and resistance around the health status of the black communities, which pose an increasing challenge to the remoteness of the NHS (McNaught, 1987: Chapter 3; Kushnick, 1988; Grimsley and Bhat, 1988).

In 1939 a widely publicized report (Spring Rice, 1939) on the health of working class married women documented in graphic detail the appalling and deteriorating health status of working class women in the inter-war years. The report noted that

the national health insurance system makes no provision for the wife of an insured man, she has still to call in a private doctor when she feels ill . . . The

> greater . . . her fortitude . . . and the lower . . . her financial resources, the
> longer will she defer seeking the advice she needs. (Spring Rice, 1939: 198)

The introduction of the NHS in 1948 was unquestionably an enormous step forward in improving the access of working class women to health care, and contributed to the great improvement in maternal mortality rates after the war. However there is evidence of continuing class inequalities amongst women both in their health status and in their effective use of the NHS over the post-war period (Doyal, 1985: 238–45). Women in general are more likely than men to experience chronic and degenerative illnesses, whose treatment has been underresourced in the NHS compared with treatment for acute illnesses (Pascall, 1986: 193). The incidence of cancers and heart disease has been increasing faster amongst women than amongst men in recent years.

Over the past two decades a fragmented but influential women's health movement has emerged in Britain, informed by feminist critiques of health care and adverse personal experiences of the NHS. In addition to the struggle for reproductive freedom discussed above, attention has focused on issues such as inadequate and inefficient cervical and breast cancer screening, the provision of well-woman clinics (Foster, 1989), the medicalization of childbirth, and the inferior status of women workers at all levels of the NHS. Although about 75 per cent of NHS workers are women, the higher-status specialties and senior administrative posts continue to be dominated by men (Doyal and Elston, 1986: 193–203). Given the enormous power of the medical profession in the NHS bestowed by government, the continued male dominance has fundamentally influenced priorities and practice within the service. Nowhere is the alliance of male dominance and scientific medicine more powerful than in the management of childbirth (Graham and Oakley, 1981) – routine ultrascanning, the virtual ending of home delivery, induced delivery, the subordination of midwifery to the medical profession, increasing numbers of forceps deliveries and Caesarian sections, foetal monitoring technology. The benefits of these and other developments have been questioned increasingly by women in Britain and elsewhere in recent years, which has presented a significant challenge to the medical orthodoxy. In Britain this conflict came to an important climax in 1985–6 when Wendy Savage, an NHS obstetrician committed to woman-oriented practice, was suspended on the insistence of her senior colleagues who supported more active, technological management of childbirth. Wendy Savage was subjected to a 'trial' of her methods in the form of an enquiry conducted by a barrister and two senior obstetricians. During the fifteen months of her suspension, an enormous wave of local community support and wider popular support for her emerged. The incident gave an almost unique insight into the hidden and unaccountable world of decision making about resources and patient care in the NHS (Savage, 1986). The eventual reinstatement of Wendy Savage was a significant and popular challenge to the power of patriarchal, medical orthodoxy in the NHS.

Conclusion

This book has been primarily concerned with the impact of social policy on 'race', class and gender divisions and with the cross-national diversity of social policy within a common structure of racialized and patriarchal capitalism. Many of these concerns seem to lie outside those preoccupying the mainstream study of social policy and policy analysis, at least in Britain. Three important academic reviews of recent policy change in Britain were published in 1990 by Hills, by Johnson and by Savage and Robins. They are all well informed and accessible, and will be widely used. However, none of them gives much more than passing attention to questions of 'race', class and gender. Generally they reflect and reinforce the valuable empirical tradition of social policy analysis in Britain. Even the use of occupational social class as a critical parameter seems to be fading out of academic fashion. There remains a huge antipathy to using and operationalizing the concept of 'class' in policy analysis, presumably for fear of its Marxist connotations. Yet, in Britain above all, class (using whatever definition) is manifestly fundamental to the social structure and therefore to analysing the functioning and impact of the welfare state.

The issues surrounding gender and social policy analysis remain somewhat peripheral to the mainstream in Britain, despite over twenty years of considerable feminist scholarship in this area. According to Maclean and Groves (1991: 2), 'mainstream social policy literature, including some well-known recent texts, . . . has continued to a surprising extent to marginalize women.' 'Women's issues' and feminism have been incorporated as a specialist area in some of the social sciences, which is hived off from the mainstream. Hence the critical literature on women and social policy in Britain is now very substantial, but it has been ignored by much of the mainstream, despite the much improved representation of women within the upper reaches of the academic social policy community.

Critical analysis of 'race' and social policy in Britain has been pursued largely outside the academic 'discipline' of social policy. There is, as yet, no generic textbook on 'race' and social policy in Britain, and there are very few black faces amongst the academic social policy community. The question of 'race' is marginalized to the edge of the social science disciplines to an even greater extent than gender and class. The race relations industry and anti-racist movements and struggles nevertheless keep the issues on the policy agenda.

This chapter has sought to demonstrate that three pillars of the post-war British welfare state – social security, health care and family policy – embraced an ideology of welfare citizenship, grafted onto the class structure and espousing patriarchal and colonial notions of Family and Nation. The Liberal Collectivist welfare state up to the 1970s was therefore built upon a series of contradictions between ideology and reality, such as: the commitment to the social minimum, and the reality of mass poverty and labour disciplinary social security measures; the commitment to a full-time domestic welfare role for women, and the reality of the demand for women's paid labour; the commitment to welfare citizenship for migrant workers from the former colonies, and the reality of entrenched subjective, institutional and structural racism. These contradictions were juggled relatively convincingly up to the early 1970s, and rather less so since. As in many other states, since the early 1970s a number of factors have forced a restructuring and retrenchment of the welfare state. These factors include the tax backlash against welfare state inefficiency and the alleged inflationary effects of welfare spending and the return of mass unemployment. The weakness of the British economy meant that these developments were experienced more intensely in Britain than in many other advanced capitalist states. Restructuring and retrenchment of the welfare state have frequently been resisted by the insistent articulation of welfare needs by welfare consumers, professionals and workers as well as by the poverty lobby and the new social movements amongst women, black people and other groups.

Under the Conservative governments since 1979 a fitful but intense struggle over the welfare state has raged, as the Thatcherites attempted with some success to move towards a more centralized version of the US welfare state with more or less publicly regulated private welfare provisions. The notion that local and central government should be a regulator and enabler of private welfare forms (both for profit and not for profit) is now widely accepted, way beyond the think-tanks of the New Right, including many on the left. The pace of policy change has been gradual and pragmatic, but it gathered momentum with the 'third term' post-1987 reforms of social security, employment training, the NHS, education and housing. Many elements of the Liberal Collectivist ideological commitment to equity and social justice in terms of welfare provision, let alone outcome, have been diluted or have disappeared. There is little doubt that occupational social class inequalities in income, health status and other welfare parameters have widened during the 1980s. In Marxian terms the division of material welfare within the working class between higher-paid and more securely employed people on the one hand, and unemployed and low-paid people on the other hand, has widened further than at any time since the war. It is less clear what aggregate changes in gender and racial inequalities have taken place since the mid 1970s. As in the US it would seem that there has been a reinforcement and strengthening of class divisions amongst women and amongst black people. An affluent minority has gained from the enterprise economy and some market-led equality of opportunity, while at the other extreme an underclass including many lone mothers and young black people has suffered increasing poverty and social isolation.

However, despite the significant shifts in such directions under Thatcherism, it can still be argued that important elements of Liberal Collectivism have survived. Thatcherism inadvertently succeeded in putting issues of welfare equality and needs further up the political agenda, alongside the important issues of welfare efficiency and effectiveness. The new social movements – the poverty lobby, the women's movement, anti-racist pressures, movements of disabled people and so on – have not been swept away and have had some successes in neutralizing the adverse effects of Thatcherite measures, and where possible in manipulating them to their advantage. Hence Taylor-Gooby (1985: 63), writing in the mid 1980s, suggested that the first five years of Thatcherite social policy showed more continuities than differences with the past. Appraisals of the Thatcherite 'experiment' in social policy range very widely. Johnson (1990), for example, emphasizes Thatcherite 'success' in reconstructing the welfare state by privatizing welfare needs and services, in promoting social inequalities and in making welfare administration less democratic and accountable. Such an analysis is akin to that offered in this chapter. In marked contrast, however, Le Grand (1990) suggests not only that the welfare state has survived Thatcherism largely intact, but that in some areas it has thrived and has made a major contribution to 'the economic gains of the 1980s'. It is perhaps not sufficiently appreciated that the momentum of Thatcherite social policy has certainly been slowed down by both organized and riotous pressure 'from below'. The urban uprisings of 1981 and 1985, and the anti-poll-tax 'riot' of 1990, were only the most prominent examples of significant riotous protest which prompted second thoughts amongst Conservatives. The hard slog of the welfare pressure and interest groups as well as the new social movements, often supported by the liberal media and the churches, helped to undermine support for Thatcherite conservatism which contributed to the demise of its leader in November 1990. At the time of writing (June 1991), the future direction of social policy in Britain is uncertain, but a moderate shift either back towards Liberal Collectivism or forward towards Social Market corporatism seems possible. Fully assessing the impact of the policy changes of the late 1980s will only be possible in the mid 1990s, so that it is too early to form a judgement as to how deep and how lasting will be the transformation of Liberal Collectivism by Thatcherism.

In the 1990s the British welfare state is likely to continue moving hesitantly away from post-war Liberal Collectivism and towards state regulated private welfare, in both for-profit and not-for-profit forms. The opposition parties profess varying degrees of commitment to greater accountability in the welfare state and greater equality of opportunity and outcome, but there is little support for the Swedish Social Democratic model. The model of the FRG is based on a mixed economy of welfare unique to the German context, which could not easily be transplanted to Britain. On the New Right there is apparently increasing impatience for a yet more radical Thatcherite approach to the welfare state for the mid 1990s and beyond. In September 1990 a prominent group of New Right Conservative MPs, apparently prompted by Mrs Thatcher, produced outline proposals for the complete privatization of the welfare state, with social security and health care to be based on private insurance and with a voucher scheme for a completely private education system (CPC, 1990). Such proposals have surfaced regularly over the post-war decades, but support for them has undoubtedly grown within the Conservative Party. However, the extent of that support within the party and amongst the electorate looks quite limited, as shown by the tentative moves of the Major government back towards consensual one nation Toryism since November 1990. One thing is certain, the struggle over the British welfare state will be long and hard during the 1990s.

6

Divisions of Welfare: Past, Present and Future

During the 1970s and 1980s the four welfare states examined here all came under increasing pressure, caught in a vice of increasing demand for benefits and services and decreasing supply of resources. In the labour market the end of 'full' employment and the growth of informal, intermittent and part-time paid employment upset the social insurance basis of benefits systems. Poverty amongst unemployed people was rediscovered. In family policy, the expansion of women's paid employment and the emergence of women's movements challenged the patriarchal basis of social policy. Increasingly women have shouldered a dual burden of paid employment and unpaid caring work at home. The costs and expectations of health care systems have expanded immensely driven by technological, professional, demographic and consumer pressure. To a greater extent in Britain and the US, and to a lesser extent in Sweden and the FRG, funding for direct public provision of welfare benefits and services has been retrenched, despite the increasing demands. Attempts to achieve greater economic efficiency in the welfare state by tighter bureaucratic regulation and elements of privatization have not had spectacular success on their own terms. The outcome is that social inequalities in welfare appear to have widened during the 1970s and 1980s. Here we have focused on social class, gender and racial inequalities. There is considerable evidence that, in the recent period, the relatively affluent middle class and skilled working class have successfully defended their share of the welfare state, while a very substantial minority of the working class have suffered a decline in their share of social welfare relative to their needs. The rights of women within the welfare states have generally improved over the two decades, but gender inequalities and segregation in the labour market have not altered significantly. A new patriarchy has emerged with women more dependent on the welfare state and/or modest income from paid employment, and less dependent on men. Racial inequalities in access to and needs for welfare benefits and services remain acute in all four states, and the evidence suggests that these have probably worsened in the past two decades. This issue hardly seems to be on the social policy agenda in Sweden and the FRG. In the US and Britain, the issue appears on the agenda but much more effective anti-racist policies are required just to correct the underlying trends. The welfare state has therefore become more socially unjust, while not apparently becoming more economically efficient. Despite retrenchment of the welfare state, sustained economic growth in the future looks uncertain in all four states for a whole number of reasons extraneous to domestic social policy. Without the cushion of the welfare state, our four regimes would have experienced much more severe social strife and resorted to much more authoritarian responses to stifle welfare demands over the last two decades. Liberal democratic regimes are utterly dependent on the welfare state for their economic and political survival. Yet, to some extent, the ideological and economic costs of the welfare state are a drain on the dynamism of corporate and competitive capitalist economic activity. This is a dilemma or, if you prefer, a contradiction which will never wither, at least in a capitalist context.

The future of all four of the welfare states examined here, viewed from 1991, looks increasingly uncertain. There seems little likelihood of a return to the political and economic conditions which sustained the post-war expansion of the welfare state; the post-war class 'settlements' embodied in the welfare consensuses continue to wither away. Sustained economic growth over a long period seems unlikely in view of ecological factors and growing pressures on the West from the peoples of Eastern Europe and the underdeveloped world. However, as for example Mishra (1990) suggests, Western governments have so far coped in diverse and sophisticated ways with the conflicting pressures of welfare demand and supply. In Sweden, the debate on the future of the welfare state has intensified with the economic crisis of the early 1990s, and there is an apparently growing acceptance that the limits of the welfare state have been reached and that further retrenchment will be required. However implementation of such measures will be gradual and firmly contested by the labour movement and the new social movements. In the FRG, the future of the welfare state will obviously be dominated by the absorption of the peoples of the former German Democratic Republic. This process is creating enormously increased demand pressures on the welfare state – notably a huge rise in unemployment and the great difference in living standards between West and East. The optimism of the moment of unification has quickly faded and it looks increasingly unlikely that the ideology of the Social Market Economy is adequate to the task of meeting the welfare demands of the East German people. In the US the retrenchment and privatization of welfare benefits and services continues under the Bush administration, while the struggle to defend welfare, civil and women's rights continues to limit the damage. The New Right has been unable fundamentally to reverse the welfare state, but welfare liberalism is also in retreat. Visibly increasing social divisions between the 'haves' and the 'have-nots' seem to provoke increasingly repressive responses from the 'haves' and increasingly criminal responses from the 'have-nots'. In Britain the shift in the social policy consensus since the mid 1970s has probably been the most dramatic amongst the welfare states examined here. The restructuring of the welfare state, particularly under Thatcherism, has increased inequalities between the social classes, as well as within the working class. The positions of women and black people within the welfare state have improved in some respects, and worsened in others. As of 1991, the future trajectory of the welfare state in Britain could take a number of different directions – pan-European corporatism, a revived Liberal Collectivism or a friendlier form of Thatcherism. Some awkward combination of the three seems most likely.

In the EC the completion of the single market by the end of 1992 and the debate around the Social Charter has prompted remarkably little discussion about their wider impact on social policy, at least in Britain. The British government has had some success in watering down the Social Charter of basic employment rights for workers to a minimum level. Nevertheless the commitment of the European Commission to the idea of a Social Charter and a *Social* Market in Europe has provided a political wedge for corporatist elements within the British labour movement and all three mainstream political parties. Over the past two decades employment-related directives from the Commission and judgements in the European Court have had some impact in progressively reforming social rights in Britain, particularly for women workers. The Swedish government has applied to join the EC, reflecting realistic fears about the withdrawal of domestic capital investment to shelter inside the twelve. No doubt Swedish capital hopes that intra-EC competition will force down Swedish taxation and the financial burden of the welfare state. On the face of it, therefore, a considerable harmonization of social policy within an expanded EC would seem likely in the near future. However in view of the great diversity of the welfare state regimes in Sweden, the FRG and Britain discussed here, such a development seems unlikely. This is particularly so, when one reflects on the socioeconomic differences between the relatively rich and economically successful regions of the EC (the Paris–Frankfurt–Milan triangle) and the relatively poor and economically less successful regions (on the geographical periphery). The latter regions can only compete with the former if they can offer lower labour costs and lower rates of taxation, which translates into lower standards of living and of social welfare. The most likely prospect is a United States of Europe with a single economic market, but a great diversity of social policies between the constituent states, a scenario discussed in more depth by Leibfried (1991). This might look very similar to the situation in the US, which in this respect is perhaps a 'working' model for the future of European social policy.

The impact of EC development and 1992 for institutional racism in Western Europe is particularly worrying. Social Europe has paid very little attention to the rights and treatment of ethnic minorities, and few states even have basic anti-discrimination legislation. The imminent implementation of tougher pan-European immigration controls and procedures is part of the development of

a common culture of European racism, which defines all Third World people as immigrants and refugees, and all immigrants and refugees as terrorists and drug-runners, will not be able to tell a citizen from an immigrant or an immigrant from a refugee, let alone one black from another. They all carry their passports on their faces. And it is these aspects of the emergence of an institutionalised racism on a pan-European basis, fomenting and fomented by popular racism, that portend the drift towards an authoritarian European state. (Sivanandan, 1991: v)

Webber (1991) and Bunyan (1991) have charted the strengthening of racist immigration controls and pan-European policing in recent years within the EC member states. The emergence of Fortress Europe therefore has immense implications for the racialized minorities resident within its walls, as well as for the peoples outside them.

In general the study of social policy in the four states examined here as well as studies on a cross-national basis tends to marginalize questions of 'race', class and gender outcomes and the shaping of the welfare state by a racially and patriarchally structured capitalist system. This is, of course, only a reflection of the wider political context within which policy analysts work and survive. There is, however, nothing inevitable or fundamentally determined about these processes of marginalization. Critical social policy analysis has made some significant inroads into mainstream traditions in the 1980s, most notably the development of feminist analysis. This has taken place despite the generally reactionary drift of capitalist society as a whole, and the academic world in particular. With the partial retreat of the New Right, the defeat of Stalinism and the growth of Social Europe, the opportunities for critical, cross-national policy analysis have never been more promising.

Statistical Appendix

Welfare Expenditure

'Real social expenditure' is a figure adjusted for price inflation in each welfare sector, including education but not including housing expenditure; it therefore adjusts for differential changes in productivity and unit input prices in each sector, and so should be a more accurate reflection of the actual services and benefits provided. 'Real GDP' is adjusted for the general inflation level in the economy. 'Real income elasticity' is given by

$$\frac{\text{average annual \% real social expenditure growth}}{\text{average annual \% real GDP growth}}$$

It is therefore a measure of how social expenditures have fared in relation to the GDP. The lower the figure the more welfare retrenchment has taken place in relation to the performance of the economy.

Table A.1 *The growth of social expenditure as a percentage of gross domestic product*

| | Real social expenditure as % real GDP | | Real income elasticity | |
	1960	1981	1960–75	1975–81
FRG	20.4	29.2	1.8	0.6
Sweden	15.9	33.5	2.0	4.0
UK	14.8	23.1	1.9	2.5
US	11.3	20.2	2.3	0.9
OECD average 19 countries	13.7	24.3	1.7	2.1

Source: OECD, 1985b: Table 4

Benefits, Taxes and Wages

Table A.2   *Relative importance of income sources, taxes and benefits, 1980, measured by the average value of the variable as a percentage of average gross income*

Variable	FRG	Sweden	UK	US
Market incomes				
Wages and salaries	63.1	64.5	72.0	75.8
Self-employment income	16.7	3.7	4.5	6.7
Property income	1.1	2.7	2.7	5.8
Occupational pensions	2.3	0.0[1]	2.5	2.6
Total	83.3	70.8	81.7	90.8
Public cash benefits				
Child benefits	1.4	1.3	2.2	0.0
Means-tested benefits	0.6	4.4	2.1	1.3
Other benefits	14.5	23.6	12.9	6.8
Total	16.5	29.2	17.2	8.0
Other cash income	0.2	0.0	1.1	1.2
Gross income	100.0	100.0	100.0	100.0
less:				
Income tax	14.8	28.5	13.6	16.5
Payroll tax (employees)	7.7	1.2	3.3	4.5
Net cash income	77.5	70.2	83.1	79.0

[1] For technical reasons, Swedish occupational pensions are included in the public cash benefits.

Source: O'Higgins *et al.*, 1990: Table 2.1

Income Distribution

Comparative data on income distribution should take into account international variations in household or family size. Families and households in Sweden tend to be smaller than those in the US, the UK and the FRG, which have roughly similar distributions of family and household size. In general households or families with low per capita incomes tend to be large households or families, and vice versa for small units. The term 'equivalent income' is used to describe data which has been adjusted for family or household size. Some data uses households as the unit basis, and other sources use families as the base unit. Table A.3 extracts some data for 1972/3 from Sawyer (1976) and Table A.4 extracts some data for 1980 from the Luxembourg Income Study (LIS). The two tables use different statistical bases and are not directly comparable, as explained by O'Higgins *et al.* (1990: 20–1). Nevertheless they yield quite similar results in many respects. However,

in Sawyer's analysis the United Kingdom appeared to be as equal as Sweden . . . while the LIS data suggest it is significantly less equal than Sweden . . . Sawyer's data also showed West Germany to be more equal than the United States, and to have a relatively higher bottom quintile income share than the LIS data show. (O'Higgins *et al.*, 1990: 37)

Tables A.3 and A.4 confirm familiar assumptions that the net income gap between poor people and middle-income groups is widest in the US and narrowest in Sweden, with the FRG and the UK in a middle-range position. They also show that the net income gap between the most affluent and the middle-income groups is highest in the FRG and lowest in Sweden, with the US and the UK in a middle-range position.

Another parameter commonly used for comparing degrees of inequality in income distributions is the Gini coefficient, a concept explained in full by Atkinson (1974). A distribution of totally equal incomes has a Gini coefficient of zero; the Gini coefficient rises with inequality, until at total inequality it reaches the value of 100. (Sometimes a scale of zero to one is used instead.) Tables A.3 and A.4 also show Gini coefficients on the same statistical base, and they yield similar conclusions to those above. Table A.5 indicates the impact of taxation and social security benefits, showing by how much the Gini coefficient is reduced when gross and net income distributions are compared. This shows that taxation and benefits have comparatively little impact on welfare distribution in the FRG, while in the US and Sweden they have a much more significant impact, with the UK once again in a middle-range position. The performance of the US in this respect may seem surprising, though the comparatively unequal *gross* income distribution there must be taken into account. Nevertheless the taxation and benefits system in the US has a much more progressive impact than that in the FRG which has a comparably unequal distribution of gross incomes.

Table A.3 *Percentage distribution of household disposable income, adjusted for household size, 1972/3*

Quintile groups of households	FRG	Sweden	UK	US
Lowest quintile	6.5	7.3	6.1	4.9
Second quintile	10.3	14.1	12.2	10.9
Third quintile	14.9	19.0	18.4	17.5
Fourth quintile	21.9	24.7	24.0	24.6
Top quintile	46.3	35.0	39.3	42.1
Gini coefficient	38.6	27.1	32.7	36.9

Source: Sawyer, 1976: Table 10

Table A.4   *Percentage distribution of family equivalent net income among quintiles of persons, 1980*

Quintiles of persons	FRG	Sweden	UK	US
Lowest quintile	7.5	10.6	9.0	6.1
Second quintile	12.7	16.1	13.5	12.8
Third quintile	16.1	19.1	18.0	18.1
Fourth quintile	20.7	23.1	23.4	24.4
Top quintile	43.0	31.1	36.1	38.6
Gini coefficient	34.0	20.5	27.3	32.6

Source: O'Higgins *et al.*, 1990: Table 2.2

Table A.5   *Impact of taxation and social security transfers, as measured by fall in Gini coefficient between distribution of family equivalent gross income and net income amongst persons, 1980*

	Numerical fall in Gini coefficient
FRG	1.2
Sweden	4.4
UK	2.4
US	4.5

Source: O'Higgins *et al.*, 1990: Table 2.2

Income Poverty

The Luxembourg Income Study (LIS) data allows for the first time some meaningful comparisons of poverty in different welfare states. The analysis of poverty by Smeeding et al. (1990) uses the 'economic distance' concept of poverty, which is computed thus:

> Equivalent disposable income is calculated for all families, and then, attributing that income to each person in the family, the median equivalent income of all the persons in the sample is established. The poverty line is defined as half of that median. Such a line is higher than the national poverty line in some countries (e.g. the United States) and lower than the line in other countries (e.g. the existence minimum in Sweden). (Smeeding *et al.*, 1990: 58)

Table A.6 shows the economic distance poverty rate before and after the effects of transfers, that is social security benefits in cash. The high pre-transfer poverty rate in Sweden is largely accounted for by the inability of the LIS to separate out the impact of occupational pensions in Sweden. Even taking this factor into account, there is little doubt that the Swedish social transfers have by far the greatest effect in reducing poverty while in the US they have the least effect, with the UK and the FRG in between. Post-transfer poverty is virtually absent amongst old people in Sweden, but remains substantial amongst old people in the US and the UK. The reduction in poverty amongst lone parent families achieved by the benefits system is very substantial in Sweden and very slight in the US, with the UK and the FRG in an intermediate position. The impact of transfers on poverty among two parent families is comparably significant in Sweden, the FRG and the UK, but is very modest in the US.

Table A.6   *Pre- and post-transfer economic distance poverty rates for persons, 1980*

	Poverty	Total	Elderly families	Single parent families	Two parent families	Other families
				Percentage of persons who are poor in:		
FRG	Pre-transfer	28.3	80.3	34.8	12.9	20.1
	Post-transfer	6.0	9.3	18.1	3.9	5.4
	% Reduction	78.8	88.4	47.1	69.8	73.1
Sweden	Pre-transfer	41.0	98.4	55.0	21.3	30.5
	Post-transfer	5.0	0.1	9.2	5.0	7.0
	% Reduction	87.8	99.9	88.3	76.5	77.0
UK	Pre-transfer	27.9	78.6	56.3	17.6	12.1
	Post-transfer	8.8	18.1	29.1	6.5	4.1
	% Reduction	68.5	77.0	48.3	63.1	68.1
US	Pre-transfer	27.3	72.0	58.5	16.0	15.4
	Post-transfer	16.9	20.5	51.7	12.9	5.5
	% Reduction	38.1	71.5	11.6	19.4	36.4

Source: Smeeding *et al.*, 1990: Table 3.5

Old Age Pensions Expenditure and the Incomes of Elderly People

Table A.7   *Expenditure on public and private sector pensions as a percentage of gross domestic product, 1980*

	Social security	Government employee	Private occupational	Individual insurance
FRG	8.3	2.2	0.5	0.8
Sweden	9.7	1.0	0.5	0.15
UK	6.4	2.0	1.0	0.1
US	5.0	1.5	1.4	0.3
Average of 18 states	6.2	1.71	0.55	0.45

Source: Esping-Andersen, 1990: Table 4.2

Table A.8   *The public–private pension mix as a percentage of total pension expenditure, 1980*

	Social security	Public employees	Private occupational	Individual private
FRG	70.4	18.6	4.2	6.8
Sweden	85.5	8.8	4.4	1.3
UK	67.3	21.1	10.5	1.1
US	60.9	18.3	17.1	3.7
Average of 18 states	68.2	18.9	4.5	6.0

Source: Esping-Andersen, 1990: Table 4.3

Table A.9   *Sources of income among households, head sixty-five years or more (percentage of total household income)*

	Work incomes	Property assets interest	Private pension	Social security transfers
FRG (1978)	11.9	11.6	3.9	68.5
Sweden (1980)	11.1	8.8	–[1]	78.1[1]
UK (1980)	23.8	9.1	5.5	54.6
US (1980)	26.8	15.4	5.5	37.3

Totals do not add to 100.0 due to other minor sources of income.
[1] For technical reasons Swedish occupational pensions are included in social security transfers.

Source: Esping-Andersen, 1990: Table 4.4

Unemployment

Standardized unemployment rates (Table A.10) as used by OECD are percentages of the total labour force, consisting of 'civilian employees, the self-employed, unpaid family workers, professional and conscripted members of the armed forces and the unemployed'. The unemployed are defined as 'persons of working age who, in a specified period, are without work, who are available for work, and who are seeking employment for pay or profit' (OECD, 1990b: 76), which is a wider definition than national definitions which usually only cover the unemployed registered at employment offices. However, those on training schemes are not included amongst the unemployed, nor are those who have permanently withdrawn from the labour market.

Table A.10 *Standardized unemployment rates*

Average for	1964–67	1968–73	1974–79	1980–87	1989
FRG	0.6	1.0	3.2	6.0	5.5
Sweden	1.6	2.2	1.9	2.7	1.4
UK	2.5	3.3	5.0	10.5	6.4
US	4.2	4.6	6.7	7.6	5.2
OECD average	2.7	3.2	4.9	7.5	6.1

Sources: OECD, 1989a: Table 2.20; OECD, 1990a: 22

Table A.11 *Percentage of the unemployed receiving unemployment insurance benefits*

	1973	1975	1977	1979	1981	1983
FRG	56	66	54	51	55	45
Sweden	N/A	50	42	48	52	60
Great Britain	39	49	42	41	N/A	31
US	41	77	53	42	41	44

N/A not available

Source: Reubens, 1989: Table 5

Women and Paid Employment

Table A.12 *Female labour force as a percentage of total labour force*

	1950	1960	1968	1974	1980	1987	Increase 1950–87
FRG	35.1	37.3	36.1	37.2	37.8	39.3	4.2
Sweden	26.3	33.6	38.1	41.8	45.2	48.0	21.7
UK	30.7	32.7	34.7	37.4	39.2	41.4	10.7
US	28.9	32.5	36.1	38.7	42.0	44.3	15.4
OECD average	N/A	33.7	34.8	36.5	38.7	40.7	N/A

N/A not available

Sources: OECD, 1989a; Table 2.3: OECD, 1985a: Table I–2

Table A.13 *Female labour force as a percentage of the female population aged from fifteen to sixty-four*

	1950	1960	1968	1974	1980	1987	Increase 1950–87
FRG	44.3	49.2	47.1	49.8	50.0	52.0	7.7
Sweden	35.1	50.1	56.6	64.9	74.1	79.4	44.3
UK	42.9	46.1	49.8	54.3	58.3	62.6	19.7
US	37.6	42.6	46.9	52.3	59.7	65.9	22.3
OECD average	38.2	45.8	46.4	49.3	53.2	56.8	18.6

Sources: OECD, 1989a: Table 2.8; Bakker, 1988: Table 2.2

Table A.14   *Male and female unemployment as percentages of the male and female labour forces*

	1960–67		1968–73		1974–79		1980–87		1960–87	
	M	F	M	F	M	F	M	F	M	F
FRG	0.9	0.7	0.8	0.9	2.9	4.4	6.1	8.1	2.8	3.6
Sweden	1.3	2.1	2.1	2.4	1.6	2.2	2.6	2.8	1.9	2.4
UK	1.7	1.1	3.2	1.0	5.2	2.5	11.9	7.3	5.7	3.1
US	4.5	5.9	3.9	5.8	5.9	7.8	7.5	7.8	5.5	6.8
OECD average	2.4	3.1	2.5	3.5	4.0	5.5	6.6	7.8	4.0	5.0

Source: OECD, 1989a: Tables 2.16, 2.17

Table A.15   *Percentage labour force status of women with children under five*

	Not in labour force	Unemployed	Total employed
FRG (1985)	61	7	32
Sweden (1983)	18	–	82[1]
UK (1985)	61	11	29
US (1986)	46	6	48[2]

[1] Proportion of women with children under seven; school begins at seven years old.
[2] Proportion of women with children under six; school begins at six years old.

Source: Moss, 1989: Table 2

Lone Parenthood

Table A.16   *Families with children headed by a lone parent*

	Lone parent families as % of all families with children	Approx. % of lone parent families headed by a woman
FRG (1982)	11.4	84
Sweden (1983)	19.0	N/A
UK (1984	13.0	91
US (1984)	25.7	89

N/A not available

Source: Millar, 1989a: Table 1.5

Table A.17 *Percentages of lone mothers and
married mothers in paid employment*

Country	Lone mothers	Married mothers
FRG (1982)	60	42
Sweden (1979)	86	64
UK (1982–4)	39	49
US (1980)	71	60

Source: Millar, 1989a: Table 7.2

Table A.18 *Net income per adult equivalent unit
for lone parent families as a percentage of that for
two parent families,*[1] *1980*

FRG	78
Sweden	87
UK	76
US	57

[1] This provides a measure of the relative economic welfare position
of families, correcting for differences in household size.

Source: Hauser and Fischer, 1990: Table 6.2

Health Care Expenditure and Health Status

Table A.19 *Public expenditure on health care as a
percentage of total health care spending*

	1960	1975	1980	1984
FRG	67.5	80.2	79.3	78.2
Sweden	72.6	90.2	92.0	91.4
UK	85.2	90.3	90.2	88.9
US	24.7	42.5	42.5	41.4
OECD mean	61.0	76.2	79.0	78.7

Source: OECD, 1987: Table 18

Table A.20 *Total health care spending as
percentage of gross domestic product*

	1960	1975	1980	1984
FRG	4.7	7.8	7.9	8.1
Sweden	4.7	8.0	9.5	9.4
UK	3.9	5.6	5.6	5.9
US	5.3	8.6	9.5	10.7
OECD mean	4.2	7.0	7.2	7.5

Source: OECD, 1987: Table 18

Table A.21   *Public health expenditure per capita in US dollars at current prices*

	1970	1984
FRG	163	844
Sweden	309	1176
UK	140	585
US	135	678

Source: OECD, 1987: Tables 18 and 20

Table A.22   *Real elasticities of total health care expenditures to gross domestic product[1]*

	1960–75	1975–84	1980–84	1960–84
FRG	1.2	0.9	0.1	1.3
Sweden	2.4	1.6	0.02	2.7
UK	2.1	1.0	0.4	2.1
US	1.8	1.2	0.9	1.7
OECD mean	1.6	1.3	0.5	1.6

[1] Total health care expenditure is a 'real' figure, deflated by the health care price index, including both private and public spending. Gross domestic product is 'real', deflated by the GDP deflator (i.e. overall inflation). Elasticity is the ratio of real health care expenditure growth to real GDP growth in the periods specified.

Source: OECD, 1987: Table 21

Table A.23   *Health status assessed by seventeen age- and sex-specific mortality rates and infant mortality rates*

	Standardized mortality index[1] 1975	Rank	Infant mortality[2] 1983/8
FRG	1.23	10	9.1 (1988)
Sweden	0.76	1	6.8 (1985)
UK	0.91	4	9.4 (1985)
US	1.18	9	10.4 (1986)
Netherlands	0.80	2	
France	1.11	8	7.0 (1986)
Australia	1.01	5	9.2 (1984)
Italy	1.04	6	10.9 (1985)
Canada	1.08	7	9.1 (1983)
Switzerland	0.86	3	6.9 (1985)

[1] For each age- and sex-specific measure, the rate for each country has been divided by the mean for the ten countries. The standardized index is then calculated as the average of these indices for all seventeen measures.
[2] Deaths in the first year per 1000 live births.

Sources: Maxwell, 1981: Table 3-4; OECD *Economic Surveys* (annual for each country)

References

ÅBERG, R., SELÉN, J. and THAM, H. (1987) 'Economic resources' in ERIKSON, E. and ÅBERG, R. (eds.) *Welfare in Transition*, Oxford, Oxford University Press.

ACHDUT, L. and TAMIR, Y. (1990) 'Retirement and well-being among the elderly' in SMEEDING, T., O'HIGGINS, M. and RAINWATER, L. (eds.) *Poverty, Inequality and Income Distribution in Comparative Perspective*, Hemel Hempstead, Harvester Wheatsheaf.

ADAMS, C. and WINSTON, K. (1980) *Mothers at Work: Public Policies in the United States, Sweden and China*, New York, Longman.

ADAMS, P. (1989) 'Family policy and labour migration in East and West Germany' *Social Service Review*, 63, 2.

ALBER, J. (1983) 'Some causes of social security expenditure development in Western Europe 1949–1977' in LONEY, M., BOSWELL, D. and CLARKE, J. (eds.) *Social Policy and Social Welfare*, Milton Keynes, Open University Press.

ALBER, J. (1986) 'Germany' in FLORA, P. (ed.) *Growth to Limits*, vol. 2, Berlin, de Gruyter.

ALCOCK, P. (1987) *Poverty and State Support*, London, Longman.

ALFORD, R. (1975) *Health Care Politics*, Chicago, University of Chicago Press.

ALLSOP, J. (1989) 'Health' in McCARTHY, M. (ed.) *The New Politics of Welfare: An Agenda for the 1990s?* Basingstoke, Macmillan.

AMENTA, E. and SKOCPOL, T. (1989) 'Taking exception: explaining the distinctiveness of American public policies' in CASTLES, F. (ed.) *The Comparative History of Public Policy*, Cambridge, Polity Press.

ANDERSON, O. (1972) *Health Care: Can There Be Equity?* New York, John Wiley.

ARDAGH, J. (1987) *Germany and the Germans*, London, Hamish Hamilton.

ASCHENBAUM, W. (1986) *Social Security: Visions and Revisions*, Cambridge, Cambridge University Press.

ASHFORD, D. (1986) *The Emergence of the Welfare States*, Oxford, Blackwell.

ASRAT-GIRMA (1986) 'Afro-Caribbean children in day care' in AHMED, S., CHEETHAM, J. and SMALL, J. (eds.) *Social Work with Black Children and their Families*, London, Batsford.

ATKINSON, A.B. (1974) 'Poverty and income inequality in Britain' in WEDDERBURN, D. (ed.) *Poverty, Inequality and Class Structure*, Cambridge, Cambridge University Press.

ATKINSON, A.B. and MICKLEWRIGHT, J. (1989) 'Turning the screw: benefits for the unemployed, 1979–1988' in ATKINSON, A.B. (ed.) *Poverty and Social Security*, Hemel Hempstead, Harvester Wheatsheaf.

BAKKER, I. (1988) 'Women's employment in comparative perspective' in JENSON, J., HAGEN, E. and REDDY, C. (eds.) *Feminization of the Labor Force*, Cambridge, Polity Press.

BALDWIN, P. (1990) *The Politics of Social Solidarity: Class Bases of the European Welfare State*, Cambridge, Cambridge University Press.

BALL, W. and SOLOMOS, J. (1990) *Race and Local Politics*, Basingstoke, Macmillan.

BARRETT, M. and McINTOSH, M. (1982) *The Anti-social Family*, London, Verso.

BAWDEN, D.L. and PALMER, J. (1984) 'Social policy: challenging the welfare state' in PALMER, J. and SAWHILL, I. (eds.) *The Reagan Record*, Cambridge (MA), Ballinger.

BAXTER, C. and BAXTER, D. (1988) 'Racial inequalities in health: a challenge to the British National Health Service' *International Journal of Health Services*, 18, 4.

BEECHEY, V. and PERKINS, T. (1987) *A Matter of Hours: Women, Part-time Work and the Labour Market*, Cambridge, Polity Press.

BEN-TOVIM, G., GABRIEL, J., LAW, I. and STREDDER, K. (1986) *The Local Politics of Race*, Basingstoke, Macmillan.

BERFENSTAM, R. and WILLIAM-OLSSON, I. (1973) *Early Child Care in Sweden*, London, Gordon and Breach.

BERGSTRAND, C. (1982) 'Big profit in private hospitals' *Social Policy*, Fall.

BERNSTEIN, B. (1984) 'Welfare dependency' in BAWDEN, D.L. (ed.) *The Social Contract Revisited*, Washington DC, Urban Institute Press.

BJORKLUND, A. and HOLMLUND, B. (1990) 'Unemployment policy: lessons from Sweden' *Economic Review*, January.

BJÖRKMAN, J.W. (1989) 'Politicizing medicine and medicalizing politics: physician power in the US' in FREDDI, G. and BJÖRKMAN, J.W. (eds.) *Controlling Medical Professionals*, London, Sage.

BLOCK, F. (1987) 'Social policy and accumulation: a critique of the new consensus' in REIN, M., ESPING-ANDERSEN, G. and RAINWATER, L. (eds.) *Stagnation and Renewal in Social Policy*, Armonk (NY), M.E. Sharpe.

BODENHEIMER, T. (1989) 'US health policy in the austerity era' *Social Science and Medicine*, 28, 6.

BORCHORST, A. and SIIM, B. (1987) 'Women and the advanced welfare state – new kind of patriarchal power?' in SASSOON, A. (ed.) *Women and the State*, London, Hutchinson.

BRANDES, S. (1976) *American Welfare Capitalism 1880–1940*, Chicago, University of Chicago Press.

BRAUNS, H.-J. and KRAMER, D. (1989) 'West Germany: the break up of consensus' in MUNDAY, B. (ed.) *The Crisis in Welfare*, Hemel Hempstead, Harvester Wheatsheaf.

BREUGHEL, I. (1989) 'Sex and race in the labour market' *Feminist Review*, 32, Summer.

BRINDLE, D. (1990) 'Firms "cannot afford child care" ' *The Guardian*, April 25th.

BROBERG, A. and HWANG, P. (1991) 'Day care for young children in Sweden' in MELHUISH, E. and MOSS, P. (eds.) *Day Care for Young Children*, London, Routledge.

BROWN, E.R. (1979) *Rockefeller Medicine Men*, Berkeley, University of California Press.

BROWN, J. (1990) *Child Benefit: Options for the 1990s*, London, Save Child Benefit and Child Poverty Action Group.

BROWN, J. and SMALL, S. (1985) *Occupational Benefits as Social Security*, London, Policy Studies Institute.

BRYAN, B., DADZIE, S. and SCAFE, S. (1985) *The Heart of the Race: Black Women's Lives in Britain*, London, Virago.

BUNYAN, T. (1991) 'Towards an authoritarian European state' *Race and Class*, 32, 3.

BURGHES, L. (1987) *Made in the USA: A Review of Workfare*, London, Unemployment Unit.

BURTON, J. (1988) 'Workfare: ethics and efficiency' *Economic Affairs*, April/May.

CARENS, J. (1988) 'Immigration and the welfare state' in GUTMAN, A. (ed.) *Democracy and the Welfare State*, Princeton (NJ), Princeton University Press.

CARR-HILL, R. (1989) 'Inequalities in health: the country debate' in FOX, J. (ed.) *Health Inequalities in European Countries*, Aldershot, Gower.

CASTLES, F. (1982) 'The impact of parties on public expenditure' in CASTLES, F. (ed.) *The Impact of Parties*, London, Sage.

CASTLES, F. (1989) (ed.) *The Comparative History of Public Policy*, Cambridge, Polity Press.

CASTLES, S. (1984) *Here for Good: Western Europe's New Ethnic Minorities*, London, Pluto Press.

CASTLES, S. and KOSACK, W. (1973) *Immigrant Workers and Class Structure in Western Europe*, Oxford, Oxford University Press.

CLARKE, S. (1988) 'Overaccumulation, class struggle and the regulation approach' *Capital and Class*, 36, Winter.

COCKBURN, C. (1987) *Two-Track Training: Sex Inequalities and the Youth Training Scheme*, Basingstoke, Macmillan.

COHEN, B. (1988) *Caring for Children: Services and Policies for Childcare and Equal Opportunities in the United Kingdom*, London, Commission of the European Communities.

COHEN, S. (1982) *From Ill Treatment to No Treatment*, Manchester, Manchester Law Centre Immigration Handbook 6.

COLLINS, S. (1983) 'The making of the black middle class' *Social Problems*, 30, 4.

COOK, J. and WATT, S. (1987) 'Racism, women and poverty' in GLENDINNING, C. and MILLAR, J. (eds.) *Women and Poverty in Britain*, Brighton, Wheatsheaf.

CPC (1990) *Choice and Responsibility: The Enabling State*, London, Conservative Political Centre.

CRE (1990) *Commission for Racial Equality: Annual Report 1989*, London, CRE.

CSO (1988) 'The effects of taxes and benefits on household income, 1986' *Economic Trends*, December.

CSO (1989) *Social Trends 1989*, London, Central Statistical Office, HMSO.

CSO (1990a) *Social Trends 1990*, London, Central Statistical Office, HMSO.

CSO (1990b) 'The effects of taxes and benefits on household income, 1987' *Economic Trends*, May.

DAHLERUP, D. (1987) 'Confusing concepts – confusing reality: a theoretical discussion of the patriarchal state' in SASSOON, A. (ed.) *Women and the State*, London, Hutchinson.

DAHLGREN, G. and DIDERICHSEN, F. (1986) 'Strategies for equity in health: report from Sweden' *International Journal of Health Services*, 16, 4.

DANIEL, W. (1980) *Maternity Rights: The Experience of Women*, London, Policy Studies Institute.

DAVID, M. (1983) 'Sexual morality and the new right' *Critical Social Policy*, 2, 3.

DAVIDSON, N. (1987) *A Question of Care: The Changing Face of the National Health Service*, London, Michael Joseph.

DEPPE, H.-U. (1989) 'State and health' *Social Science and Medicine*, 28, 11.

DERBYSHIRE, I. (1987) *Politics in West Germany*, London, Chambers.

DES (1972) *Education: A Framework for Expansion*, White Paper, Cmnd 5174, London, Department of Education and Science, HMSO.

DEX, S. and SHAW, L. (1986) *British and American Women at Work*, Basingstoke, Macmillan.

DHSS (1976) *Low Cost Day Care Provision for the Under Fives*, London, Department of Health and Social Security, HMSO.

DIDERICHSEN, F. (1982) 'Ideologies in the Swedish health sector today' *International Journal of Health Services*, 12, 2.

DIDERICHSEN, F. and LINDBERG, G. (1989) 'Better health – but not for all' *International Journal of Health Services*, 19, 2.

DiNITTO, D. and DYE, T. (1983) *Social Welfare: Politics and Public Policy*, Englewood Cliffs (NJ), Prentice-Hall.

DOH (1989) *Working for Patients*, White Paper, Cm 555, London, Department of Health, HMSO.

DONOVAN, J. (1986) *We Don't Buy Sickness, It Just Comes: Health, Illness and Health Care in the Lives of Black People in London*, Aldershot, Gower.

DOYAL, L. (1985) 'Women and the National Health Service: the carers and the careless' in LEWIN, E. and OLESEN, V. (eds.) *Women, Health and Healing*, London, Tavistock.

DOYAL, L. and ELSTON, M.A. (1986) 'Women, health and medicine' in BEECHEY, V. and WHITELEGG, E. (eds.) *Women in Britain Today*, Milton Keynes, Open University Press.

DOYAL, L., HUNT, G. and MELLOR, J. (1981) 'Your life in their hands: migrant workers in the National Health Service' *Critical Social Policy*, 1, 2.

DSS (1990) *Support for Lone-Parent Families*, Department of Social Security, House of Commons Paper 328, London, HMSO.

DUENSING, E. (1988) *America's Elderly: A Sourcebook*, New Brunswick (NJ), Centre for Urban Policy Research.

DUNLEAVY, P. (1989) 'The United Kingdom: paradoxes of an ungrounded statism' in CASTLES, F. (ed.) *The Comparative History of Public Policy*, Cambridge, Polity Press.

EC (1989) *Poverty in Europe*, unpublished study, European Commission.

ECONOMIST (1990) 'School desegregation: magnet bribes' *The Economist*, April 28th.

EDSALL, T. (1984) *The New Politics of Inequality*, New York, W.W. Norton.

EDYE, D. (1987) *Immigrant Labour and Government Policy*, Aldershot, Gower.

EHRENREICH, B. and ENGLISH, D. (1979) *For Her Own Good: 150 Years of the Experts' Advice to Women*, London, Pluto Press.

EISENSTEIN, Z. (1984) *Feminism and Social Equality*, New York, Monthly Review Press.

ELLIS, K. and PETCHESKY, R. (1972) 'Children of the corporate dream: an analysis of day care as a political issue under capitalism' *Socialist Revolution* (San Francisco), 2, 6.

ERIKSON, R. (1987) 'Disparities in mortality' in ERIKSON, E. and ÅBERG, R. (eds.) *Welfare in Transition*, Oxford, Oxford University Press.

ERLER, G. (1988) 'The German paradox: non-feminization of the labor force and post-industrial social policies' in JENSON, J., HAGEN, E. and REDDY, C. (eds.) *Feminization of the Labor Force*, Cambridge, Polity Press.

ESPING-ANDERSEN, G. (1990) *Three Worlds of Welfare Capitalism*, Cambridge, Polity Press.

FARLEY, R. (1984) *Blacks and Whites: Narrowing the Gap?*, Cambridge (MA), Harvard University Press.

FEDERATION OF GERMAN PENSIONS INSURANCE INSTITUTES (1988) 'Evolution in the structure of employment and its consequences for general pensions schemes' *International Social Security Review*, 3.

FEINMANN, J. (1989) 'Doctors' dilemmas' *New Statesman and Society*, March 17th.

FIELD, F. (1982) *Poverty and Politics*, London, Heinemann.

FINER, M. (1974) *Report of the Committee on One-Parent Families*, vol. 1, Cmnd 5629, London, HMSO.

FINN, D. (1987) *Training Without Jobs: New Deals and Broken Promises*, Basingstoke, Macmillan.

FORMAN, M. (1983) 'Social security is a women's issue' *Social Policy* (US), Summer.

FOSTER, P. (1989) 'Improving the doctor/patient relationship: a feminist perspective' *Journal of Social Policy*, 18, 3.

FRANCOME, C. (1986) *Abortion Practice in Britain and the US*, London, Allen and Unwin.

FRIEDMAN, R., GILBERT, N. and SHERER, M. (eds.) (1987) *Modern Welfare States*, Brighton, Wheatsheaf.

FURMANIAK, K. (1984) 'West Germany: poverty, unemployment and social insurance' in WALKER, R., LAWSON, R. and TOWNSEND, P. (eds.) *Responses to Poverty*, London, Heinemann.

GEBHARDT-BENISCHE, M. (1986) 'Family law, family law politics and family politics' *Women's Studies International Forum*, 9, 1.

GEORGE, V. and WILDING, P. (1985) *Ideology and Social Welfare*, London, Routledge.

GIBBON, P. (1990) 'Equal opportunities policy and race equality' *Critical Social Policy*, 28, Summer.

GIDDENS, A. (1979) *Central Problems in Social Theory*, Basingstoke, Macmillan.

GILDER, G. (1981) *Wealth and Poverty*, New York, Basic Books.

GILROY, P. (1987) *There ain't No Black in the Union Jack*, London, Hutchinson.

GIMENEZ, M. (1989) 'The feminization of poverty: myth or reality?' *International Journal of Health Services*, 19, 1.

GINSBURG, N. (1979) *Class, Capital and Social Policy*, London, Macmillan.

GINSBURG, N. (1989) 'Institutional racism and local authority housing' *Critical Social Policy*, 24.

GLASGOW, D. (1980) *The Black Underclass*, San Francisco, Jossey-Bass.

GLAZER, N. (1986) 'Welfare and "welfare" in America' in ROSE, R. and SHIRATORI, R. (eds.) *The Welfare State East and West*, New York, Oxford University Press.

GORDON, D., EDWARDS, R. and REICH, M. (1982) *Segmented Work, Divided Workers*, Cambridge, Cambridge University Press.

GORDON, L. (1977) *Woman's Body, Woman's Right: A Social History of Birth Control in America*, Harmondsworth, Penguin.

GORDON, L. (1988) 'What does welfare regulate?' *Social Research*, 55, 4.

GORDON, M. (1988) *Social Security Policies in Industrial Countries*, Cambridge, Cambridge University Press.

GORDON, P. (1985) *Policing Immigration: Britain's Internal Controls*, London, Pluto Press.

GORDON, P. (1986) 'Racism and social security' *Critical Social Policy*, 17, Autumn.

GORDON, P. and NEWNHAM, A. (1985) *Passport to Benefits: Racism in Social Security*, London, Child Poverty Action Group and the Runnymede Trust.

GOUGH, I. (1979) *The Political Economy of the Welfare State*, Basingstoke, Macmillan.

GOULD, A. (1988) *Control and Conflict in Welfare Policy: The Swedish Experience*, Harlow, Longman.

GRAF, W. (1986) 'Beyond social democracy in Germany?' in MILIBAND, R., SAVILE, J. and LIEBMAN, M. (eds.) *Socialist Register 1985/6*, London, Merlin Press.

GRAHAM, H. and OAKLEY, A. (1981) 'Comparing ideologies of reproduction: medical and maternal perspectives on pregnancy' in ROBERTS, H. (ed.) *Women, Health and Reproduction*, London, Routledge.

GREENWOOD, V. and YOUNG, J. (1976) *Abortion in Demand*, London, Pluto Press.

GRIFFITHS, R. (1983) *Report of the NHS Management Inquiry*, London, DHSS, HMSO.

GRIMSLEY, M. and BHAT, A. (1988) 'Health' in BHAT, A., CARR-HILL, R. and OHRI, S. (eds.) *Britain's Black Population: A New Perspective*, Aldershot, Gower.

GROVES, D. (1987) 'Occupational pension provision and women's poverty in old age' in GLENDINNING, C. and MILLAR, J. (eds.) *Women and Poverty in Britain*, Brighton, Wheatsheaf.

GRUNOW, D. (1986) 'Debureaucratisation and the self-help movement: towards a restructuring of the welfare state in the FRG?' in OYEN, E. (ed.) *Comparing Welfare States*, Aldershot, Gower.

HAKIM, C. (1989) 'Workforce restructuring, social insurance coverage and the black economy' *Journal of Social Policy*, 18, 4.

HALLETT, G. (1985) 'Unemployment and labour market policies: some lessons from West Germany' *Social Policy and Administration*, 19, 3.

HAMMAR, T. (1984) 'Sweden' in HAMMAR, T. (ed.) *European Immigration Policy*, Cambridge, Cambridge University Press.

HANSON, R. (1987) 'The expansion and contraction of the American welfare state' in GOODIN, R. and LE GRAND, J. (eds.) *Not Only the Poor*, London, Allen and Unwin.

HARPER, K. (1990) 'Where have all the unemployed gone?' *The Guardian*, June 8th.

HAUG, F. (1986) 'The women's movement in West Germany' *New Left Review*, 155.

HAUSER, R. and FISCHER, I. (1990) 'Economic well-being among one-parent families' in SMEEDING, T., O'HIGGINS, M. and RAINWATER, L. (eds.) *Poverty, Inequality and Income Distribution in Comparative Perspective*, New York, Harvester Wheatsheaf.

HECLO, H. (1974) *Modern Social Politics in Britain and Sweden*, New Haven, Yale University Press.

HECLO, H. and MADSEN, H. (1987) *Policy and Politics in Sweden*, Philadelphia, Temple University Press.

HEDSTRÖM, P. and RINGEN, S. (1990) 'Age and income in contemporary society' in SMEEDING, T., O'HIGGINS, M. and RAINWATER, L. (eds.) *Poverty, Inequality and Income Distribution in Comparative Perspective*, Hemel Hempstead, Harvester Wheatsheaf.

HEIDENHEIMER, A., HECLO, H. and ADAMS, C. (1990) *Comparative Public Policy: The Politics of Social Choice in America, Europe and Japan*, 3rd edn, New York, St Martin's Press.

HERNES, H. (1987) 'Women and the welfare state: the transition from private to public dependence' in SASSOON, A. (ed.) *Women and the State*, London, Hutchinson.

HESSE, B. (1984) 'Women at work in the Federal Republic of Germany' in DAVIDSON, M. and COOPER, C. (eds.) *Women at Work*, New York, John Wiley.

HEWLETT, S. (1987) *A Lesser Life: The Myth of Women's Liberation*, London, Michael Joseph.

HIGGINS, J. (1981) *States of Welfare*, London, Heinemann.

HIGGINS, J. (1986) 'Comparative social policy' *Quarterly Journal of Social Affairs*, 2, 3.

HIGGINS, J. (1988) *The Business of Medicine: Private Health Care in Britain*, Basingstoke, Macmillan.

HILL, R. (1988) 'Cash and noncash benefits among poor black families' in McADOO, H. PIPES (ed.) *Black Families*, Newbury Park (CA), Sage.

HILLS, J. (1990) (ed.) *The State of Welfare: The Welfare State in Britain Since 1974*, Oxford, Oxford University Press.

HIMMELSTEIN, D. and WOOLHANDLER, S. (1984) 'Medicine as industry: the health-care sector in the United States' *Monthly Review*, April.

HIRSCH, J. (1980) 'Developments in the political system of West Germany since 1945' in SCASE, R. (ed.) *The State in Western Europe*, London, Croom Helm.

HM TREASURY (1989) *The Government's Expenditure Plans 1989–90 to 1991–92*, Chapter 21 'Supplementary analyses and index', London, HMSO.

HOCHSCHILD, J. (1988) 'Race, class, power and the welfare state' in GUTMAN, A. (ed.) *Democracy and the Welfare State*, Princeton (NJ), Princeton University Press.

HOGWOOD, B. (1989) 'The hidden face of public expenditure: trends in tax expenditures in Britain' *Policy and Politics*, 17, 2.

HOSKYNS, C. (1988) ' "Give us equal pay and we'll open our own doors" ' in BUCKLEY, M. and ANDERSON, M. (eds.) *Women, Equality and Europe*, Basingstoke, Macmillan.

HOUSE OF COMMONS (1990) *The Income Support System and the Distribution of Income*, Report of the Select Committee on Social Services, London, HMSO.

HOUSE OF LORDS (1989) *Equal Treatment for Men and Women in Pensions and Other Benefits*, 10th Report of the House of Lords Select Committee on the European Communities, 1988–9 Session, London, HMSO.

HUHNE, C. (1989) 'Useful reforms, but the health service is still anaemic' *The Guardian*, February 15th, p. 14.

JENKINS, R. (1988) 'Discrimination and equal opportunity in employment: ethnicity and race in the UK' in GALLIE, D. (ed.) *Employment in Britain*, Oxford, Basil Blackwell.

JNPRU (1990) *The NHS Privatisation Experience*, London, Joint NHS Privatisation Research Unit.

JOHNSON, N. (1990) *Reconstructing the Welfare State*, Hemel Hempstead, Harvester Wheatsheaf.

JOHNSON, P. and WEBB, S. (1989) 'Counting people with low incomes: the impact of recent changes in official statistics' *Fiscal Studies*, 10, 4.

JONES, C. (1985) *Patterns of Social Policy*, London, Tavistock.

KAHN, A. and KAMERMAN, S. (1987) *Child Care: Facing the Hard Choices*, Dover (MA), Auburn House.

KAMERMAN, S. and KAHN, A. (1978) (eds.) *Family Policy: Government and Families in Fourteen Countries*, New York, Columbia University Press.

KATZNELSON, I. and KESSELMAN, M. (1979) *The Politics of Power*, New York, Harcourt Brace Jovanovich.

KAYE, G. (1987) 'Current regulation' in BENJAMIN, B., HABERMAN, S., HELOWICZ, G., KAYE, G. and WILKIE, D. *Pensions: The Problems of Today and Tomorrow*, London, Allen and Unwin.

KEINER, G. (1986) 'The question of induced abortion' in LIGHT, D. and SCHULLER, P. (eds.) *Political Values and Health Care*, London: MIT Press.

KERANS, P., DROVER, G. and WILLIAMS, D. (1988) *Welfare and Worker Participation*, Basingstoke, Macmillan.

KINDLUND, S. (1988) 'Sweden' in KAHN, A. and KAMERMAN, S. *Child Support: Cross-Cultural Studies*, Newbury Park (CA), Sage.

KJELLSTRÖM, S.-Å. and LUNDBERG, O. (1987) 'Health and health care utilization' in ERIKSON, E. and ÅBERG, R. (eds.) *Welfare in Transition*, Oxford, Oxford University Press.

KLEIN, R. (1989) *The Politics of the NHS*, Harlow, Longman.

KORPI, W. (1978) *The Working Class in Welfare Capitalism*, London, Routledge.

KORPI, W. (1983) *The Democratic Class Struggle*, London, Routledge.

KUSHNICK, L. (1988) 'Racism, the National Health Service and the health of black people' *International Journal of Health Services*, 18, 3.

LABOUR PARTY (1989a) *Ten years of Inequality: Britain – Europe's Poor Relation*, File on Fairness, 3, London, Labour Party.

LABOUR PARTY (1989b) *Labour Party Policy Review*, London, Labour Party.

LAND, H. (1971) 'Women, work and social security' *Social and Economic Administration*, 5, 3.

LAND, H. (1975) 'The introduction of family allowances' in HALL, P., LAND, H., PARKER, R. and WEBB, A. (eds.) *Change, Choice and Conflict in Social Policy*, London, Heinemann.

LANE, J.-E. and ARVIDSON, S. (1989) 'Health professionals in the Swedish system' in FREDDI, G. and BJÖRKMAN, J. (eds.) *Controlling Medical Professionals*, London, Sage.

LANE, M. (1974) *Report of the Committee on the Working of the Abortion Act*, vol. 1, Cmnd 5579, London, HMSO.

LARSSON, S. (1991) 'Swedish racism: the democratic way' *Race and Class*, 32, 3.

LARWOOD, L. and GUTEK, B. (1984) 'Women at work in the USA' in DAVIDSON, M. and COOPER, C. *Women at Work*, Chichester, Wiley.

LASCH, C. (1977) *Haven in a Heartless World*, New York, Basic Books.

LAWSON, R. (1980) 'Poverty and inequality in West Germany' in GEORGE, V. and LAWSON, R. (eds.) *Poverty and Inequality in Common Market Countries*, London, Routledge.

LEACH, P. (1979) *Who Cares? A New Deal for Mothers and their Small Children*, Harmondsworth, Penguin.

LEAMAN, J. (1988) *The Political Economy of West Germany 1945–1985*, Basingstoke, Macmillan.

LEE, P. and RABAN, C. (1988) *Welfare Theory and Social Policy*, London, Sage.

LE GRAND, J. (1987) 'The middle-class use of the British social services' in LE GRAND, J. and GOODIN, R. (eds.) *Not Only the Poor: The Middle Classes and the Welfare State*, London, Allen and Unwin.

LE GRAND, J. (1989) 'An international comparison of distribution of ages-at-death' in FOX, J. (ed.) *Health Inequalities in European Countries*, Aldershot, Gower.

LE GRAND, J. (1990) 'The state of welfare' in HILLS, J. (ed.) *The State of Welfare*, Oxford, Oxford University Press.

LE GRAND, J. and WINTER, D. (1987) 'The middle classes and the defence of the British welfare state' in LE GRAND, J. and GOODIN, R. (eds.) *Not Only the Poor: The Middle Classes and the Welfare State*, London, Allen and Unwin.

LEIBFRIED, S. (1979) 'Public assistance in the Federal Republic of Germany' in PARTINGTON, M. and JOWELL, J. (eds.) *Welfare Law and Policy*, London, Frances Pinter.

LEIBFRIED, S. (1991) 'Towards a European welfare state?', unpublished manuscript, Center for Social Policy Research, Bremen University.

LEUCHTENBURG, W. (1963) *Franklin D. Roosevelt and the New Deal 1932–1940*, New York, Harper and Row.

LEWIS, J. (1989) ' "It all really starts in the family . . .": community care in the 1980s' *Journal of Law and Society*, 16, 1.

LIGHT, P. (1985) *Artful Work: The Politics of Social Security Reform*, New York, Random House.

LILJESTRÖM, R. (1974) *A Study of Abortion in Sweden*, Stockholm, Royal Ministry of Foreign Affairs.

LILJESTRÖM, R. (1978) 'Sweden' in KAMERMAN, S. and KAHN, A. (eds.) *Family Policy: Government and Families in Fourteen Countries*, New York, Columbia University Press.

LINTON, M. (1984) 'By all accounts they should be bust' *The Guardian*, October 9th.

LOCK, S. (1990) 'Steaming through the NHS – time for the profession to unite' in *The NHS Review – What it Means*, London, British Medical Journal.

LONSDALE, S. (1985) *Work and Inequality*, London, Longman.

LONSDALE, S. and BYRNE, D. (1988) 'Social security: from state insurance to private uncertainty' in BRENTON, M. and UNGERSON, C. (eds.) *Year Book of Social Policy 1987–8*, Harlow, Longman.

LUBOVE, R. (1968) *The Struggle for Social Security 1900–1935*, Cambridge (MA), Harvard University Press.

LUSTGARTEN, L. (1987) 'Racial inequality and the limits of the law' in JENKINS, R. and SOLOMOS, J. (eds.) *Racism and Equal Opportunities Policies in the 1980s*, Cambridge, Cambridge University Press.

MacGREGOR, S. (1981) *The Politics of Poverty*, London, Longman.

McKINLAY, J., McKINLAY, S. and BEAGLEHOLE, R. (1989) 'A review of the evidence concerning the impact of medical measures on recent mortality and morbidity in the US' *International Journal of Health Services*, 19, 2.

MACLEAN, M. and GROVES, D. (eds.) (1991) *Women's Issues in Social Policy*, London, Routledge.

McNAUGHT, A. (1987) *Health Action and Ethnic Minorities*, London, Bedford Square Press, for the National Community Health Resource.

MACNICOL, J. (1980) *The Movement for Family Allowances, 1918-1945*, London, Heinemann.

MARABLE, M. (1983) *How Capitalism Underdeveloped Black America*, London, Pluto Press.

MARABLE, M. (1984a) 'Black families: what's in "crisis" – and what's not', *Guardian* (New York weekly), May 30th, p. 19.

MARABLE, M. (1984b) *Race, Reform and Rebellion*, London, Macmillan.

MARTIN, J. and ROBERTS, C. (1984) *Women and Employment: A Lifetime Perspective*, London, HMSO.

MAXWELL, R. (1981) *Health and Wealth*, Lexington (MA), Lexington Books.

MEACHER, M. (1989) 'Employment' in McCARTHY, M. (ed.) *The New Politics of Welfare: An Agenda for the 1990s*, Basingstoke, Macmillan.

MICKLEWRIGHT, J. (1989) 'The strange case of British earnings-related unemployment benefit' *Journal of Social Policy*, 18, 4.

MILES, R. (1989) *Racism*, London, Routledge.

MILLAR, J. (1989a) *Poverty and the Lone Parent Family*, Aldershot, Avebury.

MILLAR, J. (1989b) 'Social security, equality and women in the UK' *Policy and Politics*, 17, 4.

MILLER, S.M. and JENKINS, M. (1987) 'Challenging the American welfare state' in FERGE, Z. (ed.) *The Dynamics of Deprivation*, Aldershot, Gower Press.

MINFORD, P. (1983) *Unemployment: Cause and Cure*, Oxford, Martin Robertson.

MISHRA, R. (1984) *The Welfare State in Crisis*, Brighton, Wheatsheaf.

MISHRA, R. (1990) *The Welfare State in Capitalist Society*, Hemel Hempstead, Harvester Wheatsheaf.

MOELLER, R. (1989) 'Reconstructing the family in reconstruction Germany' *Feminist Studies*, 15, 1.

MORGAN, R. (ed.) (1984) *Sisterhood is Global*, Harmondsworth, Penguin.

MORRIS, R. (ed.) (1988) *Testing the Limits of Social Welfare*, Hanover (NH), University Press of New England.

MOSS, P. (1987) *A Review of Childminding Research*, London, Thomas Coram Research Unit.

MOSS, P. (1988) *Childcare and Equality of Opportunity*, London, The European Commission.

MOSS, P. (1989) 'The costs of parenthood' *Critical Social Policy*, 24, Winter.

MOSS, P. (1990) 'Childcare in the European Communities 1985–1990' *Women of Europe: Supplements*, 31, Brussels, Commission of the European Communities.

MOSS, P. (1991) 'Day care for young children in the United Kingdom' in MELHUISH, E. and MOSS, P. (eds.) *Day Care for Young Children*, London, Routledge.

MOYNIHAN, D. (1973) *The Politics of a Guaranteed Income*, New York, Random House.

MULLER, W. (1989) 'Germany, West' in DIXON, J. and SCHEURELL, R. (eds.) *Social Welfare in Developed Market Countries*, London, Routledge.

MURRAY, C. (1984) *Losing Ground: American Social Policy 1950–1980*, New York, Basic Books.

MURSWIECK, A. (1985) 'Health policy-making' in VON BEYME, K. (ed.) (1985) *Politics and Policy in the Federal Republic of Germany*, Aldershot, Gower.

MYRDAL, A. (1945) *Nation and Family: The Swedish Experiment in Democratic Family and Population Policy*, London, Kegan Paul.

MYRDAL, G. (1938) 'Population problems and policies' *Annals of the American Academy of Political and Social Science*, 197, March.

MYRDAL, G. (1940) *Population and Democracy*, Cambridge (MA), Harvard University Press.

NACAB (1991) *Barriers to Benefit: Black Claimants and Social Security*, London, National Association of Citizens Advice Bureaux.

NASENIUS, J. and VEIT-WILSON, J. (1985) 'Social policy in a cold climate: Sweden in the eighties' in BRENTON, M. and JONES, C. (eds.) *Yearbook of Social Policy in Britain 1984–5*, London, Routledge.

NATIONAL RAINBOW COALITION (1988) 'A national health program for the United States' *Critical Social Policy*, 22.

NAVARRO, V. (1975) *National and Regional Health Care Planning in Sweden*, US Department of Health, Education and Welfare Publication (NIH) 74-240, Washington DC, Government Printing Office.

NAVARRO, V. (1989) 'Why some countries have national health insurance, others have national health services, and the US has neither' *Social Science and Medicine*, 28, 9.

NCOPF (1990) *Barriers to Work: A Study of Lone Parents' Training and Employment Needs*, London, National Council for One Parent Families.

NECKERMAN, K., APONTE, R. and WILSON, W.J. (1988) 'Family structure, black unemployment and American social policy' in WEIR, M., ORLOFF, A.S. and SKOCPOL, T. (eds.) *The Politics of Social Policy in the United States*, Princeton (NJ), Princeton University Press.

NEIDHARDT, F. (1978) 'The Federal Republic of Germany' in KAMERMAN, S. and KAHN, A. (eds.) *Family Policy: Government and Families in 14 Countries*, New York, Columbia University Press.

NEW, C. and DAVID, M. (1985) *For the Children's Sake: Making Child Care More Than Women's Business*, Harmondsworth, Penguin.

NOLAN, B. (1989) 'An evaluation of the new official low income statistics' *Fiscal Studies*, 10, 4.

NORRIS, P. (1987) *Politics and Sexual Equality*, Brighton, Wheatsheaf.

NOVAK, T. (1988) *Poverty and the State*, Milton Keynes, The Open University Press.

O'CONNOR, J. (1973) *The Fiscal Crisis of the State*, New York, St Martin's Press.

OECD (1985a) *The Integration of Women into the Economy*, Paris, Organization for Economic Cooperation and Development.

OECD (1985b) *Social Expenditure 1960–1990*, Paris, OECD.

OECD (1987) *Financing and Delivering Health Care*, Paris, OECD.

OECD (1989a) *Historical Statistics: 1960–1987*, Paris, OECD.

OECD (1989b) *Sweden: OECD Economic Survey 1988/1989*, Paris, OECD.

OECD (1990a) *Main Economic Indicators*, April 1990, Paris, OECD.

OECD (1990b) *Quarterly Labour Force Statistics*, 1, Paris, OECD.

O'GRADY, F. and WAKEFIELD, H. (1989) *Women, Work and Maternity: The Inside Story*, London, Maternity Alliance.

O'HIGGINS, M. (1985) 'Inequality, redistribution and recession: the British experience, 1976–1982' *Journal of Social Policy*, 14, 3.

O'HIGGINS, M., SCHMAUS, G. and STEPHENSON, G. (1990) 'Income distribution and redistribution: a microdata analysis for seven countries' in SMEEDING, T., O'HIGGINS, M. and RAINWATER, L. (eds.) *Poverty, Inequality and Income Distribution in Comparative Perspective*, Hemel Hempstead, Harvester Wheatsheaf.

OHRI, S. and FARUKI, S. (1988) 'Racism, employment and unemployment' in BHAT, A., CARR-HILL, R. and OHRI, S. (eds.) *Britain's Black Population: A New Perspective*, Aldershot, Gower.

OLOFSSON, G. (1988) 'After the working-class movement: the new social movements' *Acta Sociologica*, 31, 1.

OLSSON, S. (1986) 'Sweden' in FLORA, P. (ed.) *Growth to Limits*, vol. 1, Berlin, de Gruyter.

OLSSON, S. (1987) 'Towards a transformation of the Swedish welfare state?' in FRIED-MAN, R., GILBERT, N. and SHERER, M. (eds.) *Modern Welfare States*, Brighton, Wheatsheaf.

OLSSON, S. (1989) 'Sweden' in DIXON, J. and SCHEURELL, R. (eds.) *Social Welfare in Developed Market Countries*, London, Routledge.

OPCS (1989) *Labour Force Survey 1987*, London, Office of Population Censuses and Surveys, HMSO.

OWEN, S. and JOSHI, H. (1990) 'Sex, equality and the state pension' *Fiscal Studies*, 11, 1.

PAINTIN, D. (1984) 'Late abortion – problems and possibilities' in *Abortion Services in London*, London, Women's Reproductive Rights Campaign.

PARKER, J. and MIRRLEES, C. (1988) 'Welfare' in HALSEY, A.H. (ed.) *British Social Trends since 1900*, Basingstoke, Macmillan.

PASCALL, G. (1986) *Social Policy: A Feminist Analysis*, London, Tavistock.

PEARSON, M. (1986) 'Racist notions of ethnicity and culture in health education' in RODMELL, S. and WATT, A. (eds.) *The Politics of Health Education: Raising the Issues*, London, Routledge.

PETCHESKY, R. (1984) *Abortion and Woman's Choice*, New York, Longman.

PETCHESKY, R. (1985) 'Abortion in the 1980s: feminist morality and women's health' in LEWIN, E. and OLESEN, V. (eds.) *Women, Health and Healing*, London, Tavistock.

PETCHEY, R. (1989) 'The NHS Review – the politics of destabilisation' *Critical Social Policy*, 25, Summer.

PFLANZ, M. (1971) 'German health insurance: the evolution and current problems of the pioneer system' *International Journal of Health Services*, 1, 4.

PHA (1988) *Beyond Acheson: An Agenda for the New Public Health*, Birmingham, Public Health Alliance.

PHILLIPS, D. (1991) 'Day care for young children in the United States' in MELHUISH, E. and MOSS, P. (eds.) *Day Care for Young Children*, London, Routledge.

PINKNEY, A. (1984) *The Myth of Black Progress*, Cambridge, Cambridge University Press.

PIVEN, F. and CLOWARD, R. (1971) *Regulating the Poor*, New York, Vintage.

PIVEN, F. and CLOWARD, R. (1977) *Poor People's Movements*, New York, Vintage.

PLOTNICK, R. (1989) 'How much poverty is reduced by state income transfers?' *Monthly Labor Review*, July.

PLOWDEN, B. (1967) *Children and their Primary Schools: A Report of the Central Advisory Council for Education*, London, HMSO.

PONTUSSON, J. (1984) 'Behind and beyond Social Democracy in Sweden', *New Left Review*, 143.

PONTUSSON, J. (1987) 'Radicalization and retreat in Swedish Social Democracy', *New Left Review*, 165.

POWER, M. (1988) 'Women, the state and the family in the US' in RUBERY, J. (ed.) *Women and Recession*, London, Routledge.

RAFFEL, N. (1987) 'The US health system – a brief description' in RAFFEL, M. and RAFFEL, N. (eds.) *Health Policy Formulation, Implementation and Impact*, Chichester, John Wiley.

RAPAPORT, R. and MOSS, P. (1989) *Exploring Ways of Integrating Men and Women as Equals at Work*, unpublished report to the Ford Foundation.

RÄTHZEL, N. (1991) 'Germany: one race, one nation?' *Race and Class*, 32, 3.

REA, D. (1989) 'Changing the patients' role' *Critical Social Policy*, 25, Summer.

RENNER, C. and NAVARRO, V. (1989) 'Why is our population of uninsured and underinsured persons growing?' *International Journal of Health Services*, 19, 3.

REUBENS, B. (1989) 'Unemployment insurance in the United States and Europe, 1973–83' *Monthly Labor Review*, April.

RILEY, D. (1981) 'The Free Mothers: pronatalism and working mothers in industry at the end of the last war in Britain' *History Workshop Journal*, 11, Spring.

RIMLINGER, G. (1971) *Welfare Policy and Industrialization in Europe, America and Russia*, New York, John Wiley.

ROBINSON, R. (1990) *Competition and Health Care*, London, King's Fund Institute.

ROCHERON, Y. (1988) 'The Asian Mother and Baby Campaign: the construction of ethnic minorities' health needs' *Critical Social Policy*, 22, Summer.

RODRIGUEZ-TRIAS, H. (1982) 'Sterilization abuse' in HUBBARD, R., HENIFIN, M. and FRIED, B. (eds.) *Biological Woman – the Convenient Myth*, Cambridge (MA), Schenkman.

ROSE, R. and SHIRATORI, R. (1986) *The Welfare State East and West*, New York, Oxford University Press.

ROSENBERG, P. and RUBAN, M. (1986) 'Social security and health care systems' in LIGHT, D. and SCHULLER, P. (eds.) *Political Values and Health Care*, London: MIT Press.

RUBERY, J. (1988) 'Women and recession: a comparative perspective' in RUBERY, J. (ed.) *Women and Recession*, London, Routledge.

RUBERY, J. and TARLING, R. (1988) 'Women's employment in declining Britain' in RUBERY, J. (ed.) *Women and Recession*, London, Routledge.

RUGGIE, M. (1984) *The State and Working Women*, Princeton (NJ), Princeton University Press.

RUGGIE, M. (1988) 'Gender, work and social progress' in JENSON, J., HAGEN, E. and REDDY, C. (eds.) *Feminization of the Labor Force*, Cambridge, Polity Press.

RUGGLES, P. and O'HIGGINS, M. (1987) 'Retrenchment and the New Right' in REIN, M., RAINWATER, L. and ESPING-ANDERSEN, G. *Renewal and Stagnation in Social Policy*, Armonk (NY), M.E. Sharpe.

RUZEK, S. (1978) *The Women's Health Movement*, New York, Praeger.

SAFRAN, W. (1967) *Veto-Group Politics: the Case of Health Insurance Reform in West Germany*, San Francisco, Chandler.

SALMON, W.J. (1985) 'Profit and health care: trends in corporatization and proprietization' *International Journal of Health Services*, 15, 3.

SASSOON, A. (1987) *Women and the State*, London, Hutchinson.

SAVAGE, S. and ROBINS, L. (eds.) (1990) *Public Policy under Thatcher*, Basingstoke, Macmillan.

SAVAGE, W. (1986) *A Savage Enquiry: Who Controls Childbirth?*, London, Virago.

SAVAGE, W. and FRANCOME, C. (1989) 'Gynaecologists' attitudes to abortion' *The Lancet*, December 2nd.

SAVAGE, W. and WIDGERY, D. (1989) 'Working for patients?' *New Statesman and Society*, February 10th.

SAWYER, M. (1976) *Income Distribution in OECD Countries*, Paris, Organization for Economic Cooperation and Development.

SCHMIDT, M. (1978) 'The politics of domestic reform in the Federal Republic of Germany' *Politics and Society*, 8, 2.

SCHMIDT, M. (1989) 'Learning from catastrophes: West Germany's public policy' in CASTLES, F. (ed.) *The Comparative History of Public Policy*, Cambridge, Polity Press.

SCOTT, H. (1982) *Sweden's 'Right to be Human'*, London, Allison and Busby.

SCRIVEN, J. (1984) 'Women at work in Sweden' in DAVIDSON, M. and COOPER, C. (eds.) *Women at Work*, Chichester, John Wiley.

SERNER, U. (1980) 'Swedish health legislation' in HEIDENHEIMER, A. and ELVANDER, N. (eds.) *The Shaping of the Swedish Health System*, London, Croom Helm.

SIEGRIST, J. (1989) 'Steps towards explaining social differentials in morbidity: the case of West Germany' in FOX, J. (ed.) *Health Inequalities in European Countries*, Aldershot, Gower.

SIIM, B. (1987) 'The Scandinavian welfare states – towards sexual equality or a new kind of male domination?' *Acta Sociologica*, 30, 3/4.

SIIM, B. (1988) 'Towards a feminist rethinking of the welfare state' in JONES, K.B. and JÓNASDÓTTIR, A.G. (eds) *The Political Interest of Gender*, London, Sage.

SIMMS, M. (1985) 'Legal abortion in Britain' in HOMANS, H. (ed.) *The Sexual Politics of Reproduction*, Aldershot, Gower.

SIVANANDAN, A. (1988) 'Introduction' to WALRAFF, G. *Lowest of the Low*, London, Methuen.

SIVANANDAN, A. (1991) 'Editorial' *Race and Class*, 32, 3.

SKOCPOL, T. (1987) 'America's incomplete welfare state' in REIN, M., RAINWATER, L. and ESPING-ANDERSEN, G. (eds.) *Stagnation and Renewal in Social Policy*, Armonk (NY), M.E. Sharpe.

SMEEDING, T., RAINWATER, L., REIN, M., HAUSER, R. and SCHÄBER, G. (1990) 'Income poverty in seven countries: initial estimates from the LIS database' in SMEEDING, T., O'HIGGINS, M. and RAINWATER, L. (eds.) *Poverty, Inequality and Income Distribution in Comparative Perspective*, Hemel Hempstead, Harvester Wheatsheaf.

SOLOMOS, J. (1987) 'The politics of anti-discrimination legislation: planned social reform or symbolic politics?' in JENKINS, R. and SOLOMOS, J. (eds.) *Racism and Equal Opportunities Policies in the 1980s*, Cambridge, Cambridge University Press.

SOLOMOS, J. (1989) *Race and Racism in Contemporary Britain*, Basingstoke, Macmillan.

SONTHEIMER, K. (1972) *The Government and Politics of West Germany*, London, Hutchinson.

SPRING RICE, M. (1939) *Working Class Wives: Their Health and Condition*, Harmondsworth, Penguin.

STACK, C. (1974) *All Our Kin: Strategies for Survival in a Black Community*, New York, Harper and Row.

STAPLES, C. (1989) 'The politics of employment-based insurance in the United States' *International Journal of Health Services*, 19, 3.

STARK, T. (1988) *A New A–Z of Income and Wealth*, London, Fabian Society.

STARR, P. (1982) *The Social Transformation of American Medicine*, New York, Basic Books.

STARR, P. and IMMERGUT, E. (1987) 'Health care and the boundaries of politics' in MAIER, C. (ed.) *Changing Boundaries of the Political*, Cambridge, Cambridge University Press.

STATISTISCHES JAHRBUCH (1989) *Statistisches Jahrbuch 1989 für die Bundesrepublik Deutschland*, Stuttgart, Metzler-Poeschel.

STEELE, J. (1988) 'The high price of a country's health' *The Guardian*, January 25th.

STEPHENS, J. (1979) *The Transition from Capitalism to Socialism*, London, Macmillan.

STONE, D. (1980) *The Limits of Professional Power*, Chicago, University of Chicago Press.

SUNDQVIST, K. (1987) 'Swedish family policy and the attempt to change paternal roles' in LEWIS, C. and O'BRIEN, M. (eds.) *Reassessing Fatherhood*, London, Sage.

SWEDISH INSTITUTE (1988) 'General facts on Sweden' *Fact Sheets on Sweden*, Stockholm, Swedish Institute.

TAYLOR, D. (1989) 'Citizenship and social power' *Critical Social Policy*, 26, Autumn.

TAYLOR-GOOBY, P. (1985) *Public Opinion, Ideology and State Welfare*, London, Routledge.

TCRU (1990) *Under Fives Services: Provision and Usage*, London, Thomas Coram Research Unit.

THERBORN, G. (1989) ' "Pillarization" and "popular movements" ' in CASTLES, F. (ed.) *The Comparative History of Public Policy*, Cambridge, Polity Press.

THERBORN, G. and ROEBROEK, J. (1986) 'The irreversible welfare state' *International Journal of Health Services*, 16, 3.

TINGSTEN, H. (1973) *The Swedish Social Democrats: Their Ideological Development*, Totowa (NJ), Bedminster Press.

TITMUSS, R. (1958) *Essays on 'the Welfare State'*, London, Unwin.

TITMUSS, R. (1974) *Social Policy*, London, Allen and Unwin.

TOWNSEND, P. (1979) *Poverty in the United Kingdom*, Harmondsworth, Penguin.

TOWNSEND, P., DAVIDSON, N. and WHITEHEAD, M. (1988) *Inequalities in Health*, Harmondsworth, Penguin.

US BUREAU OF THE CENSUS (1979) *The Social and Economic Status of the Black Population in the US: An Historical View 1790–1978*, Washington DC, US Department of Commerce.

US BUREAU OF THE CENSUS (1987) *Statistical Abstract of the United States 1987*, Washington DC, US Department of Commerce.

VALENTINE, C. (1968) *Culture and Poverty*, Chicago, University of Chicago Press.

VALKONEN, T. (1989) 'Adult mortality and level of education: a comparison of six countries' in FOX, J. (ed.) *Health Inequalities in European Countries*, Aldershot, Gower.

VOGEL, J. (1987) 'The victims of unemployment: labour market policy and the burden of unemployment' in FERGE, Z. and MILLER, S. (eds.) *The Dynamics of Deprivation*, Aldershot, Gower Press.

VOGELHEIM, E. (1988) 'Women in a changing workplace: the case of the Federal Republic of Germany' in JENSON, J., HAGEN, E. and REDDY, C. (eds.) *Feminization of the Labor Force*, Cambridge, Polity Press.

WALKER, A. (1987) 'The poor relation: poverty among old women' in GLENDINNING, C. and MILLAR, J. (eds.) *Women and Poverty in Britain*, Brighton, Wheatsheaf.

WALKER, M. (1990) 'The thin white-collar line' *The Guardian*, April 21st.

WALKER, M. (1991) 'Sentencing system blights land of free' *The Guardian*, June 19th.

WALKER, R., HARDMAN, G. and HUTTON, S. (1989) 'The occupational pension trap' *Journal of Social Policy*, 18, 4.

WALLRAFF, G. (1988) *Lowest of the Low*, London, Methuen.

WEBBER, F. (1991) 'From ethnocentrism to Euro-racism' *Race and Class*, 32, 3.

WEINSTEIN, J. (1968) *The Corporate Ideal in the Liberal State*, Boston (MA), Beacon Press.

WEIR, M., ORLOFF, A.S. and SKOCPOL, T. (1988) *The Politics of Social Policy in the United States*, Princeton (NJ), Princeton University Press.

WHITEBOOK, M., HOWES, C. and PHILLIPS, D. (1989) *Who Cares? – Child Care Workers and the Quality of Care in America*, Oakland (CA), Child Care Employee Project.

WHITTLE, C. (1977) *Social Assistance in the Federal Republic of Germany*, mimeo, background paper for the Review of Supplementary Benefit, London, DHSS.

WIDGREN, J. (1982) 'The status of immigrant workers in Sweden' in THOMAS, E.-J. (ed.) *Immigrant Workers in Europe: Their Legal Status*, Paris, The Unesco Press.

WILENSKY, H. (1975) *The Welfare State and Equality*, Berkeley, University of California Press.

WILENSKY, H., LUEBBERT, G., HAHN, S. and JAMIESON, A. (1985) *Comparative Social Policy: Theories, Methods, Findings*, Berkeley, University of California Institute of International Studies, Research Series 62.

WILLIAMS, F. (1989) *Social Policy: A Critical Introduction*, Cambridge, Polity Press.

WILSON, D. (1979) *The Welfare State in Sweden*, London, Heinemann.

WILSON, D. (1987) 'The welfare state in America' in FORD, R. and CHAKRABARTI, M. (eds.) *Welfare Abroad: An Introduction to Welfare Provision in Seven Countries*, Edinburgh, Scottish Academic Press.

WILSON, W.J. (1978) *The Declining Significance of Race*, Chicago, University of Chicago Press.

WILSON, W.J. (1987) *The Truly Disadvantaged*, Chicago, University of Chicago Press.

WOODALL, P. (1990) 'Survey – the Swedish economy' *The Economist*, March 3rd.

WOOLHANDLER, S., HIMMELSTEIN, D., SILBER, R., BADER, M., HARNLY, M. and JONES, A. (1985) 'Medical care and mortality: racial differences in preventable deaths' *International Journal of Health Services*, 15, 1.

WRENCH, J. (1987) 'The unfinished bridge: YTS and black youth' in TROYNA, B. (ed.) *Racial Inequality in Education*, London, Tavistock.

WRRC (no date) *Sterilisation*, mimeo, London, Women's Reproductive Rights Campaign.

YOUNG, H. (1988) 'Stark dreams of the American way' *The Guardian*, March 16th.

ZAPF, W. (1986) 'Development, structure and prospects of the German social state' in ROSE, R. and SHIRATORI, R. (eds.) *The Welfare State East and West*, New York, Oxford University Press.

Index